New Letters Reader I

CONTENTS

4

New Letters Reader One

An Anthology of Contemporary Writing

**Edited by DAVID RAY
with JUDY RAY**

A *New Letters* Book
University of Missouri - Kansas City

SWALLOW PRESS
OHIO UNIVERSITY PRESS
Chicago   Athens, Ohio   London

ISBN 0-8040-0850-7

Ohio University Press/Swallow Press
Scott Quad, Dept. FRDR
Athens, OH 45701

Editorial

"The artist creates a single, a singular thing, out of his solitary labor; but the editor creates a small unanticipated community that has never existed before and will never exist again."

—JOYCE CAROL OATES

Little magazines are part of the great Alternative—to a world progressively gobbled up by slick formulas, a world of pulp and vinyl, of third-hand opinion and cacophonous hype. God save us from the resonant voices, Heinrich Böll says somewhere (or one of his despairing soldiers says to himself on his way to a futile death on the battlefield): the resonant voices are everywhere, selling us the world that hems us in, with all its inescapable products. Little magazines, on the other hand, survive as an endangered species. Few have a use for them: they turn up at garage sales, next to old mink collar-pieces and soft-hued satin glass. Their causes are, admittedly, quixotic. Some editors hope to stop Armageddon with a haiku. Others believe in good writing as Adelle Davis believed in vitamins. Possibly the idea of publishing work just because it's good (rather than "exploitable") occurs more often to little magazine editors than to others.

We know the name game and the name of the game. But little magazines struggle on, as part of an alternative world; and their editing, like other subtle interactions, is a complex and often painful experience. The editor must empty his mind and experience what the writer is saying. And that's a difficult job, for there are many writers, and they are saying a great many different things, and they never stop saying them. The editor's job is that of a catalyst, bringing writer and reader together. If his editing has the quality of art, he succeeds in offering the readers of his magazine work that is truly worth the sharing—work that moves a reader sometimes to tears or laughter, work that can make whiskers stand up, work that seems fresh and relevant to life. If the editor must read a thousand pages to find one he wishes to share and endorse, then that is his affliction, for good writing is inspiriting, but the literature of limbo offers a sea of perplexity and groping, with an occasional spine-chilling passage or pure Eros or Thanatos.

8

I once belonged to a coffee klatch in a corner drugstore in Chicago where each morning a friend shared with us the Miss Lonelyheartish letters sent to a famous advice columnist for whom my friend was a ghostwriter. (The advice columnist was too busy on the lecture circuit to write her own responses.) The experience of reading those letters left me with the feeling that the reader (consumer of literary wares) never truly faces reality: it is too bleak and despairing. The world is full of girls who think they were impregnated by snakes, of the dying who want to whisper their last words abroad, of quiet psychopaths who sip whiskey as they contemplate mass murder while they watch daily soap operas: it is too ugly to behold or share. Like toxic hot potatoes, the letters had been passed along to a ghostwriter who deferred them still again. So much for what doesn't get published. Which is not to say we don't make mistakes—our values are, perhaps, so out of touch with current fashions that one of our rejects may well get the National Book Award in due time—Rhadamanthine certainty is the privilege of mythic demi-gods, not of mere mortals.

We have been fortunate that good writers have wanted their work to appear in *New Letters*, despite our ability to pay only a meager honorarium from our small budget. Thus our offering here, in this first of our retrospective anthologies, is rich; and I have no hesitancy in advocating this book as a companion of many forays into the art of shared discovery. Our small *New Letters* community feels that it has been present at the creation now and then.

If I have one regret from these twelve years of discovery and struggle it is that we may have tried too hard to survive, to urge support. You see, there's a terrible risk in being mistaken for another of the resonant voices.

The buck has always stopped on my desk. But I have solicited and obtained advice of many kinds on many occasions. Both our staff and our volunteer group, New Letters Community Associates, have selflessly shared their time, energies, insights. I could not have carried on without this help, and I wish to acknowledge here with deep gratitude all the assistance received throughout the first dozen years of *New Letters*.

—DAVID RAY

University of Missouri—Kansas City,   June, 1983

Named for Victoria, Queen of England

CHINUA ACHEBE

I was born in Ogidi in Eastern Nigeria of devout Christian parents. The line between christian and non-christian was much more definite in my village 40 years ago than it is today. When I was growing up I remember we tended to look down on the others. We were called in our language "the people of the church" or "the association of God." The others we called, with the conceit appropriate to followers of the true religion, the heathen or even "the people of nothing."

Thinking about it today I am not so sure that it isn't they who should have been looking down on us for our apostasy. And perhaps they did. But the bounties of the christian God were not to be taken lightly — education, paid jobs and many other advantages that nobody in his right senses could under-rate. And in fairness we should add that there was more than naked opportunism in the defection of many to the new religion. For in some ways and in certain circumstances it stood firmly on the side of humane behaviour. It said, for instance, that twins were not evil and must no longer be abandoned in the forest to die. Think what that would have done for that unhappy woman whose heart torn to shreds at every birth could now hold on pre-cariously to a new hope.

There was still considerable evangelical fervour in my early days. Once a month in place of the afternoon church service we went into the village with the gospel. We would sing all the way to the selected communal meeting place. Then the pastor or catechist or one of the elders having waited for enough heathen people to assemble would address them on the evil futility of their ways. I do not recall that we made even one conversion. On the contrary I have a distinct memory of the preacher getting into serious trouble with a villager who was apparently notorious for turning up at every occasion with a different awkward question. As you would expect, this was no common villager but a fallen christian, technically known as a *backslider*. Like Satan, a spell in heaven had armed him with unfair insights.

My father had joined the new faith as a young man and risen rapidly in its ranks to become an evangelist and church teacher. His maternal grandfather who had brought him up (his own parents having died early) was a man of note in the village. He had taken the highest but one title that a man of wealth and honour might aspire to, and the feast he gave the town on his initiation became a byword for open-handedness bordering on prodigality. The grateful and approving community called him henceforth Udo Osinyi — Udo who cooks more than the whole people can eat.

From which you might deduce that my ancestors approved of ostentation. And you would be right. But they would probably have argued if the charge was made by their modern counterparts that in their day wealth could only be acquired honestly, by the sweat of a man's brow. They would probably never have given what I believe was the real but carefully concealed reason, namely that given their extreme republican and egalitarian worldview it made good sense for the community to encourage a man acquiring more wealth than his neighbours to convert that threat of material power into harmless honorific distinction, while his accumulated riches flowed back into the common-wealth.

Apparently the first missionaries who came to my village went to Udo Osinyi to pay their respects and seek support for their work. For a short while my great grandfather allowed them to operate from his compound. He probably thought it was some kind of circus whose strange presence added lustre to his household. But after a few days he sent them packing again. Not, as you might think, on account of the crazy theology they had begun to propound but on the much more serious grounds of musical aesthetics. Said the old man: "Your singing is too sad to come from a man's house. My neighbours might think it was my funeral dirge."

So they parted — without rancour. When my father joined the missionaries the old man did not seem to have raised any serious objections. Perhaps, like Ezeulu, he thought he needed a representative in their camp. Or perhaps he thought it was a modern diversion which a young man might indulge in without coming to too much harm. He must have had second thoughts when my father began to have ideas about converting him. But it never came to an open rift; apparently not even a quarrel. They remained very close to the end. I don't know it for certain but I think the old man was the very embodiment of tolerance insisting only that whatever a man decided to do he should do it with style. I am told he was very pleased when my father, a teacher now, had a wedding to which white missionaries (now no longer figures of fun) came in their fineries, their men and their women, bearing gifts. He must have been impressed too by the wedding feast which might not have approached his own legendary performance but was by all accounts pretty lavish.

About ten years ago, before my father died he told me of a recent dream in which his grandfather, long long dead, arrived at our house like a traveller from a distant land come in for a brief stop and rest and was full of admiration for the zinc house my father had built. There was something between those two that I find deep, moving and perplexing. And of their two generations — defectors and loyalists alike — there was something I have not been able to fathom. That was why the middle story in the Okonkwo trilogy as I originally projected it never got written. I had suddenly become aware that in my gallery of ancestral heroes there is an empty place from which an unknown personage seems to have departed.

I was baptised Albert Chinualumogu. I dropped the tribute to Victorian England when I went to the university although you might find some early acquaintances still calling me by it. The earliest of them all — my mother — certainly stuck to it to the bitter end. So if anyone asks you what Her Brittanic Majesty Queen Victoria had in common with Chinua Achebe, the answer is: they both lost their Albert! As for the second name which in the manner of my people is a full-length philosophical statement I simply cut it in two, making it more businesslike without, I hope, losing the general drift of its meaning.

I have always been fond of stories and intrigued by language —first Igbo and later English which I began to learn at about the age of eight. I don't know for certain but I probably have spoken more words in Igbo than English but I have definitely written more words in English than Igbo. Which I think makes me perfectly bilingual. Some people have suggested that I should be better off writing in Igbo. Sometimes they seek to drive the point home by asking me in which language I dream. When I reply that I dream in both languages they seem not to believe it. More recently I have heard an even more potent and metaphysical version of the question: in what language do you have an orgasm? Which would settle the matter if I knew.

We lived at the crossroads of cultures. We still do today; but when I was a boy one could see and sense the peculiar quality and atmosphere of it more clearly. I am not talking about all that rubbish we hear of the spiritual void and mental stresses that Africans are supposed to have, or the evil forces and irrational passions prowling through Africa's heart of darkness. We know the racist mystique behind a lot of that stuff and should merely point out that those who prefer to see Africa in those lurid terms have not themselves demonstrated any clear superiority in sanity or more competence in coping with life.

But still the crossroads does have a certain dangerous potency; dangerous because a man might perish there wrestling with multiple-headed spirits, but also he might be lucky and return to his people with the boon of prophetic vision.

On one arm of the cross we sang hymns and read the Bible night and day. On the other my father's brother and his family, blinded by heathenism, offered food to idols. That was how it was supposed to be anyhow. But I knew without knowing why that it was too simple a way to describe what was going on. Those idols and that food had a strange pull on me in spite of my being such a thorough little christian that often at Sunday services at the height of the grandeur of Te Deum Laudamus I would have dreams of a mantle of gold falling on me while the choir of angels drowned our mortal song and the voice of God Himself thundering: This is my beloved son in whom I am well pleased. Yes, despite those delusions of divine destiny I was not past taking my little sister to our neighbour's house when our parents were not looking and partaking of heathen festival meals. I never found their rice to have the flavour of idolatry. I was about ten then. If anyone likes to believe that I was torn by spiritual agonies or stretched on the rack of my ambivalence he certainly may suit himself. I do not remember any undue distress. What I do remember was a fascination for the ritual and the life on the other arm of the crossroads. And I believe two things were in my favour — that curiosity and the little distance imposed between me and it by the accident of my birth. The distance becomes not a separation but a bringing together like the necessary backward step which a judicious viewer may take in order to see a canvas steadily and fully.

I was lucky in having a few old books around the house when I was learning to read. As the fifth in a family of six children and with parents so passionate for their children's education I inherited many discarded primers and readers. I remember *A Midsummer Night's Dream* in an advanced stage of falling apart. I think it must have been a prose adaptation, simplified and illustrated. I don't remember whether I made anything of it. Except the title. I couldn't get over the strange beauty of it. A Midsummer Night's Dream. It was a magic phrase — an incantation that conjured up scenes and landscapes of an alien, happy and unattainable land.

I remember also my mother's *Ije Onye Kraist* which must have been an Igbo adaptation of *Pilgrim's Progress*. It could not have been the whole book; it was too thin. But it had some frightening pictures. I recall in particular a most vivid impression of *the valley of the shadow of death*. I thought a lot about death in those days. There was another little book which frightened and fascinated me. It had drawings of different parts of the human body. But I was only interested in what my elder sister told me was the human heart. Since there is a slight confusion in Igbo between heart and soul I took it that that strange thing looking almost like my mother's iron cooking pot turned upside down was the very thing that flew out when a man died and perched on the head of the coffin on the way to the cemetery.

I found some use for most of the books in our house but by no means all. There was one Arithmetic book I smuggled out and sold for half-a-penny which I needed to buy the tasty *mai-mai* some temptress of a woman sold in the little market outside the school. I was found out and my mother who had never had cause till then to doubt my honesty — laziness, yes; but not theft — received a huge shock. Of course she redeemed the book. I was so ashamed when she brought it home that I don't think I ever looked at it again which was probably why I never had much use for mathematics.

My parents' reverence for books was almost superstitious; so my action must have seemed like a form of juvenile simony. My father was much worse than my mother. He never destroyed any paper. When he died we had to make a bonfire of all the hoardings of his long life. I am the very opposite of him in this. I can't stand paper around me. Whenever I see a lot of it I am seized by a mild attack of pyromania. When I die my children will not have a bonfire.

The kind of taste I acquired from the chaotic literature in my father's house can well be imagined. For instance I became very fond of those aspects of ecclesiastical history as could be garnered from *The West African Churchman's Pamphlet* — a little terror of a booklet prescribing interminable Bible readings morning and night. It had the date of consecration for practically every Anglican bishop who ever served in West Africa; and, even more intriguing, the dates of their death. Many of them didn't last very long. I remember one pathetic case (I forget his name) who arrived in Lagos straight from his consecration at St. Paul's Cathedral and was dead within days, and his wife a week or two after him. Those were the days when West Africa was truly the white man's grave, when those great lines were written, of which I was at that time unaware:

Bight of Benin! Bight of Benin!
Where few come out though many go in!

But the most fascinating information I got from *Pamphlet*, as
we called it, was this cryptic entry for the month of August:

Augustine, Bishop of Hippo, died 430

It had that elusive and eternal quality, a tantalizing unfamiliarity
which I always found moving.

I did not know that I was going to be a writer because I
did not really know of the existence of such creatures until
fairly late. The folk-stories my mother and elder sister told me
had the immemorial quality of the sky and the forests and the
rivers. Later, when I got to know that the European stories I
read were written by known people it still didn't help much.
It was the same Europeans who made all the other marvellous
things like the motor-car. We did not come into it at all. We
made nothing that wasn't primitive and heathenish.

The nationalist movement in British West Africa after the
Second World War brought about a mental revolution which
began to reconcile us to ourselves. It suddenly seemed that we
too might have a story to tell. *Rule Britannia*! to which we had
marched so unself-consciously on Empire Day now stuck in our
throat.

At the university I read some appalling novels about Africa
(including Joyce Cary's much praised *Mister Johnson*) and decided that the story we had to tell could not be told for us by
anyone else no matter how gifted or well-intentioned.

Although I did not set about it consciously in that solemn
way I now know that my first book, *Things Fall Apart*, was an
act of atonement with my past, the ritual return and homage of
a prodigal son. But things happen very fast in Africa. I had
hardly begun to bask in the sunshine of reconciliation when a
new cloud appeared, a new estrangement. Political independence
had come. The nationalist leader of yesterday (with whom it
had not been too difficult to make common cause) had become
the not so attractive party boss. And then things really got

going. The party boss was chased out by the bright military boys, new idols of the people. But the party boss knows how to wait, knows by heart the counsel Mother Bedbug gave her little ones when the harrassed owner of the bed poured hot water on them: "Be patient," said she, "for what is hot will in the end be cold."

One hears that the party boss is already conducting a whispering campaign: "You done see us chop," he says, "now you see *dem* chop. Which one you like pass?" And the people are truly confused.

In a little nondescript coffee shop where I sometimes stop for a hamburger in Amherst there are some unfunny inscriptions hanging on the walls, representing a one-sided dialogue between management and staff. The unfunniest of them all reads —poetically:

> Take care of your boss
> The next one may be worse.

The trouble with writers is that they will often refuse to live by such rationality.

Remarks

RICHARD HUGO

from an interview with Susan Zwinger

Usually late at night . . . around ten o'clock until three in the morning . . . I drink a lot of coffee when I write and smoke a lot of cigarettes. And I'm extremely concentrated, almost single-minded. That is to say, everything is out but the words. I just play with phrasing, and hope something . . . something good enough.

* * *

A while back I said what a poet did for a living wasn't very important. I was asked out in Colorado how a poet should make a living . . . this is a game a lot of people play. I was feeling less perverse than usual, so I made up a job that would be ideal for a poet. He would work in a warehouse on swing shift, and he would be the only one working there. He would work from four in the afternoon until midnight. The job would consist simply of hauling boxes on dollies and putting them on shelves. He would receive his instructions by written note when he went to work. When he went home at night, he would lock up the warehouse. There would be nobody else there. That would be my ideal job for a poet.

* * *

In essence, I grew up in a static world, and one day it began to change very violently and very rapidly. I saw all of my boyhood play areas wiped out. Salmon Creek, which ran through a virgin forest all the way through the city, was developed for houses. The swamp that used to have an old dugout canoe in it was wiped out by houses. I grew up with a sense of permanence . . . with the coming of WW II in 1939, and for America in 1941, that was when everything began to change.

* * *

In grammar school . . . one of our teachers used to read aloud
to us. I was in the eighth grade, and she read Tennyson's "The
Brook." I thought that was such a pretty poem, and I remember
feeling then, I was twelve years old, I remember thinking "gee,
I'd like to write a poem that pretty about a stream some day."
Well, I don't know that I've ever written a poem that pretty,
but I think I've outdone him in number . . . I've got a lot of
river poems. I grew up on rivers and creeks.

*   *   *

One poet who influenced me quite a bit . . . not a very well
known poet . . . is a British poet named Bernard Spencer who
died in 1962 or '63 because of a freak accident in Vienna. He
fell off a moving train. He wrote a book called *Aegean Islands
and Other Poems* which was published in 1947. It's a book that
influenced me quite a bit. It's hard for me to talk about influences
because I don't like to read. The biggest influence on my poetry
(I didn't realize this till years later) wasn't poetry at all, but
was swing music.

*   *   *

This is how I developed the idea of moving on very rapidly from
thing to thing in my earlier poems. There was no poetry in the
house, and since poetry is an auditory art form, this would make
sense: learning sound from swing music. Generally I don't like to
read and I'm not much influenced by it.

*   *   *

When I was a boy in the Thirties, my grandparents who raised me
were anything but literary. Almost no books in the house. The
first art, auditory art I heard that had any value were the big swing
bands on the radio . . . Benny Goodman, Bob Crosby, later on,
Artie Shaw. Now what Swing music did was develop sort of a go
quality to music, and this is where I developed the idea of getting
something going before the thing now going died out. Which is
what Swing bands did. Just as one series of rifts which was coming
to an end, something else would start. So you never had the idea
of anything stopping.

*   *   *

The only way you can be a good public poet is to be extremely bright and clever like Auden, because you are at all times entertaining your audience. If you're not entertaining your audience you will sound pontifical. The same reason a father can no longer lecture his son on morality . . . because he can't think fast enough to keep his son entertained while he's giving him the word.

*   *   *

Finding out what you love is literally finding out a way to say it. All loving is stating it for a poet. . . . For example, if you fall in love with a crocodile it is simply a matter of finding out that you have, and then admitting it. That's very difficult.

*   *   *

I studied under a man named Redford. Under Redford I was in prose. He was my first college creative writing teacher. Incidentally he came to Washington from Montana. I never had the patience for prose. I couldn't sense the form. You don't have it all in front of you at once. I'm very immediate-minded, and in order to work, I almost have to have it on one page. I don't have recall. It is hard for me to pace prose.

*   *   *

I often write about things that are ignored . . . or I think they are ignored. I like that assurance that I'm the only one who ever saw it. This is once again just being able to emotionally possess something. I think that urban poets quite often don't emotionally possess their materials, and one reason is that they grow up knowing that what they see is shared by multitudes. I think this is a distinct disadvantage. Of course, there are wonderful urban poets. . . . Weldon Kees, for example. I know that urban poets have well developed lives of fantasies, and these are things to be tapped, but that emotional possession of one's material belongs more to country people.

*   *   *

There's no doubt that there is always sadness in my poetry . . . always has been and always will be . . . I will always see life as a sad business.

It's something I'm obsessed with . . . this idea of being accepted. Of self acceptance. Of being worthy of being loved. Problems that I guess are always with us, with humanity. Problems that don't change.

*   *   *

I've had good students . . . students who are so good that they make the teacher look good . . . and if you're a teacher, of course, you've got to be corrupt and take the credit for it even if you don't deserve it.

*   *   *

I often deal with someone who has stayed there all his life and cannot get out . . . indeed, at one time, I was told this by other people and I believe it to be true. . . . I had an amazing gift of being able to walk into a town I'd never been in before and within a few minutes know exactly what that town would mean to someone who had lived there all his life. I cannot do this any more.

*   *   *

Because I was an unstable person and very unsure of myself, I would hit outrageous stances. That is to say, hold hammy, melo-dramatic, romantic poses and so forth. Not necessarily that other people would see, but they were there. Roethke did this too. He did this in his poems. His was the poetry of overstance. That's what I learned from him in sort of an indirect way. I realized that you could literally be outrageous, take an outrageous stance and create something beautiful out of it. That gave me that con-fidence. And that was just exactly what I needed. So it was the sheerest luck that I happened to have him as a teacher.

*   *   *

And of course a lot of my early poems are just roaring at times. Poems like "Digging is an Art" and "The Way a Ghost Dissolves." They're booming poems . . . hopefully you get away with it.

*   *   *

Young writers title a poem something like "Autumn Rain," and then when they run out of interesting things to say about autumn rain, they strain to find something else. The mistake they're making is that they think that they have to go on talking about autumn rain because that's the subject that started the poem. What starts the poem is never really the subject of the poem because you never really know what that is until the poem is written. This is why you should never title a poem early. Until you've got the poem finished, at least for young people, don't title it. I don't have this problem any more.

*   *   *

Thirty-five combat missions, and I returned to the United States and was discharged prior to the surrendering of Japan in 1945. I was 21.

*   *   *

It takes quite a few years before you can take emotional possession of those things that are really yours.

*   *   *

In fact, I think poets should call things by names . . . by their right names.

*   *   *

Around my middle thirties, around twelve or fifteen years ago. What happens when you finally catch on to what it is you love and what it is you own emotionally . . . this is really finding your style.

*   *   *

Roethke did not come till the fall of 1947, and I managed to get into his first poetry writing course, and then I repeated it for credit. In March 1948 I got my BA and was out of school for 15 months. When I started graduate school in summer 1949, I had Roethke as my thesis advisor. Then he was ill, and I had to find another advisor.

Then I left school in December of 1950, and in 1951 I hired into the Boeing company and worked there for thirteen years.

*   *   *

Most of my poems are slower now. I'm letting more air in between the words, between the lines. They're more tender now. I don't think tenderness is a weakness the way I used to, and I'm not afraid of having emotions that I used to think were too sloppy to admit to.

I was too much Humphrey Bogart in my early days. My look was hard. What I was trying to do, I realize now, was literally trying to create a person who was acceptable, a person who deserved to have friends and a home. At one time the kind of person I thought this would be was a person who was hard enough and brave enough to look the dangerous world right in the face . . . to see things the way they were . . . to be totally unsentimental . . . to be totally hard and courageous. So I wrote hard and courageous poems. In real life, of course, I was not hard and courageous. I was a sissy. But now I'm in my Leslie Howard period.

*   *   *

There's a part of me that's sort of a stay at home, and I hope some day to buy a house and to live in it the rest of my life. Indeed I lived in the same house for almost twenty-five years.

*   *   *

I'd like to think that I've never written a poem with an uninteresting opening line. In other words, I would just be appalled if the first line didn't grab. Grab people. Grab your ears. In fact, I'm more addicted to that than Roethke was. Some of Roethke's first lines are just moderately good, just fairly interesting. I want to be interesting from the very first syllable, and never want to stop. Stop being interesting and making interesting sounds and movements until the poem stops. Because I think you can be anything but boring. To be boring is unforgivable.

* * *

In my second book, I have a poem called "Index" that no one understands. In fact, I don't think I understand it anymore. But I will say this, I have never let a poem go unless at least for a period of time I could understand it.

* * *

I think that the person that is deserving of friends and is deserving of a home is a nice tender polite man, warm and friendly.

* * *

However, I was a humor writer at one time, and wrote humor for the University of Washington campus magazine. It came rather easily for me. I didn't spend much time on it. Just tore it off and gave it to the editor and she published it.

When I was twenty-one, I sent a couple of things to the Saturday Evening Post and almost got taken for the old humor page. I think I could probably have been a humor writer and a successful one.

* * *

Auden says that everyone is trying to become somebody else, and the poet makes it for the duration of the poem. This maybe is the best explanation, and it is true that each person, except for subnormal people, is trying to be someone else every waking moment.

* * *

I write about unpeopled worlds. Very seldom does a person in my poems have a relationship with anybody else. If he does, it's nearly always someone who's dead. I see the world as a sad place without any people in it. Decaying shacks, abandoned ranches, desolation, endless spaces, plains, mountains, ghost towns. They are right for my sensibilities.

* * *

It is lonely . . . and this is a good place for me as a poet.

Two Poems

RICHARD HUGO

Camas Prairie School

The schoolbell rings and dies before
the first clang can reach the nearest farm.
With land this open, wind is blowing
when there is no wind. The gym's so ugly
victory leaves you empty as defeat,
and following whatever game
you will remember lost, you run fast
slow miles home through grain,
knowing you'll arrive too late
to eat or find the lights on.

Flat and vast. Each farm beyond
a gunshot of the next. A friend
is one you love to walk to, 28 below.
A full moon makes this prairie moon
and horses in a thick night
sound like bears. When your sister's raped
help is out of range. Father's far
from Mother and a far bell's
always ringing you can't hear.

The teacher either must be new each year
or renewed forever. Old photos
show her just as gray beside the class
of '35. Indians rehearse
the Flag Salute, and tourists
on their way to Hot Springs wave.
The road beside the school goes either way.
The last bell rings. You run again,
the only man going your direction.

The Tinker Camp

for Susan Lydiatt

Whatever they promise for money, luck,
a lifetime of love, they promise empty.
They beg us cruel ways, forlorn hand
stuck at us, pathetic face, or watch us
with dead eyes through rags they hung to dry.
They have cheated the last two centuries,
have lied and are hated, have stolen from
the unorganized poor. Even pans they sell
seem made of mean tin, and their wagons
gypsy as kisses you imagine when young.
Always the necessary, dreaded 'move on'.
They never park where we might picnic,
but camp on bare ground, just off roads
where dust from traffic cakes food,
police can eye and insult them, and access
to that long road out of scorn is near.
Our accent and our rental car are signals:
Steal. Beg. Don't feel anything. Don't dream.
They sleep well with our money. We
are the world that will not let them weep.

Words to a Young Revolutionist

HAYDEN CARRUTH

Yes, it is exhilerating, I remember of course
how you find the target so unexpectedly
in words so unexpectedly speaking
the focus of your heart's desire.

Yes, it is liberation, that is
the shining word—for you, for them.
I say it myself, even now
over and over.

Yes, we will go on, our work
lies before us, as our knowledge lies
behind us.

Yes, when the assassination
had been completed the people,
men and I hope some women,
rushed to the Forum
and toppled the statues from the pedestals,
Caesar's head rolled in the debris
with its nose broken.

Yes, let me take you down
through the levels of your city, the levels
of debris, to the place I know
there around the corner
from Astor Place, where the fire
of crates burns in the old drum
with a smell of oil, a smell of paint
and we stand in the dark wind warming
our bellies. I see an old woman
marching along in the shadowy
firelight, clutching her shawl,
her other fist raised,
I see her shouting but I do not hear

because I hear her breasts where they lie
slack and thin on her belly
muttering to each other.

Yes, I am up to my neck
in the dust this dark wind is blowing
and I cannot move though the women
are moving down below and they try,
they try. Even now one of them,
Héloisa or Eurydice,
strokes my belly and lays her cheek
on my penis but she is
cold. The wind is cold, the fire
is cold. I turn my head
and see here next to me on the dust
Caesar's head lying sideways with its broken nose,
staring from empty eyes.

Yes, I hear the words on Caesar's tongue.
I hear your words, I hear your feet
walking, running somewhere in your city,
stirring the dust with your ankles.

Liberation, liberation, an endless rhythm,
cold women, warm women
and the women growing cold as I
grow cold, muttering
into the wind and dust.

Yes, I hear the words on Caesar's tongue
in this long, long filthy street
that is filled with words
for the words are penetrated by the wind
but not dispersed, they are buried by the dust
but they rise again—liberation, liberation
spoken by the living and the dead,
they will never cease, they will never be able
to cease.

Yes.

Old Men on Their Way to Pick Up the Morning Mail

ROBERT GIBB

In the morning the fog recedes
Like tentacles. Shapes become
What they will in the emerging

Light; a gathering of solidities
To be discovered as a shell
Might be — curved against the

Day. The old men move into
The streets, the veil of
Sleeping water lifted from them.

Septuagenarians in the Age of
Aquarius, they are half again
As frail as this feeble light.

Their thin shins are bent, their
Lungs as laced as an old corset.
They seem almost to dissolve in

The lingering pockets of fog. This
Half-light they hold like mushrooms,
Bent towards some damp purpose.

A bite in the air should kill them,
Yet they are resilient as tar-babies.
They have learned to mingle with

The air as an element in it.
They have learned to be something
More, or less, than human.

Three Poems

PATRICIA GOEDICKE

The People Gathering Together

All over the earth I can see them,
In every city and town
The people gathering together,

Sailing the dark waters
In great glowing patches of brightness,
Islands of floating flowers.

Once a week they swing
And dip and bend together,

Garlands of party-going faces
Wallowing in the troughs
Or high up on the crests

Refusing to think about their feet
Dangling beneath them,

The long, wavering roots
Loose now, forever

They are as dazzlingly brave
And brilliant as coats of arms

All week they work hard,
Each in the boat of himself commands
As much of the ocean as he can

So that thinking of it I could weep,
For now none of us knows where he is going

Over the blank, heaving waves
There are these huge distances between us,

Therefore we stick to the surface,
Floating along like huge colonies of blossom

Whether it is Paris or London
Or a primitive tribe in New Zealand

All over the earth we keep coming together,
We keep giving each other these parties,
These heartbreakingly beautiful parties.

Greyhound

Sometimes I think I am not a car but a bus
And not a Greyhound but a Chihuahua,
Second-class, Mexican, hairless.

Lambs, pigs, people
Like parts of myself, stumbling
Inch up and down the aisle

Wheeling around mountains I hold on
To all my hopes, my passengers
Search the highway ahead . . .

Whizzing through beds of flowers,
Flying across deserts, ignorant
Stopping and starting
Where are we going? Inside

Galaxies of men women and children
Wave from every porthole

For the women inside me are my rubber tires
Milking me, milking me
Back to the playpen, the huge breast

For the children inside me are no strangers
In the West, in the South, in the North
Flying the same flag

For wherever I go I have been there already
From one filling station to the next

For the people inside me are a logjam
Of golden lumberjacks, whales in schools
Each with the same shining face:

Love's open house like an army
Surging up the passage to unseat me:

Pouring through Washington, Chihuahua, Veracruz
Crowding my corridors with bedazzled flowers

Sunfaced, moonfaced, waving from every corner
Heading for new horizons where we've been before

Until They have Consumed Me Utterly

All night, in slow motion
The clapboards of old age

Keep falling on me, the backstairs,
Pieces of the front porch, the attic

And there is nowhere to turn,
No soft thing

All night it is stone country,
Slab country, all heavy edges

For now everything is broken,
Lurching like a locomotive in a station

It is all stopping and starting,
There is no swiftness anywhere,
Everything is so slow I could cry

Except that this is my life and I'm interested in it:
Some people can watch the roof fall in

And hardly notice, they are in such a hurry
To hand themselves over to a junk heap
But I swear I will slip out of it

Like smoke from a destroyed chimney
Thin as paper I will slide out under the ramshackle door

Somehow I will carry my spirits and my clothes with me
Bag and baggage I will move out into the cold

And though I am no longer beautiful
Nor fleet footed, nor able to fly

I will not give up,
Until they have consumed me utterly

Even at the end I will stay awake
As long as I can, between drugs
And the suffocating rubble of time

When one can no longer run
Walking has a strange fascination

When one can no longer walk
Crawling keeps one close to the ground.

Indolence in Early Winter

Jane Kenyon

A letter arrives from friends . . . .
Let them all divorce, remarry
and divorce again!
Forgive me if I doze off in my chair.

I should have stoked the stove
an hour ago. The house
will turn cold as stone. Wonderful!
I won't have to go on
balancing my checkbook.

Unanswered mail piles up
in drifts, precarious,
and the cat sets everything sliding
when she comes to see me.

I am still here in my chair,
buried under the rubble
of failed marriages, magazine
subscription renewal forms, bills,
lapsed friendships . . . .

This kind of thinking is caused
by the sun. It leaves the sky earlier
every day, and goes off somewhere,
like a troubled husband,
or like a melancholy wife.

Siege at Stony Point

Horace Gregory

Three Voices Speaking

Birds, birds—birds, birds, birds—
A darkening of wings across the sky,
A half a million birds dropped from the air
Flying through sleep, through half-lit dawns and hours,
Black myrmidons in passage everywhere.
Starlings and crows, ferocious wrens,
Voracious hawks, and vultures drinking oil
Empty our lamps while foraging rooks
Deplete our fruits and strip the willows bare.

Some say, 'The birds are sent by Eskimos,
From antique Crees in Arctic wildernesses,
From stark Siberia, or Greenland's glassy waters,
From dark-skinned countries, fast in endless cold.'
Others insist that they took flight from County Clare
Straight up from fallen cottages, wrecked iron,
Moss-ridden stones, and broken angels
Lying among dank stubble and the thorn.
And ravens, fifty thousand strong and heady,
Are among the lot, their red eyes glaring.

Aristophanes once knew the birds as brothers,
He half implied this transient universe
Was theirs to wander, cherish, or remake—
The voluble Hoopoe, or raging parakeet—
But what of Earth?
                    that strange, elusive,
Far distant apparition of orange light,
Seen from a cockpit on the rim of outer space?
The gods may well desert it.
It is there for anyone to take.

Main Street Morning

NATALIE L. M. PETESCH
For M.N.

"Nor must you dream of opening any door
Until you have foreseen what lies beyond it."
Richard Wilbur, *Walking to Sleep*

You have come all this way to find out the truth about yourself, not the self you have carefully devised for over thirty-one years, but the self which split involuntarily into chromosomes, giving you his dark, curled hair but not her fern-green eyes—those mutual gifts which existed before you did, and which subsequently She gave away as if their love had not existed and therefore you, Marie, did not exist either.

A long search and a longer doubt have brought you to this ridiculous point, where you watch through your binoculars like a would-be assassin as *She* (Cecilia Roche née Cecilia Niall) goes to work, the woman who once either hated you or loved you, or both, but could not have been indifferent. She is about to leave Sears Roebuck where she is employed during the evening hours in Drapes & Fabrics, Custommade. She has gone in just now only to collect her check or perhaps to exchange a few words with her fellow employees and emerges, clutching her handbag. She does not trouble to straighten her skirt: perhaps she is indifferent to such matters. A few doors down on Main Street, she pauses at the window of a shoe store where they are offering (you recall) two pairs for five dollars: you wonder if that means she still has no money: for long ago you decided that it was money and only money which could have wrenched you away from her, sobbing. Yes, sobbing: you will not have it any other way.

You'd be the first to admit that this is a crazy way for you to spend your vacation. Cooped up in a room of the Manor Hotel, facing Main Street. Of course, every small town in the U.S. has its Main Street, but only this one has Cecilia Niall Roche in it. She has lived here for thirty years, ever since World War Two, as her generation refers to it—as if World War Three were already included in their plans. She (naturally) has had other children, though none of them could look like you, with that share of your genetic inheritance which belongs to Jules Blaine. Natural though it may be, the fact wrenches from you a spasm of loneliness, reminding you how quickly one's pendulum swings from being glorious Prince Hal to Falstaff snuffling in his bed. The moral of this comparison, Marie, you admonish yourself, is that a woman who plans to spy on her own mother ought to remain calm and not drink too much coffee. Already you're too nervous to handle the binoculars, which bear the sweating imprint of your fingers. But at least since you bought the binoculars you've been able to see her face, clearly framed like an antique portrait, and you accept the fact that she is (as they say), "lovely." (Suddenly you become "lovelier" to yourself.)

It's a round saucer of a face, with smooth puffed out cheeks, precisely the sort of face you would smile at for its Campbell Soup innocence, if she were someone else. If you were to meet that cherubic face at a party, would you ever imagine that she had lain in a ward, labored thirty-eight hours, and finally given birth to a nameless little gnome (yourself)? That, carefully adjusting her mask, she had gone back to Duluth, Boise, Davenport, Sheboygan—back to this very Main Street, the home of her fathers: absolved, pardoned, excused, by all except the main character of this drama, yourself? Nobody has yet asked your pardon.

Adjusting the binoculars like a telescopic sight, you think: suppose you were now to take the elevator down, walk out the revolving door, and trap her as she emerges from, say, the bakery, and walking toward her, in face to face confrontation you say: "Mother? . . . " You practice it a moment, repeating in various inflections: QUESTION: Mother? . . . EXCLAMATION;

SHOCK OF RECOGNITION: Mother!!!! . . . SARDONIC: Mothe*rrr*! EXPLETIVE: Mother!

You turn away from the window, understanding very well· that what you've tried to do is destroy your feelings. Good: you've destroyed them, Marie, how clever of you—now what are you going to do with the bits and pieces? You get up from your aching knees (you should have placed a pillow in front of the window, but you were too nervous and you forgot). You decide to go out . . . to actually *see* her. You'll follow her, till you catch her metaphorically in the till. You'll then inform her she's under citizen's arrest. *J'accuse*, Cecilia Niall Roche. . . . So you go down the hall which smells like a subway urinal: it's that roach killer they use, an invisible fluid which destroys the nervous system, they paint it along the baseboards. In the elevator the elevator operator (no orange-eyed electronic robots in Main Street) looks warily down at his feet: you're a stranger here, he can tell that, but he doesn't want to be nosy, you've paid for your privacy and there've been no big-city habits, no men in your room, no strange activities— unless the long silences during which you are on your knees at the window waiting for Her to come out have seemed to him portentous. It is a small local hotel where people know each other and are friendly; there's no protocol of deliberate silences separating Each from the Other, as in big cities. Still, you feel he'd like to penetrate your mystery. Not *my* mystery, you defend yourself sardonically; *my* life is a dull and open secret: *her* mystery.

But you think your bitterness may show on your face, so quickly you cross over the uneven step (he doesn't even say tonelessly, "Watch your step"—here on Main Street they don't warn you every time of what's right before your eyes). Out in the sun you're momentarily blinded. You've left your binoculars upstairs and for a moment you panic, as if without those defensive shields you'll not be able to bear the evidence of your eyes.

Out here on the street—so quiet one wonders where all the population explosion that demographers murmur about has exploded to—there is no possibility you will lose sight of her.

There she is, walking very slowly this Monday morning. Well, if she's not in a hurry, neither are you. You have the advantage this time, there's no programmed period of gestation, after which you must "show," willie-nillie. Now you may show and be damned. The woman ahead of you is a bit shorter and stouter than the one you spied upon from the window: you take that in as though it's merely one more response to a random sample you're doing on Main Street.

She's gone into a Rexall's. Although it's still early (10:30 a.m.) the three or four booths in the small drug store are already filled except for the one nearest the cash register and lunch counter: she takes it. Across the aisle from her sits an old man, alone and unshaven. He's spread himself around the booth with a newspaper borrowed from the rack, looking as much at ease as if he were in the neighborhood library. She checks the time with the red and black electric clock above the lunch counter which reads, instead of the hours: S U N R I S E   B R E A D.

As for you, Marie, nearly a third of your face covered by wide sunglasses, you head for the lunch counter, your back turned to her. Actually, you see her quite clearly in the round sign facing you which has a mirror finish and a Bicentennial sticker glued like a bull's eye at the center, offering you Home-made Apple Pie. You promptly order pie and coffee, although you can see the bakery label on the pan, and you know it will be too sweet and taste not at all of apples. Still, it's something to shut your mouth on while waiting for the person she is waiting for.

You've not long to wait—they're punctual on Main Street, with no subway hang ups or traffic jams to slow them down—there she is. Her appointment is with no Jules Blaine, of course, no dashing young lover in khaki, but only another middle-aged woman like herself (wearing—somewhat to your surprise—real Indian moccasins such as are popular in the Southwest). Her housedress, however, is predictable—a pale blue cotton with some sort of trimming at the sleeves, a starched strand of which is coming loose near the rounded forearm. No matter: she's smiling a warm greeting and already they're into something you can't share, you've no idea what they're talking about. The occasional clink of money, the ring of the cash register or an eruption of news from a small radio on the counter chops up their conversation into secret semaphores and codes: you have to strain to hear them.

The woman in blue greets Cecilia with a sort of calm delight. You're somehow shocked to hear Her addressed so personally yet casually—rather like the *tu* instead of the *vous* coming from a street vendor once as you browsed among the bookstalls along the Seine. It had frightened you, as though someone had meant to insult you: it had in fact been only a boy about ten years old, selling plastic replicas of Notre Dame and Sacré Coeur: he'd stared at you, challengingly, enjoying his own insolence. Still, you'd bought one, pretending not to understand his rudeness. . . .

Already Cecilia's begun to pull out some snapshots she's taken somewhere, and her friend of course thinks they're wonderful pictures. She even says it: "These are just wonderful."

"Neil took them. We said he shouldn't have to take pictures at his own wedding, but he insisted. He wanted some done by himself. He said he was the best wedding photographer in the State, he wasn't going to start married life by letting somebody else take pictures of his own wife!"

The woman in blue erupted into a delighted, mischievous laugh.

"But Sandy, he's not at his own wedding!"

Sandy! Somehow you'd never thought of that. But peering into the mirror across from you, you imagine you do see a few faint freckles along the nose, rather like the vein of cinnamon deep in your apple pie. Well: so her hair has not always been corn-colored but rather (you now embellish the antique photo in your mind), a desert color, a sunset color, something Jules would certainly have preferred to his own coarse black hair cropped close by the Army so that one saw the pale olive skin against the hair, curling like knotholes.

" . . . so exciting, I thought I'd never make it . . . and not to cost me anything either."

"And what about? . . . " Her friend looks at her tentatively.

Sandy glances around to see if anyone is listening, sees only the rounded indifference of your back, hunched addictively over the apple pie. You hardly notice that in your excitement you have spilled hot coffee over your hand.

"Oh, I guess they'll be all right." Then defensively, "He might have done a lot worse, I guess. He might have married . . . " Her voice lowered, Sandy whispers the unmentionable. Then her tone changes. "But it'll work out, I'm sure. Besides, it's their affair, not mine . . . Why don't you take these and show them to Phil? I've got to do some more errands . . . " She glances again at the red and black clock on the wall. Yourself, you have difficulty with the clock: it reads to you like a concrete poem:

BREAD

READ

AD

Or, if you blur your eyes a second, DAD, or even D EAD.

Sandy's friend murmurs something like "not losing a son but gaining a daughter." You strain your ears, you *think* you hear her say she knows what it's like to lose a daughter, but it must be your imagination, you can't pin the words down, Sandy's voice disappears into a kind of murmuring protest or enumeration, you're not sure which. Finally you hear it " . . . getting used to it, you know . . . daughters-in-law and one grandson."

You now experience a totally irrational pride in your sex. But that she does actually have such an Item as a grandson is a bit of a shock to you: it puts her in danger of getting lost again just when you've "found" her, as if she could suddenly disappear at that point where the parallel lines between past and future meet. And now you're experiencing something else. Somehow the fact of her grandson is wrapped up like those Japanese *origami*, a design within a design, with the fact that you will soon be thirty-two years old. You feel suddenly hollow and wasted, as if the long struggle to resist entrapment by your own body (as Sandy was entrapped) has put you exactly there and nowhere else.

But now here she is: bright-yellow hair, and around her eyes criss-crosses, like those on your apple pie: lines so deeply slashed into the cheeks they might have been deliberately grooved there, as on some carefully crafted mask of clay about to be fired in the kiln. You try to imagine what she looked like back then—when you were presenting her with that historic moral choice: reject and survive or accept and be damned. In your now-corrected script of the Forties you see Sandy was "titian-haired": You even enjoy the cliché which at other times would have struck you as laughable.

In your new script Sandy is meeting her lover, your father Jules Blaine, in New York. She has told her parents that she is "taking a holiday" from the government office on Main Street (where several months ago she met Jules Blaine, who came to inquire about a friend of his who is missing in action. . .) Part of Sandy's work at the big government office is typng up casualty reports: it's a job that fills her mind with nightmares, and when Jules enters her office she already sees him as a casualty of the war.

But she has come to New York to be with him, with Jules. Where did she discover the cunning, the duplicity, during The Biggest War on Earth to escape from Main Street to do this? Impossible for you, in the Present, to understand how she managed it. Although for a while you helped run a radio program in New York, and have written television commercials, you've never had to make your audience understand why they should purchase cars, curtains, cough syrups . . . all you had to do was invent a catchy slogan, retain their attention.

Thus, it's difficult for you to imagine what she is saying to Jules as they climb the Fifth Avenue bus. You understand the feeling though: it's summer, they're sitting on "top-of-New York," looking down. There is a slight breeze as they head crosstown toward Riverside. Her hair is not coarse and curled into knotholes like yours, like Jules', but soft and curved around the ears like the mouth of a cream pitcher (they call it a "page boy"). Jules is singing something from *Oklahoma*. If you listen carefully, you can almost hear his voice: *People will think we're in lo-ove* . . . There are tears in Sandy's eyes, perhaps of joy?—no, of grief, because Jules is going down South before being shipped overseas. "No," he says, he "doesn't know which 'Theater.'" They smile bitterly at the word *theater*. She begs: won't she be able to be with him again before they send him away? (Sitting in the drug store you almost urge them on: yes, yes, they *must* see each other!)

All is quickly decided—ecstatically, spontaneously, as if no lovers in time of war had ever thought of it before . . . She will join him in a week. Not a word to Sandy's parents waiting on Main Street of course: so far as they know she will still be in New York, visiting Sandy's best friend. "Will Melissa cover for you?" asks Jules. She nods; they are utterly delighted with the conspiracy (Oh what a joy it is to fool one's parents, *isn't it? isn't it? isn't it?*) They are as ecstatic as if there were not yet to be endured in this war a Battle of the Bulge, an Iwo Jima, an Okinawa.

They are on their way to Melissa's apartment: during the summer Melissa's family are not there, they are at the Cape, only Sandy is there with Jules—hour after hour, whenever he can escape to her. After which he returns to the barracks, where he becomes again the property of the State. He and Sandy have a special arrangement for calls, so that when the phone rings it can only be him: to the rest of the world the occupants are permanently out of town. In a city of seven million Sandy recognizes only one person. When one evening while they are celebrating Jules' nineteenth birthday at Rockerfeller Center they run into some of Jules' relatives, they brazen it out. Jules makes up a story on the spot: he is good at making up stories, as Sandy, obviously, is not.

Indeed Sandy is having trouble right now explaining to her friend in the booth how she feels about it all—about her daughter-in-law, or her former daughter-in-law, it's not clear which. " . . . it breaks my heart, though to see . . . " and she goes on. It has something to do with the way her grandson is being treated or not treated, loved or not loved, ignored or spoiled or both. He's being deprived of something, that's obvious. And Sandy's grief is as keen as if it were her own child being singled out by fate for unjustifiable suffering. (You pause to wonder: is there *justifiable* suffering?) But no, what Sandy is protesting is not her grandson's suffering but her son's,

his loneliness . . . You decide it must be the older son, not
Neil, since Neil is the boy from whose wedding she's just returned.

While Sandy's present life continues under your ear like a
pizzicato, you suck at the rim of your now-empty cup and gaze
sideways at the clock which seems to your blurred vision to be
reading the hour of D EAD. You continue to watch Sandy and
Jules descend the Fifth Avenue bus. They are now returning to
Melissa Levin's Riverside apartment. Again, there's an elevator—
not much different from the one on Main Street, and they're
going up, up, up: with your coffee cup in hand you are trans-
fixed by the vision, which blurs as she steps quickly into the
apartment. As they shut the door in your face, you can feel the
melting of their bones.

It's been a long cup of coffee and you know you're beginning to look out of place, a young unmarried woman like you,
having no job to go to on a Monday morning on Main Street.
But you're afraid to get up, afraid your body will reveal how
like a shuttlecock it's been tossed between two women, both of
them Sandy. You now notice, with a combination of relief and
panic, that Sandy's friend has gotten up to leave. That leaves
you and her alone (at least from your point of view). Now
would be the moment, the sweet and catastrophic moment to
say . . . to say . . . Instantly you destroy your impulse by a
rescuing gesture of absurdity . . . to say: *Mother come home.
All is forgiven.* Love, Marie.

Fortunately for you Sandy has decided it's time to hurry on
to her appointment. For a few moments you're too weak to move,
you'll have to let her leave without you. But a faint grind of
electricity from the B R E A D clock reminds you that if you
lose sight of her now you won't see her again till she goes back
to work; and there you will be able to observe her only as she
measures the fabrics, snipping away at yards of muslin, corduroy
or denim like one of the Three Fates cutting away lives. So,
leaving some money on the counter, you hurry out to the opposite side of Main Street. Ah, there she is, going into the local
bank. So: she lives in the "real" world after all, complete with

savings, mortgages, escrows and overdrawn accounts. You follow her inside. The bank is surprisingly crowded for such a small town and there're only two windows open for service. It's obvious that people are just as busy with banks in Main Street as everywhere in America . . . and what's this? Sandy is buying a U.S. Savings Bond for someone's birthday, for the grandson whose neglect she was protesting at the drug store.

You now get into a parallel line, ostensibly to cash a traveler's check and to get some small change for the parking meter. While waiting in line your mind wanders: waiting is for you (and for Sandy) one of the more draining rituals in our still unpredictable technology. It was to avoid Waiting that Sandy got on that train to the army base in Carolina (S.). You glance down at the modest hemline which presently hides her legs, and you contrast it with her appearance on that train in August of 1944. She is going to meet Jules, where she will sit in the sweltering heat (there is no air conditioning) for twenty-eight hours, the perspiration trickling down her back, while the train crawls along with its fantastic overload of servicemen (by this time next year the lists will be in the thousands who will never return).

It is the first train Sandy could get to—as the blue carbon share of her ticket assures her—CAROLINA (S.). There are no seats. All night long Sandy and about six other people sit on the suitcases piled between the cars, guarding their feet as the coupled trains grind again and again to a halt. At these stops a few teenagers called Soldiers climb down, their duffle bags on their shoulders. Always they have this dazed look, as if they do not recognize the town they have come to visit.

Eventually Sandy's train does arrive in Carolina S., late in the afternoon. She is faint with sleeplessness and from the shock of the heat, which is something she has never experienced on Main Street. Jules cannot get away in time to meet her, so there she stands, feeling exhausted and lightheaded but also enjoying an odd excitement at the sight of a mule standing at the train station, its cart loaded with bales of hay. It stands patiently, only its ears flick in protest whenever there's a whoosh of steam from the locomotive (no diesel on this ancient train, though we are only a year away from Hiroshima).

Sandy takes a cab to the hotel Jules has instructed her to go to. She showers and changes her clothes, but she is too restless either to sleep or read (there is no radio in her room), so she goes out to the street. In spite of her fatigue and her awe at the sun which glowers down like some wrathful Jehovah making good His threat of destruction by fire, she strolls down their Main Street which is only a few blocks from the hotel. She is filled with a romantic curiosity about the town, which is exciting to her because Jules "lives" there. She presently notices a line of black people, extending all the way around the corner: they are waiting at the Colored entrance to see a film with Cary Grant. At the front of the movie house there is another ticket taker, sitting idly, waiting for the First Show to begin.

Sandy does not wish to wander far from the hotel: what if Jules should arrive early and not find her? She begins—somewhat reluctantly, as she is enjoying her first stroll in a Southern town—to trace her steps. She is rewarded for her small sacrifice, because as the hotel comes again into view she sees Jules standing outside, obviously looking up and down the street for a slender girl with bare legs and honey-colored hair. They are at once in each other's arms: through the khaki shirt Sandy can feel the warm sweat of Jules' body.

The bank teller now holds the U.S. Savings Bond tentatively above her typewriter and asks Sandy, "Who •should I make it out to?" Sandy replies, "Make it out to Jules B. Roche II."

Jules? You can scarcely believe the effrontery of it. What a cunning hypocrite, to name her firstborn son for her lover— to have this perpetual reminder of her love which is at the same time *her fault, her fault, her most grievous fault.* . . . She has managed, apparently, to repress the memory of how she tried to destroy everyone and everything associated with Jules Blaine. How in late March of 1945 she rode out to the Armbruster farm, which is about four miles south of Main Street: that is as far as the municipal bus line will go.

March 1945

The bus driver looks at Sandy oddly as she descends—a girl of eighteen, with no shopping bags, no suitcase, no boots or scarf or gloves, nor (he glances down) stockings. And it is snowing, sleeting; a bruising March wind whips about the pools of water left by the boots of previous passengers standing at the driver's change box. He looks again, confirming his first impression: the girl steps down one step at a time, bearing the heavy weight of her curving belly against herself as she grips the edge of the doorway, she makes her way clumsily out of the bus: the driver peers out the window on his side to see where she might be going. He sees only a weathered cowshed for somebody who may have a dairy animal or two and a water pump nobody uses any more. The old Armbruster farmhouse is still in use, though he does not presently see any smoke from their chimney: he has the impression that the Armbrusters are away visiting folks in Canada.

The driver watches while the girl whose honey-colored hair seems to be darkening as it becomes wet with sleet, makes her way to the farmhouse as if she knows where she's going and why. Certainly she must know the Armbrusters: she has a key and opens the front door easily. The driver is tempted to shrug away the incident, but the curve of the belly haunts him all the way back to the garage where he places a tentative call to the police. Not wanting to be nosy or cruel, "but not everyone who *looks* like a nut is crazy," he apologizes.

In the farmhouse Sandy does not bother to light a lamp or turn on the heat. Instead she goes methodically to the linen closet where she knows she will find all the sheets, dishtowels, bath towels and facecloths (she has been here many times, baby-sitting for the Armbrusters), and begins very expertly to lay the bath towels across the window sills, blocking out the air. She even admires the colorful towels, their creamy texture, towels which the Armbrusters received as a wedding present and which have lasted a decade: now they're soft and flannel-like, suited for swaddling bands . . . Every window plugged, Sandy now lays the folded sheets at the base of the doors, sealing up all drafts: the sheets are very white and glint in the semi-darkness like the eyes of animals. She is beginning to feel cold and at the same time somewhat feverish: yet it is not boring, this final domestic chore, there is even a tidiness about it: she opens the gas jets neatly so that their tiny porcelain arms all extend parallel to one another. Then she goes to a rocking chair where almost at once she achieves a slow rhythmical rock; the wood creaks slightly, gradually shading to a hum like a lullabye, to which she falls quietly asleep. . . . When the screaming sirens stop in front of the farmhouse and the firemen smash the windows Sandy is sleeping soundly, her body soft, yielding to unconsciousness. At once she is carried out, given oxygen.

Well: she has made an attempt to get rid of you, Marie, and of herself too. But it's useless. After that fiasco, you grow and grow visibly, invincibly, for good or evil—until at last God repents of his wrath and washes you out with her blood.

You're glad you don't remember the trauma of your birth. It's bad enough reliving her trauma at the Home for Unwed Mothers. There's no such place on Main Street, they don't have unwed mothers on Main Street, so to spare Sandy the pain of neighborly curiosity, Sandy is shipped off to a benevolent institution in Philadelphia, where two months after her failure at the Armbruster farm, you, Marie, are born. Once in a sociology class you took part in a panel, along with three other undergraduates on "The Unwed Mother." Eventually all four of you decided it would be an excellent idea to visit the local hospital, where you taped intervews with the women there, who made surprisingly fierce statements about the right to keep their child.

Sandy's opinion on this subject, however, is not being asked. Instead, now that she has carried "full term," she has been lying all night covered by a coarse army blanket, her hands on her belly, her eyes closed. She is praying, praying, praying. For this ordeal to be over. For the wisdom and the strength to know what to do. For some word from Jules who is hidden away somewhere in Iwo Jima, hidden so well that he will never be found except by Japanese children looking for relics of the victorious invading army.

Finally a nun enters the room; it is dawn; she pulls the curtains apart, and smiles at Sandy. Impossible to know whether her cruelty is intentional when she says what she says to all her girls every morning, "And how are you feeling today?"

At last you have gotten through the line: it has taken, it seems to you, an incredibly long time. But this is a small town; what would have been a quick and businesslike affair in any other place is here a social event. You clutch your change, pocket the money from your traveler's check and move slowly toward the door.

"Put his father's name on it too, please," says Sandy. "Jules A. Roche. I mean, not his mother's name. His mother—"

"Yes, I know . . . " the teller says sadly. "It nearly broke my heart to hear it. Like your son got to be a father and a widower both at once. Like God didn't know which way to treat him, hardly."

Sandy bows her head, pulls out a handkerchief which she doesn't need but uses to conceal her pain at hearing her life counted out by the teller like so much small change.

The teller goes to type up the U.S. Bond while you loiter nearby, looking over some information about how the government is now insuring your savings up to $40,000.

Sandy now puts her grandson's gift into her handbag: you hear that he is six, going on seven, and the teller adds: "Well, you tell him 'Happy Birthday' for me, will you?" Sandy is perceptibly happier now that her list of woes, like the plagues of Egypt, have been named and numbered and she is momentarily free to forget them, including the one she will never forget and cannot share with anyone—not with the teller, nor with her husband, nor with her sons, nor with anybody but you, Marie. Who now share her sorrow as she leaves by the electronic door.

Outdoors she stands again in the August sun, squinting at the clock which is suitably cloistered in a church steeple. She feels the need to move quickly now, as the moment she has been planning for has arrived, and she must hurry to meet it. Ah . . . you see at once to whom she is hurrying. It is Jules B.

Roche II, descending now from a bus, holding a sheet of paper on which you can see as he waves it at her whorled circles of dark blue fingerpaint. "It's a storm! A storm!" he informs her. Diffident, anxious to assure the artist that his success is clear and striking, she says simply, "Oh what a beautiful painting!"

You now apprehend that for Sandy love is always terminal, always something for her life to be lost in . . . Overcome by her failure to express her perfect admiration for his painting, she swoops down, capsizes the artist in her arms, covers him with kisses. "Did you have a nice day?" she asks at last: respectfully.

Your knees are weak as you lean against the freshly painted red, white and blue fire hydrant. Your impulse is to run toward them crying out, *me too! me too!* You can now taste your own long denial; you want to run and tell her all about your thirty-one years without her and have her cry out with absolving certainty: *Oh what a beautiful daughter you are!* have her insist with incontrovertible passion: *Oh what a beautiful life you have!* Which will give you the courage to go on, to go back into the ugliness of your century where life begins with television commercials and ends with nursing homes. But, as they pass you, Jules is trying to guess what they will do together to celebrate his birthday and Sandy is laughing. *Laughing.* It is the first time in all your imagined scripts that you have heard her laugh and it is real laughter, not something you have projected onto invented memories. Hearing it now for the first time, you lean weakly against the fire hydrant, standing aside to let them pass.

Stephen Wunrow

Nuclear Madness

51—62

On Nuclear Power

George Wald

George Wald is Higgins Professor of Biology Emeritus, Harvard University, Cambridge, Ma. Nobel Laureate in Physiology or Medicine, 1967.

Nuclear power is life-threatening in all its forms—not only all its present forms, but all future developments that are contemplated. It represents a development that can't be tamed, a wrong turn in human history. Expensive as it would be to shut down the 70 nuclear plants now licensed in the US, in the long run it will prove more expensive to keep them going, and not just in money or convenience, but in the lives and health of this and future generations.

As long as they continue operating they will present dangers of malfunction and accident, and will continue to accumulate radioactive wastes that no one knows how to dispose of safely and that will remain dangerous for tens of thousands of years. Add that the longer those plants run the harder they themselves will be to dispose of: the neutron flow in the course of operation eventually turns the entire structure radioactive. The most prudent and responsible procedure would be to shut them down now. Business and government are doing all they can to gloss over this reality, but that's the way it is.

June 3 is anti-nuke day all over the developed world. The only effective grass-roots politics now operating in the developed world is the anti-nuclear movement. During the past months I have been over much of the world, and everywhere I go, there is the anti-nuclear movement. All over Europe, Japan, Australia, the graffiti on the walls are anti-nuclear. I have asked myself in all those places, what are these people trying to say? I think they are always trying to say the same thing: "THIS COUNTRY IS OUR HOME—NOT YOUR BUSINESS. A home for us to live in, not for you to exploit and degrade for profit."

The Australians have the slogan, "KEEP THE URANIUM IN THE GROUND," and after long and careful thought I believe that is the only proper place for it.

Nuclear power is life-threatening not only through the probability of accident; but also through the production as by-product of plutonium 239, at once perhaps the most toxic substance known and the most convenient material from which to make atom bombs; and through the production of radioactive wastes.

It is less well known that *nuclear power is an economic disaster.*

We are often told that nuclear power costs about as much as coal-firing and about one-half as much as oil firing. Such estimates reckon only the costs of construction and operation. To them must be added a long series of major costs unique to nuclear power. One doesn't talk about them much, for the entire game now is to unload all those costs on the taxpayer. Congress is now doing that, bill after bill.

What are those hidden costs?

First, the tailings, the highly radioactive residues from uranium mining. The old AEC committed the strange blunder of letting them be used as land fill and in building foundations. Hence sections of Denver, Salt Lake City, and Grand Junction and Durango, Col. are highly radioactive. This material is to be removed or buried, at taxpayers' expense.

Second, enrichment of the uranium ore, all done by the "government"— i.e., the taxpayers—and sold to power companies at bargain prices.

Third, since the American insurance companies refused from the beginning to insure nuclear power plants, the Price-Anderson Act lays the bulk of the liability in the event of accident on — the taxpayers.

Fourth, policing. Every step in moving radioactive material or storing it and in the operation of nuclear plants requires special policing. An industry statement has said that proper security "could run into billions" (UPI, Oct. 19, 1977). And the Barton Report commissioned by the NRC in 1975 pointed out that we cannot expect to maintain our present civil liberties along with widespread nuclear power.

Fifth, reprocessing, recovering uranium and plutonium from the spent fuel rods. There is no commercial reprocessing going on in the US; all of it is done by "the government" under private contract.

Sixth, the disposal of nuclear wastes. Up to the present they have mainly been stored where produced; but by now 11 power plants are threatened with shutdowns because of lack of further storage space. "The government" has taken over this problem, and now plans—at taxpayers' expense—to start a shell game of moving them about to temporary repositories while hoping to achieve some permanent solution, which, judging from suggested schemes, is likely to be fantastically expensive.

And last, what happens when a nuclear power plant has run its course? The rated life is 30 to 40 years; and then what? The most favored plan now is to bury the entire plant, the entire structure of which is by then radioactive, under a mountain of earth, at a cost of $300 to $500 million, and then stand guard over it for 100 years. Why 100 years? Why not 500 or one thousand years? The US now possesses the oldest continuous government on the Earth; and we have just celebrated its 200th anniversary. Where can one hope to find the political or geological stability this situation demands?

It is in part for these reasons that the business of building nuclear power plants has gone under. At its peak in 1973, 41 new reactors were ordered in this country; then in 1974, 23; in 1975, 4; in 1976, 3; in 1977, 4; and in 1978, 2 (*Wall St. Journal*, Feb. 7, 1979).

It is in fact a dead industry, kept alive only by tube feeding and artificial respiration. The irony is that we who would like to pull the plug have to pay the bill.

Accident At Three Mile Island

" . . . how everything turns away/Quite leisurely . . . "
—W. H. Auden

JIM BARNES

The island steams under the opening sky.
All around the narrow length of land
the river flows as it always has, and late

birds heading north to Canada notice
nothing unusual about the air.
There may, or may not, have been a disaster

among the undergrowth: what birds may tell
is augured late at best, and fish homing
upstream are mainly interested in falls.

Who knows? At any rate the land was calm.
Nothing surprised farmers off their tractors
or knocked the rheumy cattle off their hoofs,

though something surely must disappear every
time the earth shakes or the sky moves an inch
or two to right or left. Still there will always

be a boy fishing from some river bank
who doesn't especially want anything to happen
except summer and a dog scratching at his side.

Psalm: People Power at the Die-in

(The anti-nuclear die-in,
Washington, D.C., and the
official shutdown of the
Seabrook Plant, June 1978)

DENISE LEVERTOV

Over our scattered tents by night
lightning and thunder called to us.

Fierce rain blessed us,
catholic, all-encompassing.

We walked through blazing morning
into the city of law,

of corrupt order, of invested power.

By day and by night
we sat in the dust,

on the cement pavement we sat down and sang.

In the noon of a long day, sharing the work of the play,
we died together, enacting

the death by which all
shall perish unless we act.

*　　*　　*

Solitaries drew close, releasing
each solitude into its blossoming.

We gave to each other the roses
of our communion —

A culture of gardens, horticulture not agribusiness,
arbors among the lettuce, small terrains.

*　　*　　*

When we tasted the small, ephemeral
harvest of our striving,

great power flowed from us,
luminous, a promise. Yes! . . .

great energy flowed from solitude,
and great power from communion.

Extreme Unction In Pa.

DAVID RAY

No, not the last *Last Supper*, and yet
for the sake of the world I mumbled all
the holy poems I knew. They too
were dying. Outside the silver diner
rain fell and fell, and from the South
came wind that bore the glowing mask,
danced the silly saffron masque of hell.
And though I dreaded walking out,
inhaling tiny drifts from Satan's mills
that stood upon the earth like pots
of clay, turned on a loving wheel,
I'd try to tip my hat to the waitress
to keep her calm. *Go down gentle,*
I hoped to say, stay still upon your stools,
all you chubby drivers, innocent and hungry,
and feathered ladies on some worldly journey.
The sky went dark. Trees were trembling.
We had our share of cobalt blue,
but heavy lead had followed, and iodine
like that blind Homer kicked upon the shore, seaweed.

Newspaper Hats

Jim Howard

They are no substitutes for gas masks
Or lead helmets. But you can shape them
any way you want yourself. Here is one:

the Bishop's hat, and maybe if you make up
a prayer in your head, this one will funnel it up
and save something. Fold this here

and back over, tuck it in: the soldier's dress cap.
The headlines might rub off in your hair,
but that would be part of the job. Unfolding,

back to the original triangle hat—when the sun
blasts through what was an atmosphere, the brim
could provide a brief shade. I had a friend

who taught me these. He lives two states west now,
under the shadow of a mountain on giant shock absorbers,
a hollowed-out mountain no one climbs. Uniforms

with men in them go about their business there,
driving dark trucks over fluorescent streets
underground. Their families pass the food

and talk sometimes at dinner. The way they look
at each other is a story. I sit tonight,
give instructions to no one but the room,

and make newspaper hats for those people, for a friend
I had, for myself. And I try them on, hoping to see
how we wear the things that happen in the world.

Poem To The Sun

MORTY SKLAR

You want to sit here and write a poem,
here in Rossi's Cafe on Gilbert,
main drag trucks early a.m.
across from end of March puddle empty lots
across from sun

You want to sit across from empty puddle lots,
sun hop skip and jump from
rooftop shingle to puddle to semi windshield
shatter, in the dust diffused in window,
home fries eggs sunnyside grease air in Rossi's,
ninety-three million miles

    beamed down, twenty-five feet from a
puddle, a puddle, ye gads, ninety-three
million miles to a puddle, no, not yet
O Great Starship, don't beam me
back

    . . . the snow
has just melted here,
light spreading like a cosmic *good* virus,
glinting off auburn coffee, splashed on
the floor tossed around in mop
with radio wave mix from shelf
transistor

    . . . You want to sit here,
a living crystal receiver, here,
goddamn,
    40 billion trillion miles from nowhere,

next to a puddle,
next to the sun.

Rose Bay Willow Herb

Judy Ray

The willow herb, the
rose bay willow herb,
sweeps woods and commons
with pink sunset stripes.
It rises from black
aftermath of fire
that crackled through thick
undergrowth of trees.
Even after war
it flourishes in
empty lots, in bomb
craters, and like a
phoenix of flora
rises tall and wild,
true fireweed, indeed.
Should the air it spikes,
water it drinks, ash
it grows from become
radioactive,
the invisible
aftermath of a
great folly, perhaps
the willow herb, the
rose bay willow herb,
will still grow wild with
pink sunset stripes and
bloom abundantly.
But who will there be
of our coughing, skin-
flaking, misshapen
kind to perceive a
symbol of hope? And
perhaps the only
phoenix to arise

from that blind folly
will be some tiny
flung molecule of
untainted earth with
no memory of
tall willow herb, wild
rose bay willow herb.

The Plumber Arrives At Three Mile Island

ROBERT STEWART

A plumber's price is high because he uses
equipment that can channel what diffuses—
since heavy duty's standard on some jobs,
and augers, threaders, clamps and come-alongs
can bring our flooded dreams another turn.
Unless a plumber has somewhere to stand
he'll wade right in among the toilet fish
and fumble with the break below the wastes,
among those places we will not admit,
where all our bright ideas turn to shit.
But now the whole trade's dirty—used to be
just septic tanks and sewers; it used to be
a plumber always had a place to wash
when he was through to tally up the costs.

Nuclear Land

ELLEN TIFFT

Salvador Dali almost foresaw it.
In his pictures ghostly part-buildings stand
the way alleys made the backdrop
for the stage of Diocletian's palace.
Now, even these are ruled completely flat.

The condition is global.
Nearly half a world away
a bent blind man with twigs on his back,
hoping to arrive in time for trumpets announcing
twilight of his Himalayan village,
finds his mountain gone.

For all of us the hill, the mountain to
which we could turn, is gone.
Even the mind's inner landscape
is sealed off. There is no quay
no caique with taut sail,
not even an underworld ferry.

We see it. It is not a dream or sci fi.
Numbness or guilt keeps us from acting, voting
against nuclear power. The global
nightmare compounds as once in Germany.

Can't we change directions, walk back
to the original mother-father sun, for God's
sake and our own can't we?
Or *is* the above to be our planet?

According To Latest Reports

GEOF HEWITT

Anyone who saw a picture of the bomb's mushroom
took radiation through the eye, perhaps a lethal dose
so the next generation wears two broken yokes
floating in a pan of blood for eyes.

And the family twitch returns
like a runaway daughter
with her issue, linked like chain
to lies that drive their brains on fire.

So fallout and the thunder blend
like dandruff on the expert's shoulder.
His voice is heavy water steaming through
the flames and curing those red eggs.

I Am Dreaming

DAVID IGNATOW

I am dreaming of the funeral of the world, watching it go by
carried in an urn, reduced to ashes, and followed by a horde
of mourners, a million abreast, across the broadest lands and
all chanting together, "We are dead, we have killed ourselves.
We are beyond rescue. What you see is not us but your thoughts
of us," and I who am observing in terror of it being real hope
not to have to wake up so as to let myself discount it as a
dream.

Hiroshima's Nails

BROWN MILLER

I wish I could drop these nails
back where they came from
all the way back in time
where they held houses together

I want to know how many nails
were melted   the specific number
might let me rest   or numb me

I want to compute how many blows
accomplished the inevitable
driving of metal into
departing substance

though it would be wiser
to count the heartbeats quickened
by each strike of dead precision

these nails help me come to
they put me through a hoop
of occult therapy   making me
small enough to fit inside the

sparks flung from impact of hammers
against nails against time
diminishing me in the
angular   cry of   friction

WHERE THE DEER LIVE · WANG WEI

In These Quiet Mountains Far From Men ·
One Hears Only Faint Sound Of Human Voice ·
The Late Afternoon Sunrays :
Filtering Through The Deep Woods :
Cast Long Shadows On The Green Moss ·

Wang Hui-Ming

Wang Hui-Ming

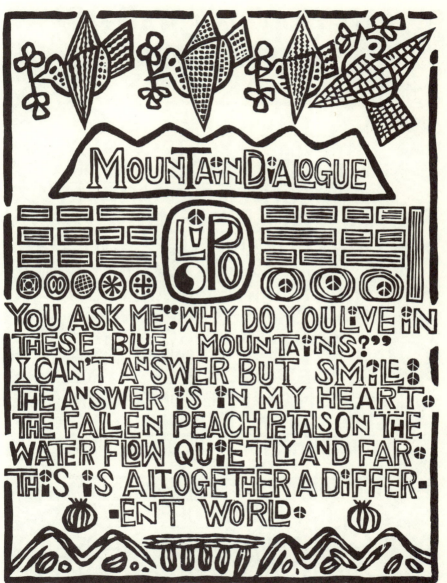

MOUNTAIN DIALOGUE

LI PO

YOU ASK ME: "WHY DO YOU LIVE IN
THESE BLUE MOUNTAINS?"
I CAN'T ANSWER BUT SMILE:
THE ANSWER IS IN MY HEART.
THE FALLEN PEACH PETALS ON THE
WATER FLOW QUIETLY AND FAR.
THIS IS ALTOGETHER A DIFFER-
-ENT WORLD.

Wang Hui-Ming

REPLY TO CHANG SHAO-FU·THE KEEPER OF ARCHIVES

WANG WEI

IN MY EVENING YEARS · I ENJOY
NOTHING BETTER THAN DOING NOTHING.
THE WORLD'S MULTITUDINOUS AFFAIRS
ARE NO CONCERN OF MINE ·
I HAVE NO PLANS IN LIFE · NO
DESIGNS FOR LIVING ·
MY MIND IS SWEPT CLEAN OF ALL BURDENS ·
I HAVE RETURNED TO THE WOOD-
LANDS I KNOW SO WELL ·
A GENTLE BREEZE FLOWING THROUGH
THE PINE TREES CARESSES MY ROBE
AND THE MOON ABOVE THE MOUNTAIN
SHINES ON MY ZITHER WHILE I PLAY ·
YOU ASK ME: WHAT IS THE TRUE MEANING
OF LIFE?
THE SOUND OF FISHERMEN SINGING
INVADES THE DEEP COVE

Wang Hui-Ming

A Wandering Monk

BILGE KARASU

(Translated from the Turkish by Fred Stark)

At the beginning, mid-point, and end of all, one image: that man wearing his˙ animal. All things mass about this image, here all things order, breathe life, uncoil and go.

The image: an *abdal* from medieval times, a wandering monk wrapped in his mantle. His eyes are lost beneath a kind of high cloth helmet, which, having shed through decades of wear its original abstraction, has ended by taking the shape of his head. His bare feet huge and purple, he is shrunken by the cold down to a hunch and a sash; and he must have decided that when dark follows these blinding needles of sun he won't be able to sleep in the open, for he forges toward the *han* that looms like slumped camels at the base of a far hill. If he can reach there, even as night is falling, and find a nook to huddle in at the foot of some wall, it will do.

At sun's decline this monk will not have reached the *han* gates. The dust from his weary-dragging feet rises now waist high. He is the only traveler on this road, which kicks up dust only where he is walking. Now and then he seems to start or shudder. The steppe is cold with evening, and all day his guts have not had one speck of bread. But only he knows that what makes him shudder is not the cold, and what makes him clench is not the cramp of hunger. No one could guess the piercing, ripping pain as teeth and claws tear the mantle, then bite through the skin to his flesh. For no one has seen yet that he carries in the folds of his sash that animal, pinkish-furred, half jerboa half mongoose, whose teeth are those of a rodent, and whose paws are a carnivore's. For years now he has carried this animal, which once when he was young and asleep in some hollow rock on a mountain had crawled into his sash and settled there. Beating had not driven it away, running had not left it behind, nor had he had the heart to kill it. It could hardly be said they share their food — the animal has so far partaken of just one in three morsels. And it attacks him only when, as now, it grows famished. The monk is so used to living with this animal that he no longer feels any surprise even at its immortality.

This evening, besides shelter, he must find a bit of bread. Having walked for days across the steppe, he is left without a single crumb in his scrip.

Now those who will spend the night at the *han* belong to a different age. Travelling together, a noisy, carefree crowd of men, they have come over the steppe to this deserted lodging — which knows no other mount than the camel — on low-slung, wind-speed, metal-plated steeds. After herding these into the courtyard, they have taken up whatever space the *han* affords. They are probably tired, for they have all eaten from their sacks and flopped down to sleep. The gates when the monk reaches them will have been shut, and darkness fallen, long since. In his time, gates once shut do not open before daybreak. But the sleepers inside live in an age when not opening the gates to let someone out — letting someone in is still, let us say, a different matter — has become incomprehensible.

The monk is before the gates, but outside in the cold. The last thing he saw before darkness closed in was this: the *han*, which since morning had seemed to his long gaze to lie up against the hill, is in fact a good way from it, exposed on all sides. So it offers no shelter, because there is no breeze either, only the downward-bearing, dry, withering cold, all around. He may choose to pace in front of those gates or not. They won't open. The claws rend his flesh, before long will be in at his bowels. He has to feed the animal, or else it makes no difference if he beats it, kicks it, throws it away by the scruff — anything. He's been trying for years and it's no use.

He's hunching up into one of the high honeycombed recesses that rise in stone on either side of the gate.

Inside, they've all lain down on the wooden benches, which

look much like tables. Sleeping, they have nothing under them. Their covers, fished from those metal-plated steeds, resemble blankets, some of them, others not. One of the benches is vacant, but a rumpled blanket lies at the foot. Whoever was there couldn't sleep, it seems, and is up wandering in the dark.

First he moved among the sleepers, then out in the court-yard to have a look at the sentries. At a guess he's young, his hair still free of gray, no sag to his shoulders, and he walks erect. But considering that he hasn't been able to sleep, he must have left his youth some way behind.

He's the one who saw, at red evening, how all alone the monk raised dust on that deserted road. When the gates of the *han* were shutting, he's the one who told the *han* master he had seen someone coming up the road not long before, who asked that the shutting of the gates be delayed for just a while. But the *han* master too lives in the monk's time. His orders are to have the gates shut before the sun sinks below the horizon. There is nothing he can do.

The risen sleeper is looking for a way to let in the monk, who must by now have reached the gates. That's why he *is* checking on the sentries.

To let in the monk would require finding the gap which years and centuries later will open in the *han* wall. At present the only worn spot is the inner corner of one leg of an arch that maintains the tower in the center of the courtyard.

He wanders about, keeping to the walls and under arches, not to be seen by the sentries. In the end he finds what he wants.

By ranging walls solid-seeming as a fortress. For some reason the earth has fallen away, though only slightly, at a point where the main body of the *han* meets the inner courtyard. There, one stone is all-but-imperceptibly out of place, but it will take centuries for a gap to open. Since coming to the *han*, on its boundless steppe between mountains, since taking, together with his companions, his first step through the gate, this man has been caught in the same time as the monk outside — who must, like himself, be shivering with the cold.

But suddenly — amazed — he'll see a man-sized gap open

inward, and the person in monk's garb slip into the courtyard, voicing a whisper that seems to come from beneath many layers of dust.

That whisper: to understand it will mean a job of intricate analysis, like decoding an ancient text. As the silent strides of the monk carry him almost to where the sleepers are, the man running to catch up will labor at the same time to comprehend his words, formulating something like, "The walls seemed hale, but circling them I found a newly-opened breach. It wasn't there my first time around — as though it appeared later." And now, for this reason, he offers praise to God.

Reaching the monk, the man finds him looking about, searching. He must be hungry, he thinks, and runs to his bench, at the head of which is a sack. From this he takes cheese- and meat-stuffed bread in transparent wrappers. He brings and offers them.

The monk, instead of holding the bread to his mouth, held it to his sash. Out from the dusty layers of cloth poked a muzzle flanked by two paws. The rest of the animal stayed hidden, but between paws and muzzle the bread gradually disappeared.

He watches in sheer amazement. The monk is silent, eyes fixed on the feeding animal. It drew back, full no doubt, into the folds of the sash, letting a small morsel of bread fall to the ground. This the monk, bending, picks up, blows on respectfully, and puts into his mouth. The man hands him some more bread, which is silently taken. Sitting on the wall-length stone block which forms a bench, munching slowly and laboriously, the monk begins to eat. There must not be a single tooth in his gums.

The sleepers snore in swelling, dying volume. Is that then how the winds blow here? The monk chews, the man watches.

Then he found the moonlight too dim. Returning through the archway to where the others were, he went to the bench and took a torch from his bag. He came back to the monk, lighting his own way and striding surely.

In the yellow light of the torch he began to sketch the bread-chewing monk. With his hands, in the air. Looking at his subject, he was sketching in the air with hands and fingers. The picture was slowly taking shape, while the monk behind it gradually went flat.

The man must have thought his picture complete, for he lowered the torch which had been clipped between his knees, held the completely flattened monk as if to frame him, and laid him on the ground. He thought for a moment, in the planing beam of the torch, where he might sign, then took something like a skewer-length etching tool from his pocket. He pressed it to the monk's flank and began signing. Then something utterly unexpected: he had not even finished signing when the monk opened his toothless mouth — but without rising, almost without moving — and began to heave ear-rending coughs. The man drew his tool away from the monk's flank, but the coughing didn't stop. It turned to vomiting. First cuds of bread spewed out around the monk's face onto the ground. Then he vomited blood, black clots, and his lungs in blood-black bits.

Terrified, the man fled. But he didn't forget to grab his torch as he was going. Hurling himself onto his bench, he pulled the blanket up to cover his face. When the roar inside him died down somewhat he was able to listen to the outside again. The coughing was gone, the retching came less often. Then that stopped too. A short while later footsteps seemed to approach. Inside the man a childish fear, huddled and blotted out all these years, reared its head again. "What if the master comes and sees my signature there. He'll blame me . . . " The men, or rather the footsteps, drew nearer. Night watch. The man went silent within. Outside it was quiet too. There was no accounting for what had happened. He could almost believe it had been a dream.

But suddenly something sharp hooked into his leg and started moving up. He knew without looking what it was. Taking the animal's throat in both hands he began to squeeze, and squeeze, and bellow. Hurried trampling of the sleepers. *Han* master rushing up with the night watch. They tore the animal off his hip. Blood could be seen oozing through rents in his clothing. Past the arch they went, he following them all, till out where stone benches lined the walls he saw on the ground in the light of their lanterns and flaming torches — nothing. To drag the animal off him they had run a rope round its neck. It now hung swinging at the end. In the courtyard, someone whirled the animal around his head and flung it, like a rock from a sling, away. Over the wall it flew, with the rope on its neck, and out of sight. The *han* master sent everyone back to bed.

When his companions set out the next morning the man stayed behind. They tried hard to persuade him, but he wouldn't budge. He told them he could not step out of the *han* yet. After travelling a good deal in the area, they were to return to a town not very far away. They agreed on a meeting with him there in five days, and left.

He stayed four days and four nights. On the morning of the fifth day he climbed his metal-plated steed, said farewell to all, and rode out through the gate. He planned to reach the town where he would join his friends by noon.

Out the gate and around the corner toward the road. But something flew out of a rock and struck to his lap like lightning. He didn't have a chance to cry out, the animal had already snuggled into his pocket. But this time without hurting him. They turned onto the road. His mind constantly on the claws that might reach out of the pocket and tear his midriff or sides, he reached the town toward twelve o'clock. Nothing happened. Something was there in the pocket of his flimsy summer jacket, like a wadded handkerchief. When he joined his friends no one noticed the animal there. He had decided to succeed where the monk had failed. The moment he felt those claws in him his hand would dive in to bring out the animal, and he would strangle it there in front of his friends. Sore at him that night — the night he had cried out — for being woken up, they had given him a hard time. Then when he hadn't wanted to leave the *han* they had put it down to shaky nerves and simply kidded him. Now they could watch him squeeze the life out of this animal. If it wouldn't die then he'd cut its throat or crack open its skull with a rock.

He was waiting. Only towards evening of that day did it dawn on him that there was no need waiting for the animal to hurt him before choking or smashing it. He was crazy to act as though it would ride forever in his pocket. Though unaware of why or how long the monk had carried this animal, still he had supposed it to be all the monk's lifetime. He was acting as though he supposed that.

They were eating. There was a big knife there on the table all ready. He put his hand in his pocket and with no effort drew out the animal. As he laid it on the table and, seizing the knife, made to cut its throat, his friends shouted, yelled at him, pinned his arms. They'd have him locked up, they said. Had he gone insane? Instead of going and killing it, why didn't he feed the poor thing? Since he did carry it around in his pocket.

They dragged him up by the armpits and put him to bed.

That night when all was still the animal, which had slipped away in the confusion, found the man's bed, clawed open his belly, tore up his bowels, gnawed at him, broke off pieces. That's how they found him the next morning. A blood track could be made out till half-way down the stairs, at which point the paws must have dried.

They buried their friend. Everything had been spoiled, and they decided to go back to their own city. They climbed their metal steeds. After a few hours they saw in the middle of the road a man dressed like a wandering medieval monk, in the corners of their eyes as they hurtled past. The monk-garbed man was walking swiftly, but seeing a cloud of dust roll toward him he lunged off the road. He watched the creatures go past at lightning speed, shook his head thoroughly, rubbed his eyes, and looked to see again. But there was nothing. Only, far in the distance, a slowly-dispersing cloud of dust.

But there was no time to linger, or he'd never make it to the *han* before the gates shut. He hastened forward, then put his hand in the folds of his sash. The warm, furry back seemed to him once again the surest proof that things were real.

At the Photographer

AYSE SARPER

Seconds of a smile
Stiffened for the camera
With someone else's child on my lap
And I remember
The wheat fields . . .
Last summer
When my eyes lingered on the nearest stalk
As it swayed with the ocean
With its seeds on the lap of foreign soil
Growing with its windblown lot
Doing its work
As I do mine
My seeds cast in another room, another house.

As the wheat knows the cry of the wind and bends
So do I
Except for this moment
With this frozen smile
I cannot bend.

So Help Me God

IFEANYI MENKITI

There are pioneer souls that blaze a trail
            where highways never ran . . .
And there are souls like stars that glow and burst
            'midst a martini firmament;
But let me live in my house by the side of the road
            and eat my salami in peace.

Early Losses: a Requiem

ALICE WALKER

Part I

Nyanu was appointed
as my Lord. The husband chosen
by the elders
before my birth.
He sipped wine with
my father
and when I was born
brought a parrot as
his gift
to play with me.
Paid baskets of grain
and sweet berries
to make me fat
for his pleasure.

Omunu was my play-mate
who helped consume
Nyanu's gifts.
Our fat selves grew
together
knee and knee.
It was Omunu I wished
to share my tiny
playing house.
Him I loved as the sun
must seek and chase
its own reflection
across the sky.

My brothers, before you
turn away—

The day the savage men came
to ambush our village
it was Nyanu who struggled
bravely
Omunu ran and hid
behind his parents' house.
He was a coward but
only nine
as was I; who trembled
beside him as we two
were stolen away
Nyanu's dead body
begging remembrance
of his tiny morsel
taken from his mouth.
Nor was I joyful that he was dead
only glad that now I would not have
to marry him.

Omunu clasped my hands
within the barkcloth pouch
and I his head
or any handy thing.
Our cries pounded back
into our throats
by handless blows we
could not see
our mothers' cries
at such a distance
we could not hear
and over the miles
we feasted on home-sickness
our mothers' tears
scurrying lizards and
the dew
all we consumed of homeland
before we left.

At the Great Water Omunu fought
to stay with me
at such a tender age
our hearts we set
upon each other
as the retreating wave
brings its closest friend
upon its back.
We cried out in words
that met an echo
and Omunu vanished
down a hole that
smelled of blood and
feces and death
and I was "saved"
for sport among
the sailors of the crew.
Only nine, upon a ship. My hair
my body a mystery
that opened with each tearing
pull. Crying for Omunu
who was not seen
again by these eyes.

Listen to your sister, singing
in the field.
My body forced to receive
grain and wild berries
and milk so I could seem
strong
a likely wench
—my mother's child
sold for a price. My father's
child again for sale.
I prayed to all our Gods
"Come down to me."
Hoist the burden no child
was meant to bear

and decipher the prayer
from within each song
—the song despised—
my belly become a stronghold
for a stranger
who will not recall
when he is two
the contours of
his mother's face.
See the men turn back
my lips
and with hot irons
brand me neck and thigh.

I could not see the horizon
for the sky
a burning eye
the sun, beloved in the shade,
became an enemy
a pestle pounding yams
that was my head.
You walked with me.
And when day sagged into night
some one of you of my own
choice
shared my rest. Omunu
risen from the ocean
out of the stomachs of whales
the teeth of sharks
lying beside me sleeping
knee and knee.
We could not speak always
of hearts
for in the morning if they
sold you
how could I flatten
a wrinkled face?
The stupor of loss

made smooth the look
that to my tormentors
was born erased.
I mourned for you. And if you died
took out my heart upon my lap
and rested it.

See me old at thirty
my sack of cotton weighted
to the ground. My hair
enough to cover a marble
my teeth like rattles
made of chalk
my breath a whisper
of decay.
The slack of my belly
falling to my knees.
I shrink to become a tiny size
a delicate morsel
upon my mother's knee
prepared like bread. The shimmering
of the sun a noise
upon my head.
To the child that's left
I offer a sound
without a promise
a clue
of what it means.
The sound itself is all
I had no one could harm.
My flight
will cause no one
alarm.

**

A sound like a small wind
finding the door of a

hollow reed
my mother's farewell
glocked up from the back
of her throat
like the gasp of a
drowning infant;
the sound itself all
I have
to remember a mother
I scarcely knew.
Omunu to me; who never knew
what Omunu meant. Whether home
or man or trusted God. Omunu.
Her only treasure
she never spent.

Three Poems

ANDREW SALKEY

A Year Afterwards

[Written after the Chile Solidarity Campaign Committee's demonstration, in Trafalgar Square, on Sunday 15th, September, 1974, which commemorated the first anniversary of the loss of Unidad Popular in Chile, during the military coup in Santiago, on Tuesday 11th, September, 1973.]

I stand and watch the green shoots
strike through the thick concrete roof.
The rain falls and softens the pain.
Chile will change.

Look out for the northern machine!
Watch how it bursts spray after spray
of copper-plated handshakes, tentacles
laced with acid drops, graveyard promises;

and watch the disappearing land!
Remember the machine's assurance!
Remember the terrible pain!
Chile will change.

When things begin to move, again,
they'll ignore the upper and middle
branches of the avenue trees, rooted
deep in the passion of the past.

They'll take, instead, the broad groundswell
and make an earthquake of all Chile;
they'll haul the peaks of the Andes flat.
Chile will change.

A Recollection of Caribbea

Her place in the New World has been deliberately squeezed and sucked dry, corner small, unnoticed as rind-twists in afternoon sunlight. Cane has become trash, hardly worth a thing in the vast, reticulated market. Even her bauxite noise is diminished. Only her oil is capable of a splash in anybody's eye.

But her people remain her constellation of importance, her pool of special treasure, her continuing resource.

And among them, the unending disatisfactions of class and client-status. Hills remaining hills without a chance of becoming mountains which might offer security of tenure, one day, some day, soon.

And the local chicanery. And the foreign chicanery. And the times.

When the big make their moves, the small suffer the shock waves.

Mountains, Rivers, and Caribbea

(For Eliot and Jason)

1

Mountains make her feel like staying;
rivers, like going,
going far away,

breaking out of the shallows,
moving sighted,
no holding on to veranda rails,

just going,
simply heading out to sea,
going with no intention of returning,

no matter what she's leaving behind,
no picking up the pieces,
no same, old, new beginnings:

2

mountains and rivers,
those large, quiet, everyday presences
of stay and go, forces she looks at,

like things,
mere raised stones and streams
she leaps over, carelessly, any early morning.

Alba

H. L. VAN BRUNT

light   the cold distances
it travels from a star
to bend through slatted blinds
and take the tallest shadows
from the corners of the room

how it stripes the chests
of children   whose small mouths
smell of stale milk
whose hands like voyagers
of the substance and the breath
have swung around like boats
moored in a running tide
whose dreams lie condensed
in sweat above their lips

innocent of death
and of one another
they lie there more alive
today than any other

Stephen Wunrow

Garcia Lorca and Desire

ROBERT BLY

Garcia Lorca's poems often begin with a simple and clear line, then all at once some incredible idea appears, the feelings open in surprise, the walls we have put up to keep things in their places collapse, instincts pour in—it's as if an animal had written some of his poems—mandible feelings come, the jokes of children, the most fantastic delicacy, the longings of the monk for the pure moon, above all desire, desire, desire. What we could call desire-energy passes through Lorca's poems as if the lines were open arteries created for it. Ortega y Gasset said once: "Europe is suffering from a withering of the ability to wish." Americans are weak in that way. Everywhere we meet people, old and young, with jaws fallen to the ground, their lower legs buckling, who when you ask them if they want this or that, answer like a dead leaf. The word I love best in Lorca is "quiero," which appears again and again: "I love, I want":

> Green, how I love you, green!
> Green wind. Green branches.
> The ship on the sea
> and the horse on the mountain.

———

> I want the water to go on without its bed,
> and the wind to go on without its mountain passes

———

> I have shut my balcony door
> because I don't want to hear the crying

I want to sleep for half a second,
a second, a minute, a century,
but I want everyone to know that I'm still alive . . .

———

When I am on the roof
what a pure seraphim of fire I want to be and am!

Many poets write about the fear of death, or monetary sys-
tems, or anxiety, or the decline of faith, but all Lorca writes
about is what he loves, what he takes delight in, what he wants,
what he desires, what barren women desire, what gypsies desire,
what brothers and sisters desire . . .

The Spanish adore Lorca, though at the moment they prefer
Antonio Machado to Lorca, and I think it's linked to this. Machado
wanted much too, but he didn't get it. His desire-energy went
straight ahead into a stone wall, as the desire-energy of many of us
does. That is what happened also to the longings Spain had in the
Thirties. Machado ended up as a French teacher in one of the
poorest villages in Spain for years, a widower after three years
of marriage. The suffering brought about when desire-energy
cannot push through makes his poetry adult. His poetry involves
not only pleasure, but what Freud calls the reality principle. The
Spanish respect that. Lorca after all died when he was thirty-seven,
just as he was beginning to feel out to the limits of his desire-
energy, in his Ghazals and Casidas.

When Lorca was thirty, in 1929, he came to the United
States, and lived here for ten months or so, mostly in a room in
John Jay Hall at Columbia. Out of that visit came *The Poet in
New York*, which I think is still the greatest book ever written
about New York. His desire-energy is astonished when it arrives in New York. In Spain these desires were always able to
find a resonating box in the creatures and landscape immediately
around him. They could express themselves easily in images of
olive groves, wind people, deaf children, unmarried women at
mass, gypsy quarrels — Lorca in an early poem, for example,
shows a young girl picking olives, and the wind has his arm
around her waist. Various boys passing, some bullfighters, try to
get her to go along. She goes on gathering olives, "the gray arm

of the wind around her waist." But in New York Lorca found
concrete and no olives. He found skyscrapers climbing like barren
stairs, cowed men working at jobs without possibility of grace,
science and people without roots. The result is that his desire-
energy becomes bottled up, becomes desperate, and bursts out in
wild images, poems of desperate power and compassion:

> In the graveyard far off there is a corpse
> who has moaned for three years
> because of a dry countryside in his knee;
> and that boy they buried this morning cried so much
> it was necessary to call out the dogs to keep him quiet.

The poems do not exclude the social, as the orthodox French
surrealists prefer them to, but show what is blocking the desire-
energy, in images of great precision:

> There is a wire stretched from the Sphinx to the safety deposit box
> that passes through the hearts of all poor children.

The Spanish critics do not know what to make of *The Poet in
New York,* and many consider it an aberration, exaggerated, or
mad. Spain being still largely unindustrialized, they do not
realize that it describes a reality. I think it is a marvellous
book, and what we need above all are clear translations of the
whole book.

Some children ask Federico Garcia Lorca in one of his early
poems why he is leaving the square where they all play, and he
says: "I'm looking for magicians and princesses!" They ask him
then if, having found the 'path of the poets,' he will go far away
from their square, and from the earth and the sea. He answers:

> I will go very far,
> farther than those mountains,
> farther than the stars,
> to ask Christ our Lord
> if he will give my old
> childhood soul back to me,
> matured by legends,
> with its feathered cap
> and its wooden sword.

There is no other poet like him in the history of poetry.
Everyone who has ever read a poem of Garcia Lorca's notices a
red ray of sunlight hit the ground a few inches from his foot,
and knows that he has a friend, and he loves him forever.

Dance of Death

FEDERICO GARCIA LORCA
(Translated by Robert Bly)

The mask. Look at the mask!
It's coming from Africa to New York!

The pepper trees are all gone,
the tiny buds of phosphorus with them.
The camels made of torn flesh are gone
and the valleys of light which the swan carried in his bill.

It was the time of dried things,
of the wheat-beard in the eye, and the flattened cat,
of rusting iron on the giant bridges
and the absolute silence of cork.

It was the grand reunion of the dead animals,
cut through by blades of light;
the eternal joy of the hippopotamus with his hooves of ash,
and the gazelle with a "live forever!" in its throat.

In the withered solitude without waves,
the dented mask was dancing.
One half of the world was made of sand,
the other half was mercury and the sun asleep.

The black mask. Look at the mask!
Sand, crocodile, and fear over New York!

Mountain passes of lime were walling in the empty sky;
you hear there the voices of those dying under the dung of birds.
A sky, clipped and pure, exactly like itself,
with the fluff and sharp-edged lily of its invisible mountains,

has finished with the most delicate stems of song,
and gone off to the flood crowded with sap,
across the resting time of the final marchers
lifting bits of mirror with its tail.

While the Chinaman was crying on the roof
without finding the nakedness of his wife,
and the bank president was watching the pressure-gauge
that measures the remorseless silence of money,
the black mask was arriving at Wall Street.

This vault that makes the eyes turn yellow
is not an extraordinary place for dancing.
There is a wire stretched from the Sphinx to the safety deposit box
that passes through the hearts of all poor children.
The primitive energy is dancing with the machine energy,
in their frenzy wholly ignorant of the original light.
Because if the wheel forgets its formula,
it might as well sing naked with the herds of horses;
and if a flame burns up the frozen plans
the sky will have to run away from the roar of the windows.

This place is not out of the question for dancing, I say this truth,
the black mask will dance between columns of blood and numbers,
between downpours of gold and groans of unemployed workers
who will go howling, dark night, through your time without stars.
O savage North America! shameless! savage,
stretched out on the frontier of the snow!

The black mask! Look at the black mask!
What a wave of filth and glow worms over New York!

I was out on the terrace fighting with the moon.
Swarms of windows were stinging one thigh of the night.
The gentle sky-cows were drinking from my eyes.
And winds with immense oars
were beating on the ash-colored lights of Broadway.

A drop of blood was looking for the light at the core of the star
in order to imitate the dead seed of an apple.
A wind from the prairies, pushed along by the shepherds,
shivered with the fear of a mollusc with no shell.

But the dead are not the ones dancing,
I'm sure of that.
The dead are totally absorbed, gobbling up their own hands.
It's the others who have to dance with the black mask and its
    guitar;
it's the others, men drunk on silver, the frosty men,
those who thrive at the crossroads of thighs and mineral fires,
those who are searching for the worm in the landscape of stair-
    cases,
those who drink the tears of a dead girl in a bank vault,
or those who eat in the corners the tiny pyramids of the dawn.

I don't want the Pope to dance!
No, I don't want the Pope to dance!
Nor the King,
nor the millionaire with his blue teeth,
nor the withered dancers of the cathedrals,
nor the carpenters, nor emeralds, nor madmen, nor corn-holers.
I want this mask to dance,
this mask with its musty scarlet,
just this mask!

Because now the cobras will whistle on the highest floors,
and the stinging weeds will make the patios and terraces tremble,
because the stock market will be a pyramid of moss,
because the jungle creepers will run after the rifles,
and soon, soon, very soon!
Look out Wall Street!

The mask, the mask. Look at the mask!
How it spits the poison of the forest
over the faulty pain of New York!

December, 1929

Death

for Isidoro de Blas

So much energy!
Energy of the horse that wants to be a dog!
Energy of the dog that wants to be a swallow!
Energy of the swallow that wants to be a bee!
Energy of the bee that wants to be a horse!
And the horse,
presses such a sharp arrow out of the rose!
It makes such a gray rose grow from its lip!
And the rose,
what a mob of lights and warnings
it ties into the living sugar of its treetrunk!
As for the sugar,
what tiny daggers it dreams of when it's awake!
And the tiny daggers,
a moon without mangers! naked bodies,
what skin, eternal and blushing, looking and looking!
And I, when I am on the roof,
what a pure seraphim of fire I want to be and am!
But this plaster arch,
how immense it is, how invisible, how tiny,
no energy at all!

Ghazal of the Terrifying Presence

FEDERICO GARCIA LORCA
(Translated by Robert Bly)

I want the water to go on without its bed.
And the wind to go on without its mountain passes.

I want the night to go on without its eyes
and my heart without its golden petals;

if the oxen could only talk with the big leaves
and the angleworm would die from too much darkness;

I want the teeth in the skull to shine
and the yellowish tints to drown the silk.

I can see the night in its duel, wounded
and wrestling, tangled with noon.

I live fighting a sunset of green poison,
and those broken arches where time is suffering.

But don't let the light fall on your clear and naked body
like a cactus black and open in the reeds.

Leave me as full of uncertainty as the darkened planets,
but do not let me see your pure waist.

Visiting Thomas Hart Benton in Kansas City

ROBERT BLY

The stone driveway is littered with chill, unswallowed leaves, damp in the November mist. The house is stone, the garage stone. We climb into the back porch, the door opens. A short man comes out, saying, Get on in there! and brushing us in with his hands. He looks like a stump, or a short tractor. This is not the carefree apartment poet typing his poems twenty minutes a day, but he is labor, the hands twisted around the brush, hours in front of the canvas, the steer driver going through snow, the wrestler wrestling with the angel lifting him and driving him down to earth again and again, the joy of hard work, the thresher defeated at dusk by the weight of the bundles.

He pulls out drinks. Curiously luminous paintings hang all around on the walls — here a small girl looks at the wolf on the path, she is hesitant, she has seen no evil, having only seen her parents (and not well) and the light brown wolf is curious to talk to her, he has met her before, in another life: she cannot remember, (though he can), she fails to remember, she is about to lose the battle again (though we know the wolf will twist away toward the river wounded at last). In the next painting water curves like lace around the island in the river that looks like an arm sleeping on a kitchen table, and the two boys in the canoe head toward the unknown falls of brightness, something they never experienced on their farm, where their lantern held up fell on the sides of the patient Guernseys standing with their heads in prison. A full-cheeked child painted — how strangely the plant turns upward, how strangely it offers in twistings upward, like hands wringing, the flower at its top, on which the butterfly of war has lit — for just a moment — and the child, who has only seen before the stable piles of stovewood, gazes at it, and feels her own blood moving so swiftly over the hills in the veins, around the curving islands in the arteries . . .

Thomas Hart Benton's wife, strong, radiant, pure, triumphant, she has survived the flesh, like the ship that has returned from the moon, and splashes down in some Russian meadow, and Tom, as she calls him, crouching down on the sofa, muttering strong feelings, "I used to go on tour . . . I've been all over this damn country . . . in 1934 . . . as far west as Lubbock, Texas . . . You from Minnesota . . . where's the university? Minneapolis, hell, I been there . . ." and his forehead 82 years old, full of Grant Wood and Vachel Lindsay, "I lived on the same floor as him in 1912, maybe it was . . . I didn't know him well . . . we were poor a lot in those days . . . " a gurgling laugh . . . he has a daughter in a commune out east . . . an amazing line in his forehead — it starts from somewhere between his nose and the right eye and goes up . . . it forks and joins, then the limb climbs steeply, and sinks finally into the upper sensual part of the brain . . . there must be water there, that has cut in and moves around the legs of chairs, the water-energy in the hips under short skirts out in the front yard as the mortgage storm comes on, the sexual energy of the travelling preacher has flowed into the girls who have known only linoleum floors and rickety kitchen tables and flat memories in the spare room bedsheets, confusing Jesus with the storms in deep sleep, thighs touching as they walk away from the cafe, that line in his forehead is the crack in the cave floor over which the spirit hunters leap, leaping like the elk, as the woman groans in labor, near seated men, who notice the storm approaching, sand blown before it . . . the wolves fade back into the woods, and the horny young girls, their hips drive the energy into the ground (just as men drive nails) and the energy flows through the dead, who carry it to the throats of trees, and up into the branches; under their shade the halfasleep mule brushes at flies, his cock hanging down like a wagon tongue, his long ears reminding men and women watching of the long river down which we all float, waking and sleeping fitfully, conscious of it at times underneath the hair line, near the shadow brain.

Ali

Thomas Hart Benton

When I got on board the steam ship "La Lorraine" at her
New York dock in late August of 1908 to go study art in Paris,
I was very uneasy. Everybody was speaking French and I didn't
know a word of the language. I was nineteen years old and while
I had had a couple of years of independent, family free, experience as a student in Chicago, and felt myself fully grown up, the
strange new world of the French ship undermined all my self
confidence. The excited chatter of the people who came to see
their departing friends and wish them "Bon Voyage" made me
feel terribly alone. I kept wishing I knew someone in New York
who could give a personal touch to my own departure.

As I stood in the line of people moving forward toward the
purser's window, to present my tickets and find my quarters, I
would have given anything for a companion, any kind of companion. But when I was shown to my second class cabin by an
English speaking steward and he pointed to some suitcases opened
up on the lower bunk and said, "Your 'compagnon' of the voyage," I did not rejoice. "What if I can't speak with him?" I
thought.

Looking about I saw a tiny wash basin in one corner of the
cabin but there were no other toilet conveniences. I asked the
steward about this. He took me down a short passage way and
showed me a room with a row of urinals and a half dozen pot
seats behind swinging doors which had no locks. There were also
a couple of tin bathtubs painted white but chipped all over.
Second class accomodations in 1908 were not as elegant as they
became later.

After the steamship got underway I went on deck and watched the New York buildings recede. When we passed Sandy Hook and I felt the first swells of the Atlantic ocean my stomach turned. I got violently sick. As fast as I could I made my way to the row of urinals below and grabbing the sides of one of them puked until I thought I was going to faint. As I struggled to keep my balance I felt a hand under my armpit and a voice came to my ears, a kindly voice, speaking in French. Then as I did not respond, it changed to English, "It's nothing" I heard, "It will pass. It don't last long, this sea sickness."

I looked around and through the haze of my misery saw a stocky thick set man something over five feet and a half tall, with large curling mustachios, waxed at the ends. He was smiling.

"Come up on deck," he said, "and you'll get over this right away. Have you a chair?"

"What chair?" I asked.

"A deck chair. You should have one. But you can use mine for the moment. Come quickly."

Sustained by my new friend's arm, I climbed back on deck and stumbled along until he sat me down and propped my feet up on his deck chair.

"I'll find your own chair," he said. "What's your cabin number?"

"My number is twenty-four," I replied.

"Why that's my number," he said. "Are you my cabin mate? Well, of course. I'm glad to meet you." He squeezed my hand. "What's your name? Where are you going?"

"I'm going to Paris to study art," I replied, "I'm an artist. My name is Benton. I come from Missouri."

"Oh, that is way out west where Jesse James and the Indians live. Yes, Yes I've heard all about it. And you are going to Paris. So am I. But you don't speak French. How are you going to get along in Paris, Artist? You have to speak French there."

"I will have to learn to do it," I said.

That is how I met Ali, Ali the Turk. He had a whole string of other names but I never fully grasped their sequences and have long forgotten them. Ali was thirty-seven years old and was balding a little above his forehead. He was handsome in a way, with shiny black eyes and a kind of dark pink skin. He was in the tobacco importing business, he told me, and was on the way to his home country, Turkey and to other places in the Middle East to buy tobacco for the cigarette makers in New York. But he was going to stop in Paris for a while, "to have a good time," he said.

Noting my total helplessness in the steam boat's French world, with its voluble, but for an alien like myself, exclusive and in-different people, he took me under his protective wing. He found my place at the dinner table and changed it so that it would be next to his own. He always called me "Artist," never using my name, and introduced me as such to the people he came to know on the ship.

I never got seasick again, in fact never again in my life. I spent the ten days or so it took to reach Le Havre quite com-fortably. Most of the time I sat in my deck chair trying to acquaint myself with a French grammar of high school vintage. Once in a while I'd ask for Ali's help but while he spoke French fluently, its grammatical foundations were beyond him. "I've forgotten all that, Artist," he said, "Anyhow, you don't need it. Just listen and learn by what you hear."

A few of those who shared our dinner table would nod to me while on their deck promenades but my only conversational mo-ments on shipboard were supplied by Ali and a disgruntled French architect who had spent ten years in America practising his trade. I judged he had not been very successful because he hated every-thing American. He would get drunk on brandy and take out his dislikes on me, reviewing bitterly, with a highly accented English, what he considered the barbarisms of America's mores. When, my patriotism aroused, I tried to defend or explain some of these, Ali always took my part. He spoke calmly, with good humor, and never, like the Frenchman, became angry or excited when opposed.

I have always remembered the intense bitterness of this French architect toward everything American. Although in later years I would come across many kindred dislikes among his com-patriots I never found any so all enveloping. There were no ideas, institutions, or ways of doing things in the United States which invited the slightest tolerance.

After we docked at Le Havre and made our things ready for the train to Paris I assumed I would be separated from Ali and started to tell him good bye. "No, Artist," he said. "I'm going to see you through to Paris. I'll tell you good bye when I get you settled among the other American students there. I can't let you try to find your way alone with no language to help."

So, as he had taken care of the first part of my overseas adventure, Ali took care of the second part. He saw that my trunk was on the Paris train, that my suitcase was put with his own baggages by the porter who carried them off the boat to our railway car. He saw to the necessary tipping on and off the ship. When I tried to reimburse him for my share of all this he waved me off. He did the same for many other later expenses which he incurred on my behalf. As long as I knew Ali, he shelled out for lunches and dinners, aperitifs and wines and just laughed when I tried to repay him.

When, in the late afternoon, we arrived at the Paris depot, Ali found a hack, picking out the one which had the sorriest looking horse because, he said, it would be cheaper. He made his bargain with its driver and had our suitcases and my trunk loaded aboard. There were few automobiles in Paris at this time and most inter-city trips were made behind horses.

Ali, who knew exactly where he was going, took me to a small left bank hotel just off the Boulevard St. Michel where he had reserved space for himself by letter. A place was also found there for me, a small room where by stretching my neck out the window I could get a glimpse of the Boulevard and its never ending flow of life. The hotel was patronized mostly by Turk, Greek, and Balkan business men but they all dressed in Parisian style and had Ali not told me I would not have known they were different from Frenchmen. Where all was strange a particular strangeness was not noticeable.

When our arrangements for the night were completed and we had beds to sleep in, pots to pee in and wash bowls, towels, and pitchers of water for our morning needs, Ali took me to dinner. We went to a café with tables on the Boulevard and others inside. It was jammed with people, young people mostly who, Ali told me, came from his part of the world, Turkey, the Balkans and the Middle East. Knowing again just where he wanted to go, Ali manoeuvred himself, with the help of a complaisant waiter, to a table in the very center of the crowded café where at adjoining tables a lot of young men were vociferously carrying on discussions. To these Ali addressed himself and after he had finished talking three swarthy young men planted themselves at our table. After they were introduced they began, to my utter surprise, speaking English to me. Though their accents were most unfamiliar and difficult to understand their friendly and sympathetic manners captured me immediately. They were students at the Sorbonne and all were studying English, which was then beginning to rival French as a necessary language for international communication. I sensed they were practising their lessons on me. They had as much difficulty with my American accent as I had with theirs but with Ali's help I managed to inquire of them about the locations in Paris where American students congregated. These, I learned, were mostly in the "Quartier Montparnasse" and were within walking distance from our hotel. The "Café Du Dôme" was said to be their favorite gathering place and directions to it were supplied us. During our conversation dinner was ordered, with our new friends invited to participate. I enjoyed this dinner very much. The good nature and warm friendliness of these students from an unknown and mysterious world greatly heightened my hopes that all would turn out well for me in Paris.

The next morning Ali had to absent himself on matters concerning his tobacco business and though he promised to return for lunch he did not show up until late in the afternoon when it was beginning to get dark. By this time I was faint with hunger. Two or three times I had gone out from our hotel and had wandered up and down the Boulevard St. Michel with the intention of going into some restaurant or café to eat but each time I lost my nerve. Speaking no French how was I to order and how was I to pay? Up to now Ali had assumed all my expenses so I had not learned to take care of them for myself. I had a substantial supply of American dollars in my pocket book, but innocently, I didn't think they would be acceptable in a French restaurant. Maybe they would not at this time. In 1908 dollars weren't circulating in Paris as they did later.

I proposed that we go back to our café of the preceding night and again have dinner with the students there. In response to this proposition Ali sat me down and gave me my first Parisian lesson. "Artist," he said, "you are young, excuse me for saying so. I know you have had some experience in the world but you don't know the student world of Paris. Those were nice young men who were with us last night but they have surely told others about their dinner with us. I am certain that the word is now around that two rich fellows from America are here and if we go back to our friends of last night they will have other friends with them who will have to be invited to dinner also. This is all right with me because I like students and don't mind the expense. But it might not be all right for you. Among the friends of our yesterday's friends, there may be one or two who are not nice and who will have ideas about us. Ideas, not so much about me, as about you. They will figure that an American student must have money—a great deal of it. And they will be right. The fifty or sixty dollars which you told me you would get every month is not much in America but it is great wealth in the student life of Paris and even greater wealth in the life of those students who come from Turkey, Greece and the Balkan countries, from my world. I am sure, as sure as I am alive, that if we go back where we were last night there will be one or two fellows added to our party who will speak better English than the others and who will be more sympathetic toward you and who will want more than the others to help you find your way in Paris. They will know just what to do for you. You will like them. They will know how to make you like them. But, Artist, remember this, the chances are great that what they will be looking for is not your welfare but a share of your monthly dollars. Before long they will get you compromised, probably through some pretty girl, and get you in a fix where you will have to give some of your dollars to them—where you might even be glad to give them. I know about this, Artist, and I don't want you to start making friends in this quarter of Paris. Find your friends among the American students that we will look up tomorrow."

Ali then took me to a quiet restaurant near the Madeleine on the right bank of the Seine far from the Boulevard St. Michel and our companions of last night. When we were settled he said, "Artist, maybe you think I'm too suspicious about the students of Paris. But there are reasons. Twenty years ago I came to study here just like you are coming now. My father was a tobacco merchant like I am, but he wanted me to be something better and he saved up enough money so that I could come to Paris and add enough to my education to make me a real person—a somebody in the world. He had a client here, a Turk like himself, who dealt in eastern tobaccos for the French and English markets. This man, as had been arranged by my father, made me a sleeping place in the back of his shop which he gave to me for staying in the place at night. I was better off than you for my Parisien début, Artist. I had a family friend and some of the security of a home.

"I did not have a bank to keep my money in like you have— a bank to care for it and give it out to me, part by part, and month by month. All the money I had for a year's study was sewed up in a shammy skin money belt which I kept fastened to my hips under my clothes. This belt had twelve little compartments of shammy sewed to it. Each compartment contained, in gold francs, what it had been calculated would be needed for a month's subsistence in Paris. I was supposed to cut the threads of one of these compartments at the beginning of each month. The first compartment had more money in it than the others, for my tuition at the Sorbonne, for the books I would need and a suit of proper French clothes. My money was not anything like what you will have, Artist, but it was a lot for a young Turkish student.

"I had been advised by my father to confide the money, belt and all, to my host, the tobacco dealer, so that he could keep it in his safe but the feel of so much wealth about my hips was dear to me and I kept putting off the day of parting with it."

Ali finished his story over coffee and cognac. It was a long story about students and people who pretended to be students, but were something else—about a party and a beautiful French girl and, of course, the loss of the money belt. I was fascinated, but as much with the way Ali told his story as by the story itself. He so obviously enjoyed it. His dark pink cheeks shone, his eyes sparkled and snapped and he twisted his mustachios vigorously at periods which needed emphasis.

"And so, Artist," he ended, "I lost my education. I was apprenticed to my tobacco dealing host and learned the business of tobacco in Paris and London and later in New York. It makes me sad to think of how easily I let my chance of being somebody in the great world of intelligence be taken away from me."

But Ali did not look sad. He looked prosperous, gay and happy with his role in life. As for me I did not quite believe his story. I had heard money belt stories before. They circulated frequently in my Missouri home country. My father himself had a couple of pretty glamorous ones. But true or not it made its point. People do take you in, I thought as I remembered a poker game during my student days in Chicago where some new found friends led me into a bet which took my monthly allowance away. So I never went back to the café on the Boulevard St. Michel even when in later moments of loneliness and curiosity I was tempted to do so.

After dinner Ali walked me up and down the fashionable boulevards with their flashy and exotic crowds. There were many young women parading there in pairs. They were all dressed much alike, a white blouse, a long black or grey skirt fitted tightly about the hips. Many had white and milky skins that seemed almost luminescent in contrast to their brightly painted red lips. My fascination with these young ladies was quickly noticed. A pair of them turned in their walk and sidled up to Ali on one side and me on the other, taking hold of our arms. Ali joked and laughed with them but I couldn't say anything. Suddenly the one on my side grabbed my hand and shoved it through a slit in her skirt down between her legs. The feel of the hair was like an electric shock and I jumped back freeing myself. I was astounded, embarrassed, outraged. I could feel the blood rush to my face. The girls shrilled with laughter. Ali laughed too but he got rid of them.

On the way back to our hotel Ali said "Artist, I've got another Parisian lesson for you. What that girl did surprised you. But the next time it won't. In a little while you may commence to invite it. Then you will want to go with one of these girls to her apartment. But don't do it, Artist. Like the students I told you about she will be thinking only about how much money she can get out of you. She may even find a way of stealing your pocket book. But that isn't the worst of it. She could give you a nice dose of syphilis especially if she has that beautiful white skin you so admire. Stay away from girls with that milky skin, Artist. They get it by taking a drug to keep their syphilis in check."

The next day Ali located my bank, and guided me there. A young English teller took my affairs in hand, changed the dollars in my pocket book into francs and gave me in addition those allocated for my September allowance. Ali asked if he knew any American students in the Montparnasse quarter. He did not know any personally but he said there was a club there called The Paris American Art Club where he was sure we would find students from the States. He hunted up the address of the place and gave it to us with minute directions about how to find it.

Ali thought the club might provide a short cut to getting me settled so we promptly set out in search of it. We found it easily and climbed a flight of stairs to a hall down which two sliding doors opened into a large room. The windows there were hung with long thick red velvet curtains making it quite dark. However we could see two young men sitting at a table conversing. Ali, exuding affability, addressed them saying I was an artist from the States, just arrived to study in Paris. He said he wanted to find a place for me to live and get me acquainted with other American students. His voluble friendliness, maybe a little boisterous, his dark pink face and flamboyant mustachios produced an effect directly opposite to that he intended. Except for a slightly startled look the young men made no response to his overtures. They just stared at him or rather through him. They didn't notice me at all. They kept their seats in frigid silence until Ali, catching the sense of things sputtered out. I then spoke up saying I was looking for a room or a little studio, asking if there was anyone at the club I could see about that. One of the young men condescended an answer. "There's a bulletin board in the hall," he said. "Sometimes there are places listed there." Then, abruptly he turned his back.

We retreated to the hall and examined the bulletin board, Ali angry and muttering. "What a rotten stuck up pair" he said. "I never knew Americans could be like that. What pricks."

There were two studio apartments listed on the board. We took their addresses and went to see them. The first, which was near at hand, was elegantly furnished. It had a kitchen and three rooms, the largest of which had a tall studio window looking down on a little garden full of late summer flowers. It was beautiful. I told Ali I couldn't wish for anything better. But after he had talked a little in French with the concierge who showed the place to us he said "Yes this is fine, Artist. But it is too much for you. You haven't got the money." So, much to my regret we left it.

The next place, also near by, was not so attractive but was still much too costly. Ali said "This is not the right neighborhood for you, Artist. We'll have to find one more suited to your pocket book. Let's go to the Café du Dôme where the American students are and make inquiries."

So we went to the café but as it was by now three o'clock nobody was there. We walked about and found a place to have lunch.

Now that I had French money I wanted to pay the bill but, as before, Ali would not let me, "Artist," he said "Maybe it is going to cost more for you in Paris than I expected. Keep your money."

After a walk about the nearby Luxembourg gardens we returned to the "Dôme," found an outside table and sat down to coffee. It was now after five and people were beginning to gather both inside the café and outside on the bit of shrubbery enclosed sidewalk where we had established ourselves. We heard English being spoken—English English and American English. But with his morning experience at the club still rankling Ali was chary about making advances to anyone. I stared at the more obviously American customers trying to attract attention but it did no good. Like Ali I was afraid of the reception I might get if I tried butting in to a conversation so we just sat and looked on as the tables filled. Finally, when our waiter passed by, Ali asked him if he knew of any studios or small apartments for rent at prices which students could afford to pay. The waiter did. He told Ali there was a young German who came to the café every evening and that he had heard him talking to people about some new studios he had built for renting at moderate prices. He generally came in about eight o'clock, the waiter said.

Ali and I went to dinner and afterwards came back to the

"Dôme" but although we sat there a couple of hours the young German did not appear. Our waiter said it was odd because he had visited the café every evening for many weeks. For four nights we haunted the Dôme without seeing our man. During the day I walked about the Louvre looking at paintings. Ali had shown me how to get there from our hotel. After breakfast I'd walk down the Boulevard St. Michel, wander along the banks of the Seine looking over the book stalls and then go into the Louvre. I was still too timid to risk myself in restaurants so I did without lunch. Ali had his tobacco business to attend to but he always came back to the hotel to take me to dinner and afterwards to the Café du Dôme. I began to feel that I was becoming a burden to him. But there was no help for it. He was determined to get me settled, he said. I don't know how but it had become fixed in his mind that the German we sought would solve my problems so we attempted no other solutions.

On our fifth night at the "Dôme" the waiter informed us that our German had returned and pointed him out. Ali, approaching cautiously, asked him if it was true that he had studios for rent. Getting an affirmative nod he explained, as he had done at the Art Club, that I was a newly arrived American art student who wanted a place in which to live and work. He added that I would remain in Paris for several years.

At the word American the young man said, "I speck English." So he did but it was in such a way, with both curious constructions and a thick Teutonic accent, that I barely understood him. He was more difficult for me than the Turkish students of the Boulevard St. Michel. However, I managed to comprehend that he did have a number of newly renovated painters' and sculptors' studios—"For rent to proper persons."

This young landlord was maybe twenty-five or six years old. He was completely self possessed, even arrogantly so. He wore thick glasses to which were attached a black ribbon reaching down under a tweed jacket. He was slim but had nevertheless a paunchy middle. His face was also fleshy and rather pale. He had a small cupid's bow mouth which seemed to pout. His habitual expression, with wrinkles on top of his nose, suggested he was smelling something putrid. I did not like him, nor did Ali.

However, we made an appointment for the next day to look at his studios which he told us were rented unfurnished and without heat, for eight to twelve dollars a month according to their size. Ali thought this was about what I could afford. As we prepared to take our leave, the young man, addressing Ali in French said, "Your little friend must come with financial recommendations if he proposes to rent." Ali satisfied him on that point but when he told me about it I was put out. "Do I look like a con guy?" I asked. "You might to him," replied Ali. What annoyed me most was the patronizing word "petit" which I understood.

We had some difficulty locating the studio building. It was at the end of a small "passage" leading off a narrow street of low houses and small gardens enclosed by high walls. The area appeared rather poor but it had some charm, with little flower beds, hedges and sycamore trees glimpsed, here and there, behind tall iron gates. I liked it well enough.

The studio building, finally discovered, was two stories high. It had an outside stairway which led to an upper balcony with an iron railing. Along this was a row of six doors about twenty feet apart. These were the doors of the painters' studios. Those for sculptors were on the ground floor. The whole building was freshly painted white and looked bright and clean. Our proprietor occupied the first studio on the balcony. On the watch for us he was at his door and invited us into a reception room, luxuriously filled with carved furniture, deep carpets and rich hangings. The room also contained a most substantial square faced, slit mouthed German lady who was introduced as "my dear mother." She, we were informed, would take care of us in "affairs of beeziness." After introducing her, the young man bowed stiffly and walked back into the studio proper, which as we could see through the door was also elegantly furnished.

"Dear Mother" led us out on the balcony and along to the next to last studio door which, sliding a key from a large ring, she opened. There was an entrance cubicle, similar to the reception room where we had met her, though smaller, which led into the studio. This was eighteen or twenty feet square, with a large window occupying most of its northward wall. A narrow stairway climbed to an overhanging balcony which could be used for storage purposes or as sleeping quarters. There was a small window in this balcony. A cast iron coal stove with a flat top, suitable for both heating and cooking, stuck out a few feet from one side of the studio wall. This stove did not go with the rent we learned but could be purchased. The place had no inside water supply or toilet facilities. However, at the end of the outside balcony, only a few steps away, was a water tap and two cubby holes each with a flush toilet. "Mother" brought our attention to the cleanliness of these facilities and told Ali she expected her tenants to keep them that way.

The lack of modern conveniences in the studio proper did not disturb me because like deficiencies were common in many houses in America at the time, and as all was new and bright and the big window filled the studio with light, I was pleased. Ali was satisfied too and advised me to rent it. Fascinated by the prospect of living in real artists' quarters, I needed no urging. I paid two months' rent, eight dollars for the first month and eight for my last month of occupancy. Ali bargained a little for the stove, and I bought it for three dollars. He said the price was high but that he would not know where to find another like it.

The next day we went shopping. Ali found me a cot bed, sheets, a couple of blankets, a table, two chairs, a small chest of drawers, a tea kettle, a coffee pot, frying pan and a bucket for water. We got all this in one block, back of the Gare Montparnasse, and then hired a push cart man to deliver it, walking beside him, the half mile or so, to the studio. We found a dealer in coal and had two bushel size sacks of "boulets" sent up. Nearby an "épicerie" was discovered and Ali taught me how to pronounce the words for my small needs for breakfast, sugar, coffee, eggs and butter. He found a "boulangerie" and a small neighborhood café where I could get a "café-croissant" in case I did not want to prepare my own breakfast. After all this we went back to the hotel, picked up my trunk and suitcase and brought them back to the studio in a hack.

Evening had now come so we prepared to go to dinner. Before doing so, however, Ali thought it would be polite to tell our landlord that we were pleased with the studio and to thank him for letting me have it, so we knocked at his door. The young man opened it but as I moved to come in he began shutting it again. I was astounded but managed to blurt out, "I just came to say that I am pleased with the studio and that I am glad to have met you. I hope we will be friends." He looked at me for a second. "Vee are pleased to half you as a tenant but you must understood that your rent money do not pay for socialization." He then bowed and shut the door sharply. Confused and shocked I backed off and hung on to the railing of the balcony. Ali, his pink face turned scarlet, was for a moment in a state of fury. Then he calmed down. "Artist," he said, "I have not done very well in finding friends for you. It was bad with those fellows in the Paris-American Club but there's something especially bad with this fellow. He isn't right, right in the head, I mean. Nobody acts this way with his tenants—especially a new one."

Ali was correct. There was really something cracked in the makeup of the young German. After this encounter I never spoke to him again. I would pass him on the stairway now and then but a perfunctory nod was the only recognition we gave one another. I paid my rent to his mother. She also was a "case." She turned out to be a screaming bullying virago despised and feared by every tradesman in the neighborhood. She hated "the French serpents" and was at all times certain they were trying to cheat her. Her strident voice became a constant accompaniment of my daily life at "Quatorze Passage Guibert."

No doubt "dear Mother" was largely responsible for her son's strangeness. Maybe her behavior, her loud vulgarity, shamed him and drove him into himself. Too weak to assert his independence of her, he protected his pride by scorning everybody. He had no friends. During the three years I dwelt at his place I never saw anyone come to see him. He stayed in his studio apartment all day, alone except for his mother, engaging himself in bookish studies of some sort. In the evening, after dinner, he dressed up and went to a café where he read the papers for an hour or so and drank sweet wine. Occasionally I would see him at the "Dôme" but this was not the only café he frequented. After he had rented all his studios I don't think he ever spoke to anyone except the café waiters and his mother. I never learned why the two had left

Germany to live in Paris.

Ali took me to dinner again. "Artist," he said "You are now set up in Paris. Let's celebrate." We had several courses with several different wines which made me a little tipsy. Afterwards we went to the "Café du Dôme" for coffee. There we got into conversation with a young artist from New York sitting alone at a table next to ours. He introduced himself with an affable grin as Abe Warshawsky. He also had just come to Paris but he had friends, he told us, to help him find his way around. Abe was a few years older than I but not in the least way patronizing. After he'd heard from Ali the story of my difficulties on the way to getting settled he offered to aid with the further development of my Parisian life. He knew how to locate The Académie Julian where I had been directed to begin my studies and promised to guide me there. He also promised to introduce me to other American students in the Quartier Montparnasse.

Ali accompanied me back to my studio and we sat there talking and sobering up after all the wine. There was no electricity in the place and as we had forgotten to purchase a "petrol" lamp we sat in darkness. Ali said "Artist, I have done all I can for you. And I believe I have found a friend for you at last. That fellow, Abe, we met at the Dôme is all right. He won't try to hook your money. You will learn from him how to get on in the Paris art world. Even if I were going to stay in Paris I couldn't help you much further with that. I don't know anything about art and artists and their world. I live in a different one. I'm going to be very busy for the rest of my stay in Paris so we won't be seeing each other so often any more."

When Ali left it came over me how much I had depended on him and how much I liked his good humored, kindly spirit. I felt very lonely and it was a long time before I got to sleep.

A week or more passed before Ali visited me again. He arrived one late afternoon, most splendidly dressed in new French tailoring, and was accompanied by a pretty and stylish young woman. He wanted to take me to dinner as usual but I had a date with my new friend Abe Warshawsky. I was glad of that because Ali's fine clothes and the young woman's elegance made me feel shabby and awkward. After this I did not see Ali for nearly a month.

In the meantime I enrolled at the Académie Julian for morning study and began painting in my studio in the afternoon. Abe Warshawsky had kept his promise and had introduced me to other American students, so there were a few people I could talk to. An artist named John Thompson, from upper New York State, had moved into the studio adjoining mine and I was developing a friendship with him. I had learned my way about Paris and was becoming more and more fascinated with the city's life. I often thought of Ali but I didn't miss him too much.

One late afternoon returning from a visit to the Louvre, I found him on the balcony by my door talking to my neighbor John Thompson. I had told Thompson about how Ali had befriended me so he was entertaining him until my return. After a little polite talk among the three of us Ali said he had something particular to say to me and we went into my studio and sat down together. "Artist" he said "I am not able to remain any longer in Paris. I must go on about my tobacco business in Turkey. But I have friends in New York, girl friends, that I want to make believe I am staying longer in the 'gay city.' " Herewith he produced an envelope full of postal cards all stamped and addressed. "Beginning next week" he went on "I want you to mail these cards. There are four names. Mail one card to each of these names once a week till they are all gone."

I said I would be glad to do so and taking the envelope of cards I put it on my table under a French dictionary I had purchased. "This is very silly" Ali said "But don't forget it. It will mean something to me when I get back to New York." After this we had dinner together, our last one.

My friend Abe Warshawsky had teamed up with me the day before to hire a girl model to paint from. She was to pose in my studio, and was to start the very next afternoon. I was much engrossed with this project. It was my first experience with so very professional a part of an artist's career and I could hardly think of anything else. As we ate dinner I told Ali all about it. He enjoyed my enthusiasm. When, after having finished eating and we were about to separate, he asked me if I had made any Parisian girl friends. I told him I hadn't. "Well, you will" he said "But don't forget the cards for my New York girls." He patted me affectionately on the back and we shook hands. I never saw him again..

A week later I thought of his postcards and went to my table to find them. They were not under the French dictionary where I had put them. Then, with my heart beating double time I had a horrible thought. When the young woman Abe Warshawsky and I had hired began her posing she complained that the studio was too cold. I hurriedly got a fire going in the stove. In my haste to do so I grabbed every piece of paper I could find about the place, including a pile of note papers on my table which I had used to write out French lessons. Had the little envelope of postcards somehow got mixed up with these? Had I burnt it? In the excitement of the moment I had done just that. So, unwittingly I betrayed the trust of my kind, helpful friend Ali.

Five years later when I began living in New York this unfortunate accident was still on my conscience and I made inquiries about Ali among the manufacturers of Turkish cigarettes down on the Eastside around Canal street, describing him minutely. Nobody there had ever heard of him. Maybe once back in his own country with renewed family connections and perhaps expanded opportunities in the Mid-Eastern tobacco business he had never returned to America.

Period Piece

BRUCE BERLIND

I stand at the window
      smoking. Across the room
         you play "Claire de lune"
con affetto
      on the grand piano.
         You are resting
after yesterday's abortion.
         Through a pane of old glass
           (the only one not yet replaced)
cars   drift   noiselessly
      slow-motion spectres in the silent snow.
         You are wearing
a red house-gown
      it is brocaded with gold
         you are very beautiful.
When our eyes meet, the
      ceiling soars like Amiens
         the room
is elegant as Versailles, my
      cigarette
         sprouts a carved ivory holder
and I know
      that we love each other
         and that
we are the last
      decadents characters
         in a Lubitsch film
dumb
      with adoration
         like Wordsworth's nun.

Elegy for 41 Whales,
Beached in Florence, Oregon, June 1979

LINDA BIERDS

—There was speculation that a parasite in the
whales' ears may have upset their equilibrium
and caused them to become disoriented—UPI

In the warm rods of your ears
forty-one parasites hummed
and you came rolling in
like tarred pilings after a hurricane.
What song were they piping for you?
What promises did you follow, past the coral
and mussels, and out from the frothy hem
of your world?

These are people.
They dance around you now like hooked marlin.
Some are weeping. Some are trying to pull you back.
Some crouch above your blow-holes
and drill their cigarettes into your skin.

All night your teeth are clicking.
All along the beach you are clicking like wind-chimes.
Is the song still piping for you?

This is sand. You cannot swim through it.
These are trees. Those houses on the cliff
are also trees. And the light that blinks
from them now is made from water.
We have a way of reworking the vital:

This is a pit. That was quicklime.
And here is fire.

Long Distance & Here

DAVID LYON

When you called from Amsterdam, the rain
was light blue against the hill & the freight
clattered like store teeth out to Montreal.

You sd   hello, the dutch are boors, etc, I miss you
        why don't you come, etc   and the wind
on the transatlantic cable whipped a neutron storm,
you in and out like some Amelia Earhart radio.

Margie, you are lost & shuffled in the world of telephones.
When your ship sails on the 17th, I won't be there
bearing roses at the dock.
There is only the rain, and the freight,
and the wind, picking up & dying.

Smoking In An Open Grave

DAVID BOTTOMS

We bury ourselves to get high.
Huddled in this open crypt we lay the bottle, the lantern,
the papers, the bag on a marble slab,
tune the guitar to a mouth harp
and choir out the old spirituals.
When the shadows of this life have grown, I'll fly away.

Across Confederate Row an owl hoots our departure
and half-fallen brick becomes a porthole filled with stars.
We lay our ears against the clay wall;
at the foot of the hill the river whispers on its track.
It's a strange place where graves go,
so much of us already geared for the journey.

Brothers Meeting

Thomas McAfee

"Voici le soir charmant, ami du criminel . . ."

The two of you stay where
You are. The street light
Won't stretch to here.
The police won't walk in
These shadows. You are brothers.
It's time you met.

Don't question me. Your mother
Sold you at birth.
Shake hands and feel the blood
Of the other. Be quick,
Then go your ways.
It's nearly dawn.

I Think Of Bread And Water
And The Roots Of A Tree All Wet

Tom Hennen

A description of the freeway
Lost
Looking for a city.
I come back
To geese.
Rain falls
On the parking meters
Glass and steel are shining
But people
Are dark
All the way through.

Five Poems

DAVID IGNATOW

Of That Fire

Inside I am on fire. Imagine, though, running up to City Hall and asking if there is a Department of Burning Need, ready for emergency, I the emergency. I can see myself being locked up gently in a madhouse and declared as finished in this world of material evidence. Are my clothes on fire? Is my hair burning? Are my cheeks aflame? Do my feet scream with pain? My voice is calm and my clothes intact, my hair and face moist with sweat and oils of my body—normal. Where is the fire, the cops ask sarcastically, giving me a ticket for speeding my brain beyond the legal limit and remanding me to court. I plead guilty and admit to it publicly, for I have no evidence but my spoken word, and all the while I know that the cop, the judge and the jury are burning inside too, without a shred of evidence either. They'd laugh and shake their heads and signify with a twirl of their fingers at their heads a crazed man before them, which would show how sane they are, not knowing they are dying in the fire that was lit in them, born of that fire.

Does this flower worry as I do though it can only spread petals to the sun as in a gesture for help? Does this tree have quarrels with itself and find it difficult to live with the others but can only express itself by rising straight up into the air? Does this ant lack love and assurance but can only run hither and yon in every aimless direction carrying a leaf in its mandibles, a token offering for its lost beloved? There is something to note about vegetable plants that have to be eaten or rot upon the ground. I would object to being eaten or left to lie upon the ground to die. Can this be said of the vegetables that maintain silence as they cling to the vine?

One Definition

I amuse myself by studying the cars
in the street, the figures walking
alongside, the shape of the trees,
the pattern formed by buildings
against the sky, my reactions
mostly of quiet enjoyment. How
does one make a poem from this,
I ask: a lift of the language,
a strong rhythm infusing a phrase
shaped suddenly out of the silence
when enjoyment is quiet. Looking
into myself, I see, beside this need
of gazing, speculation, an anxiousness
to be something other than I am
at this moment. What is it
to enjoy oneself. It is like taking milk
at the breast, but when one strikes
at the breast and grins up toothlessly
in the mother's face it evokes a smile
in return and laughter in pride
that you are not simply content
to feed, and the poem is the expression
of this change.

The Window

It was an effort at freedom from brick walls, and it succeeded,
but I do not see a face behind that window. Still, it is a window
that offers hope of another face, and from time to time when I
remember I show myself at my window, in case someone is
standing behind the curtain who needs the courage to show
himself or herself that by standing in the light I can supply.

In Peace

I am sitting opposite my psychiatrist who has just emitted a fart
with legs crossed and is now picking his nose with the forefinger
of his right hand, a homey touch, and now I can relax and tell
him things in confidence I had not been able to. At first he
had sat leaning back in his chair, observing me as I spoke, and
I spoke rather formally and in the abstract, and as I reached the
climax of a long involved sentence on perceptual knowledge he
emitted his fart and began to pick his nose. I was relieved.
What he meant was for me to let the shit flow, and so I opened
up. Of course, it was said before by others, but at least I was
one with them. He looked pleased, and so did I, and now he listens
in silence and can look at me, assured that I understand, and so
I talk on and finally it is time to go. Others are waiting at the
door for their next. We part to meet again at an appointed time
to once more go over the same ground and come up with the same
answer that in being repeated would add to our assurance that we
could live on until we had worn out our bodies and could die
in peace.

NEW LETTERS

Featuring **You Can't Lose With An Echo Harp**

by William Joyce

& the latest by

Jack Matthews

William Stafford

Anthony Ostroff

Ken McCullough

Lucien Stryk

Pati Hill

Ewart Milne

Valerie Worth

Ralph J. Mills, Jr.

& many others

A magazine of fine writing

Edited by David Ray

NEW LETTERS

A magazine of fine writing   *Edited by David Ray*

David Ray

NEW LETTERS

magazine of fine writing

India

An Anthology of Contemporary Writing

Edited by **David Ray**
and **Amritjit Singh**

NEW LETTERS

A magazine of fine writing

Edited by David Ray

$4.0(

Featuring Theodore Roethke

Freeze Dried, 16" × 24"

James Claussen

A Walk With Raschid

JOSEPHINE JACOBSEN

When the muezzin began to call, James got out of bed and went to the window. Tracy shifted as he did so, murmuring and giving a light shiver, and he pulled the sheet over her body which looked bright in the moonlight; the iron grillwork barred it.

The call, a rough, unhuman, melancholy, hornlike sound, fell and rose, with a breathstopping pause between phrases. It appeared to take up, in a strange tongue, an unsettled theme. That it referred to a god could never be doubted. It insisted, accused, identified, summoned. No matter that he couldn't get so much as his toe into Moule Idris, shoeless or shod.

They had turned off the fountain just below, and the tiled courtyard, where he and Tracy and Mr. and Mrs. Neeson had sipped mint tea at noon in a daze of color, was absolutely still. The bone-blue of the medina slept; anyway, was silent. Not a bawl, not a bark. That extraordinary voice, not like a reed or a ram's horn, but more like both than a voice, proceeded powerfully up and down its ways. Were the tanners asleep, bright yellow and red, peacefully stinking? Did the single-toothed coppersmith rise and kneel to the east? Did it wake Raschid? At the thought of Raschid asleep or awake in that visible bone-blue city, James thought immediately of Oliver, asleep or awake in a home once as familiar to James as his fingers, now distant in a variety of ways. This had happened three or four times. Beyond the fact that Raschid and Oliver both belonged to the human species, and were ten-year-old males, it was hard to see a connection.

Shivering a little in the three o'clock air, he heard the phrase end, on a wild deep braying gasp; a pause, and then a high climb.

He stared through the grill at the blaze of moonlight; all the dark seemed to have contracted into the cypresses. A small dizzy sense of ridiculousness wafted over him: James Gantry, naked, immaculately shaved, hearing the news of Allah and his Prophet, while his wife, bright as a minted penny, slept behind him, and his honeymoon rose in the blanched Moroccan night. Here every known thing seemed to have its alien echo: his feet, the brilliant geometry of the tiles; Tracy, the carved and gilded and painted bed; his son's pale-faced, square-set image; Raschid.

Raschid wore a striped djellabah; it was too small, but looked dignified. He never (when James had seen him) raised the hood. He had small bones, extended eyelashes, and a left thumb flattened in some mishap. His eyes (differing in this from his face, which was somber), were light-hearted in their darkness; unlike those of Oliver, which were of a pale and steadfast blue.

Hastily choosing the lighter confusion, James pressed down on the thought of Raschid. He didn't understand Raschid. Political prejudice aside, he did consider Arabs decorative; and then, Oliver's lack of childish charm had only lucklessly sharpened James' love of it. So he was prepared for that aspect of Raschid. But although he was gloomily convinced that the man who wasn't a scoundrel was apt to be a boob, he didn't want to be a boob, and he was alert for Raschid's angle. It could hardly be other than money, and when James found it apparently wasn't, he was thrown into unease. The whole of Fez contributed to this.

Fez was all there, close, breathing, smelling and moving, and yet he felt unsure what was real, where, exactly, the fraud began. The dyers and tanners were real; standing high above the stench, on narrow pitted steps with Tracy gamely clutching his elbow, the guide waiting, and Raschid gesticulating one step below, he saw them, inside their own lives; but, too, in some circle of Dante's. And in the cavern of trays, the coppersmith with his one tooth and serene eyes, looked at once like a tourist's artisan, and a disguised and saintly magician.

Raschid had cut himself out from the horde of children by an incident common between the sexes, and not unknown between adults and children strange to each other—a sudden wordless intimacy, based on a mutual attraction solid as an electric shock.

Raschid's reaction, James perfectly well knew, was inevitably rooted in a lack in the past, and a hunger for the future. His own, he faced with a familiar stale qualm, was at least the former. The future, now, was Tracy. He had never been truly equipped to love Oliver, if love entailed satisfaction. But, unrejected, he would have offered as fine substitutes as his nature would provide and guilt could prompt. But he *had* been rejected; first somewhere in secret, and then verbally. It was odd how clearly he knew that it was he who had been rejected, rather than Louise who had been chosen. If Louise had never found their son a very interest-compelling subject, she had maintained with him, during the periods when he attracted her attention, a mild-mannered friendliness. There were children who *did* interest her; but any comparisons which she may have made in silence, or in dreams, never resulted in maternal animosity.

It had always been hard for Oliver to speak; and it was Tracy who had got him through the ordeal of his decision, by her ability to listen, an ability as native and as finely-honed as her tennis game. How a child of his and Louise's could be that inarticulate, passed James' understanding. Though he secretly thought of Louise's articulateness as facile (perhaps because it worked so well on her newly-privileged kindergarten listeners), there it was. Oliver gave, always, the impression of weighing. He was a sort of small, human, heavily-constructed pair of scales, the results of whose balances were never disclosed. After the permissible baby age, he had been caught now and then telling stories, all involving possessions, material or animal; but until James had looked at them in the light of Tracy's sunny honesty, he had not called them lies. Like Tracy, he spontaneously believed lying to be the meanest of the vices. "Know the truth, and the truth shall make you free." It was Tracy's only biblical quotation.

One hot September afternoon she had said it to him, running her cool fingers over the pink shells of her toenails. James, waiting in his brown hateful bed-sitting room; Oliver, redelivered to the house which for twelve years had been James' home. Tracy had been standing at the window: he thought she appeared like Mercury, the gods' lissome and terrible messenger. She came over to the daybed, kicked off her pumps, curled up and seized her toes.

Over them, half humorously, half tearful, she quoted her maxim.

"Well?" said James.

"He wants to stay with Louise."

The curious shaft, like dry ice, that burned through him, he could not have diagnosed for his life.

"I don't believe it."

"He told me so. In so many words."

There was a silence. Tracy kept it; she never blundered.

"Well," he said at last. "How hard was it—for him, I mean?"

"Very, I think," said Tracy softly. She looked, for her, tired, and James rushed toward her in his mind's eye. How much she gave, how little, without denigrating herself, she asked. She had not demanded commitment. Now that she had it, she would have shaped herself to another woman's heavy and taciturn child, if that was what James and Oliver wanted. Oliver had liked her at once. He was always looking for a new thing to belong to him, James glumly thought, and it was Tracy who had lifted from all three of them that most savage incident of a split marriage— self-declaration by offspring. Louise, conditioned to consult, in her warm-soup voice, finger-painters versus block-builders, had kindly said, "Oliver should choose, himself. He's ten. It's only a limited choice, it's not as though he'd never see the other."

"A child that age, even a *frank* child," Tracy had said as she and James turned it gently over and over, "can't get words around huge things, the things its life is made of. If you ask him about motorbike parts, or batting averages, it's a piece of cake. But fool, awful questions, like 'do you love your mother?' 'are you mad at your father?' . . . What we've *got* to have is the truth, that's the only thing that'll hold up. He can say to me 'my father' or 'my mother.' To you, or Louise, he'd have to say 'you.' That's where, perhaps, I helped. Getting 'loyalty' out of it. Poor Oliver. Christ, the things people do in the name of loyalty. Pulling live tissue apart. I said it was a temporary pattern; just that. No great, per- manent decision. That you and Louise wanted to stand enough aside to give him room to breathe and think. This way, he needn't say to either, 'I don't want to live with you.' "

"It's just," said James lamely, "that he seems so remote from Louise."

Tracy laid her weary head back against the brown cushions of the daybed.

"Louise really only likes them at the pre-judgment age," she said astutely. "It makes her nervous to be sized up. Children are death on that."

"Did he say anything about me?" he after a while asked.

"Bang!" went knuckles on the door. James rose; it was their ice. Conveniently later she said gently, "He was embarrassed. He's only ten. And he sometimes finds it hard to be honest. This was one of the hard times."

James raised his amber glass and drank. Tracy, too, raised her glass. "To Oliver," she said slowly. They drank. Suddenly a wild relief—the die cast, that inn of decision in which the mind sleeps well—flooded James. "To Morocco," he said. But the second toast was too soon for Tracy. She set her glass softly by the ice-bucket, and closed her green eyes.

The chanting had stopped. The muezzin had gone back to wherever he had come from. The moonlight had withdrawn; Tracy was only a dark corner. James, who had sat down on a sighing hassock, got up. A light burst out in a kitty-cornered window in the lower garden, and Mrs. Neeson, in flamingo chiffon panels, went across it. How very gorgeous, James thought meanly. Mrs. Neeson was too much for him. The effect was flawless, but though effortless in appearance, seemed to spring from a vast hidden machinery. Surely Nubian slaves must have toiled for centuries, computers made hairline decisions, sleep, reading and eating have been forsworn for plans. Was Mr. Neeson the machinery?

Mrs. Neeson's references were too oblique and intimate to be name-dropping; nothing so cut-rate fell from her lips. The Palais Jamai, reprieved by quaintness and the lovely tokens of old Moorish lusts, amused her in an endearing way. "How we do envy you dear old number seven," she had said at once. "We cabled just too late." Tracy, with her candid gaze, had subsequently re-examined their small lustrous room. "Well, now we have the Good Housekeeping Seal," James said nastily. It had amused him that Mrs. Neeson should cause Tracy to reassess anything.

Did that flamingo vision arise, from the first sweet sleep of night, to perform esoteric rites of beautification? Or was she merely en route to the bathroom? The light still burned. The medina still slept. In an orgy of pre-dawn slackness, James wondered, abashed, if Raschid dreamed of the American who spoke French, who, infinitely powerful, infinitely just, was an enormous, sudden friend. James was as beautiful as Raschid; though, at thirty-three, it would never have occurred to him that this was true.

In the morning, the courtyard tiles shone from the hose. The fountain, released, sprang up and fell, and distant noises came from the medina.

Raschid came to the outer entrance about ten o'clock. James, who had gone out to treat with a taxi-driver, saw his striped djellabah swerve out of the medina-alley. The taxi driver said at once, "The guides will get police if he keeps does so. He can't guide. Beggars, beggars."

"He is not a beggar," said James shortly. He decided to ignore the taxi-driver's opinions. "At eleven-thirty, then," he said haughtily, and turned toward Raschid.

Day before yesterday, when he had first joined them—doubling their steps quietly along the stony way, regarded sideways by a James enchanted, apprehensive, waiting for the story, the brown small palm—he had worried about James' French. "Vous comprenez?" he asked, drawing up his short nose as though smelling language deficiencies. "Vous comprenez ce que j'ai dit?" Then he began to worry about Tracy, but not much. "Expliquez à votre femme," he said once or twice rather perfunctorily, as if she might be dangerous if too much excluded.

He made the stale standard joke, pushing a donkey aside, "Ce sont les petits taxis de la medina!" and his eyes laughing at James, at himself, at the donkeys, at the prostrate jest, took James into a dazzling intimacy.

At the end of their stroll through the bleak biblical landscape of stones, bare earth and bleached sun, James extracted a handful of change. Instantly a cloud passed over Raschid's brown eyes, muddying their color. He put both hands behind his back and looked sullenly down at his feet under the djellabah's dirty edge.

"J'ai voulu faire votre connaisance," he said. "C'était tout simplement ça."

Amazed, pleased, uneasy, James had returned his dirhams to his pocket.

"What did he say?" asked Tracy, smiling at Raschid.

"He said he wished to make my acquaintance, that was his only purpose."

They shook hands with him, first James, then Tracy, and he asked James when he would care to go through the medina. They were going the next morning, said James, but with a guide, it was already arranged. Raschid murmured something in Arabic. Then he lifted his head and said clearly in French, looking James straight in the eye, that he would like, once, to take them himself into the medina. They would go to certain places the guide would not have time for; then, when that was finished, they would go to une restaurante typique, très typique, très petite, très bonne, and there they would faire déjeuner ensemble. "Demain, peut-être?"

That they could not do, Tracy, easily snared, having committed them to lunch with the Neesons. "Alors, le jour après . . ." said Raschid.

"Hélas, nous allons à Meknes."

"Alors, le jour après ça . . ."

"But that's our last day," said Tracy, guessing.

James said to her in rapid English, "We could go in the afternoon, late, and have supper instead of lunch. I'd really like to. That would leave practically the whole day free."

"Good," she said instantly. She grinned affirmatively at Raschid; but his face, direly balanced between their glances, stayed dark until James committed them: "Eh bien, d'accord. A quatre heures et demi. Après, nous pouvons diner ensemble. Le jour après le lendemain."

The next day he came with them and their outraged guide. He pointed now and then, but did not speak except to say, with taciturn authority, "Moule Idris, c'est le plus beau de tous."

As they peered over the shoulders of a picture-snapping compatriot, into that vast, ordered, brilliant coolness, Tracy said a little crossly, "I don't see why they let people take *pictures* and not go in—if they take their shoes off, I mean. My husband went into one in Alexandria," she told the guide.

He gave them a bland frown. "Fez is a more holy city," he said. "Very holy." Raschid stared at James to see how he received this statement.

Disoriented, they trudged behind their towering and animated guide: coppersmiths, tinsmiths; souks; weavers, tanners, dyers. They debouched, helpless, into lavish rooms at the end of sinister entrances; undesired rugs, glowing like radiant signals, unfurled by rapid boys; mint tea; unstuffed hassocks, cast upon the floor to sink in gorgeous slow motion; mint tea. They flattened themselves against stone to let donkeys pass. The donkeys' aristocratic legs supported immense piles of planks, towering baskets, piles of colored cloth. "Ce sont les petits taxis de la medina," said the guide.

Tracy, all gold and green, in white linen, stayed cool and happy. James was battling a sense of disequilibrium. It seemed to have darted like a shadowy fish in deep water ever since the hour when he had heard the muezzin's raucous wandering call, when he had been alone at the window. He was summoned, yet he was not. He could touch people at any minute—indeed, it was impossible not to; but he should have been closer, or more distant. This way, it needed to be a travelogue, a chapter: the medina, Fez. The place hummed, milled, teemed; all the travelogue words. But the eyes that met his, over yaskmak and under turban, slid over human material borne past them by a guide.

His elbow was jerked; on his arm the soiled brown hand with the smashed thumbnail rested, pressing. "Voilà! C'est notre restaurante future. Quand nous faisons ensemble notre promenade."

He could see nothing but a blind darkness beyond an open doorway; and they were past it, anyway. But it was an engagement; and it was as though at last he were identified.

They had not gone to Meknes, after all. Something had upset Tracy, and she lay all day, qualmish and languid, not even much reading. She urged James to go anyway, but he suddenly realized how much he did not want to. He wanted to stay still. The Neesons *had* gone to Meknes, causing Tracy to remark, childishly, that if she *were* going to be sick, it seemed like a good day.

James sat in the shadow by the fountain and read *The Tale of Genji*. Ravished by a paragraph, he stared from his shade into a daze of sun. He jumped up, and went in to read to Tracy about the little maids going into the dim early garden, carrying their cricket-cages; but she had fallen asleep, her pale hair lightly snarled on the punched-up pillow. He stared at his future, awed. The simple, unambiguous, exquisite, and here-present future. He went back, through the cool splendors of the hall, into the court-yard, sat down and read the passage again. But this time it had thinned out. He shut the book, and then as two couples paused, staring lovingly around them, raised it.

He had not heard his muezzin again, except the night before, when, a semi-circular foursome, they were having coffee in the small bar. Then, though faint, the hard distant wail had caused them slightly to raise their voices.

It annoyed James that he did not enjoy the Neesons. He credited them with being out of the run; *more* of something, if not of something different. Mr. Neeson, who looked as though he had had his blood painlessly extracted and then been sealed again, had a small, pungent speech. It admitted of no qualifications, but it was lively. Mrs. Neeson, whose anecdotes, never blasting, were pleasantly penultimate, glowed and breathed. Perhaps Mrs. Neeson had all that blood?

A friend of hers, a more-than-promising young French film director (formerly a Godard protegé, but now intransigently individualistic), was, or might be, at Marrakesh; the Neesons were waiting for a call. Against the embroidered cushions, Mrs. Neeson appeared to have been incarnated from an absolutely first-class original. Lustrously, she leaned toward James, with a luminous-lipped air of barely pre-coital chic.

"He's very ready," she said. "Very open-ended. But there's a terrific thrust. He used color-change for mood long before Antonioni."

"Film is exciting," said Tracy. James saw with love that she felt uncertain, but not totally docile, in her habitual self-under-estimation.

"It's the camera. It's knowing how not to interfere with what the camera sees." A turbaned head appeared at her shoulder; it was the Mamounia, calling from Marrakesh.

The Gantrys were halfway up the stairs when she returned.

"Jean-Paul!" she cried softly after them. "It was! His art man is going to do some sketches of a palace in Meknes, and we're going back to Meknes, and meet him at a friend's place outside, where we can go for cocktails, and then drive on late to Rabat, all of us."

Back at the foot of the stairs again, the Gantrys glanced at each other, reapproaching the bar. Could she mean "all"?

"I've told him about you both." So she did. "And you were going to Rabat anyway, the next day."

James said at once, "How nice of him, and of you. But tomorrow, we can't." He saw Tracy's eyes cloud. "We're tied up," he nevertheless said. It sounded lame. Somehow he could not get a grip on Raschid which could produce him for the Neesons in the guise of an engagement.

But Mrs. Neeson was incurious and easy. "Oh dear, if we'd only known a bit sooner."

Behind the big carved door of Number 7, James said guiltily, "Why on earth don't you go? You can take a car back here."

Tracy had crossed to the window-grille. The fountain was still playing. "Darling, don't be ridiculous. 'Jean-Paul' doesn't want to see me. It might have been fun—but not just me, with them."

He joined her at the window. The cypresses pointed straight at a great many stars.

"I mean," said James, "he's been counting on it for three days. A kid that age . . ."

"Heavens, yes," she instantly agreed. "We couldn't change him to lunch, you don't suppose?"

He was somehow relieved that evidently it wasn't that she hankered for the Neesons in exchange for Raschid, as that she had a generous appetite for both. "We can't get *hold* of him. I've no idea where he lives, in the medina. Do you know," he said, surprised, "I can't even remember his last name. He told me twice, but Arabic names . . ." But it still seemed to him strange.

"Oh well," said Tracy mildly, and taking her kimono she disappeared into the bathroom, through whose open overhead arch he could hear her running the shower and cheerfully whistling.

He dreamed of Mercury. The god's heels, conventionally wing-tipped, barely rested on the kindergarten floor. The small black faces stared, not truly frightened. "And *this*," said Louise's breathy voice, "is *Mercury*. He is a messenger. He is the gods' *messenger*. He is a god, too. He is the god of lovers, and of thieves. We will draw that thing on his head. With our crayons. It is a helmet. A *golden helmet*. Oliver, will you turn him sideways for us, please." As Oliver moved to do so, James woke, coldly clear. Mercury had been beautiful. The small black faces had been beautiful; open, dark, turned like royal pansies toward Louise's sun. Louise's son. James' son. Not that pale, really, not in real life; not that squat, not that shut.

He had had one tantrum, Louise wrote. Only one. He bought a snake, sent from an unscrupulous snake-farm in Florida. It had to be fed live mice. Regularly. The whole thing was psychologically wrong at the moment. Cruel, stupid and inefficient. She had returned the snake, collect. Oliver had exploded. He had called her a white mouse. A white rat. For the snake to eat. He wanted to live with his father. His father was, actually, coming to take him away.

Louise, rancorless, and encouraged by this purging, had reminded him of his choice. It was a lie. He began to weep. He had never never said that, never, never. She had not said, "Then why hasn't your father come to get you?" And a little later, when she came back to the room, he hugged her violently and explained that he had said it because his snake had been returned. He had chosen her because he loved her. Since then he was friendly, and was saving for a Siamese kitten.

For an awful day James had wondered if, in his rage and frustration, Oliver had lived through minutes of believing his own invention; that he had summoned a father who, silently, never arrived; received a disprized home, nursed a secret he could never admit. Tracy had gone quite white over this story. But she did not think that, even in his rage, Oliver believed it. "That's his weak spot. It's because he's inarticulate, I'm sure. He lies sometimes, like about the racoon—because he can't fully express things."

Faces such as Raschid's did not, basically, need words; but he had them, correct, lucid, formal. It was a curious rendezvous; beyond the afternoon, the walk, the dinner, the farewell, what

did Raschid want? A different memory? A promise? A bond outside his arc? Yes, he had brothers, he had answered. Six. Two
sisters. No father. (Gone? Dead?) An aunt. A mother.

What sort of present could Raschid be given? He was extra-
ordinarily intelligent. He spoke well. He had fire, grace. He was
dirty; but small boys got dirty. But this was settled dirt. And the
djellabah was mildly ragged. Would he like James to meet his
mother? To what purpose? Was this really a friendship? Wild
as that seemed. What would they eat? What on earth would the
restaurant through that dark doorway be like? But then the inner
shops. . . . He felt a tremendous hot gaiety, a sense of some light-
hearted reprieve, that spilled into his sleep. He was amused to
find he was thinking in terms of "not letting Raschid down."

Their last day came over the gardens like a single jewel.
After lunch they went down to the lower level to say goodbye
to the Neesons, later departing for Meknes and Jean-Paul. The
Gantrys had an hour before Raschid's arrival. The lower garden
was cool and dusty; the Gantrys, faced with a long, sunny trek,
slumped peacefully in wicker chairs. Tracy thought of the postcards she had meant to get. "I could do it now," she said. "Oh sit
still," said Mrs. Neeson affably, but Tracy went on mournfully
remembering that she would *not* want to write them tonight, and
God knew, not before leaving early in the morning. Finally, she
went to get them. When she came back, some time later, she was
dissatisfied. Having searched, she had ended up with pictures
taken from curious angles, denigrating the courtyard and its views.
Nevertheless, she scribbled laxly, stopping to sigh, in the fragrant
heat.

At quarter past four, James rose. "Well," he said, "have a
fine trip. I hope . . ." But the Neesons were coming up, too. At
five, the car for Meknes would be there; they would wait by the
fountain. "Those streets must be death, in this sun," said Mrs.
Neeson. It was hotter in the upper courtyard, an intimation of
outside.

"You go and see," said Tracy to James. "He mightn't be
there yet."

James secretly had a feeling that he would have been there
for some time. He went out through the flower-beds, past the lily-

pool, along the tiled way, to the outside glare. Raschid had not yet arrived. There were two taxis (neither the one driven by Raschid's foe), a motorcycle, loiterers in the narrow shade thrown by the wall. He went back to the courtyard. Tracy had finished her cards. She stuffed them in her purse, slung it on her shoulder, and looked ready.

Suddenly James was anxious. It was like one of those dreadful, contrived stories in which at the last moment someone is run over, his mother falls dead, he is arrested, or locked in a windowless room.

"He *must* be there now," said Tracy. She had evidently explained things to the Neesons, since they looked only interested. "If your small Arab doesn't show, you'll get to Rabat with us yet," said Mrs. Neeson amiably.

"It's twenty-five to five," said Tracy. "You know he'd be there by now. Go see."

One of the taxis was gone. The shade along the wall had widened. He could not see Raschid. Perhaps he had come during James' return to the courtyard and dashed away for a minute. James' breath felt odd. I am *not* meeting a general to negotiate for peace, he reproved himself, a little amused and puzzled. The taxi-driver stared at him. James looked fiercely at the ground; the man knew perfectly well that his cab was not wanted. Then he raised his eyes quickly to his watch. It was a quarter to five, and a weight like a concrete block fell on him. Something *had* happened. And he would never know. That was the only part that was really bad. The truth, he thought, joking, can't make me free if I don't know it. Couldn't Raschid have sent him word? But he knew that an alley tart would have had more chance of penetrating the late sultan's harem, than Raschid or a friend, of penetrating the courtyard.

A taxi drew up, and two black and enormous women got out, one magnificent in royal blue, the other towering in a bone-crushing pink. They were mammoth, handsome, ferociously powerful. They began pulling bundles from the taxi, roped huge mounds, baskets, bags with knotted necks. Their driver had disappeared into the medina. James looked gratefully at this diversion. Raschid had no watch. Time, to an Arab child . . . But he did not believe it.

The taxi-driver reappeared from the medina entrance, followed by a man in a soiled white djellabah, leading two donkeys. The man and the driver began to load the bundles onto the donkeys, higher and higher; last came a roped trunk. Finally, when only the hung heads and delicate legs were visible, the man struck each donkey a blow with a large stick and they lurched, and then swayed, sagging, forward down the sloping alley and out of sight. The taxi backed, ground gears, rushed off. The driver of the parked taxi addressed James.

"Berbers," he said. "Berbers. No damn good." He spat from the taxi window. "Bad people around," he said.

James looked at him. The man stared into his eyes. "Bad boys, too," he said. "That boy, he kicked your wife."

"What?" said James.

"He kicked her," repeated the driver. "Police fix him soon, I say it. She speak to him nice, and he yelling, Non, non, non. And then she try to give him something. Give him American money. Goddam fool, he kick and yell."

"I don't know what you are talking about," said James.

"Not one hour gone by," said the taxi-driver with care. "Not one hour. He yelling at her, *menteuse, menteuse!* That's 'liar' he says. In French, crying and yelling. Then he pull up his hood, and kick her leg and run away. She smile at me, this way," he lifted his shoulders to his ears. "Very nice lady, not to get police."

James went over to the alley and looked down it. The Berbers and their donkeys had disappeared; other figures, other donkeys, strode and swayed. Hooded heads turned corners. Under a djellabah-hood, dark eyes, now turned a light, steadfast blue, raced away, raced away. The wall had cut off the sun, and a faint fresh coolness rose from the stones. As the taxi-driver watched him, he turned back and went toward the courtyard.

My Mother

ATTILA JÓZSEF

(Translated from the Hungarian by Nicholas Kolumban)

Mother held a coffee mug in both hands
late afternoon on a Sunday
and sat with a quiet smile
in the half-darkness.

She brought home her supper
from the baron's house.
We went to bed and I wondered
why they had a whole potful.

She was my mother, was small
and died very young. Washerwomen
die young. Their legs totter
from the weight of the wash.

Ironing gives them a headache.
The dirty laundry rises like the highlands;
clouds of steam soothe their nerves
and the attic offers a change of climate.
I can see her with an iron in one hand;
her fragile waist becoming thinner,
her body being crushed in the jaws of money.
Just think about it!

Her back was bent from constant work
and I never knew that she wore
a clean apron in her dreams, and in her dreams
the mailman tipped his hat to her.

A Winter Memory

Gyula Illyes

Translated from the Hungarian by Nicholas Kolumban

We ate you up, little pig!
the luckless farmer stabbed you

in the throat while you squealed with joy
as you heard his footsteps.

You danced behind the boards,
yet the people cornered you.

For even at the start of November
there was no feed left for you.

They dragged you by the ears
no matter how much you implored them.

Mother held your feet,
she who nursed you like her own son,

who fed you weeds and corn
and scratched your back.

I heard your screams
from under the warm quilts.

Wept and plugged up my ears.
Embraced my older brother.

I imagined all the horrors
when it's our turn!

But later I attended cheerfully
the singeing of your skin,

watched the up-shooting flames
and pulled your nails over my fingernails.

I chewed on your roasted, tiny tail
under the smoke-laden, ash-filled sky.

Your Song

JAMES ANDERSON

In a small bar in Los Angeles is a man
Who plays the piano and will write you a song,
Your very own song, lyrics and all
Composed on the spot for the price of a drink
And a five dollar bill, ten dollars on weekends.
I asked him once how he did it
And for the price of a drink and a five dollar bill,
The day being Tuesday, he told me to watch:
To begin, he said, it's Tuesday, it's seven o'clock,
You're already drunk, and you were drunk before you arrived.
My first decision is your song will be in a minor key.
He brought his arm down on the lower registers.
Now, if I can have your name, first name only,
We'll see how it sounds set to music.
He sang my name flat while bringing his big arm to bear
Down on the lower registers. Again.
Come on, now, he said. You know the words
So sing along with me. This is your song,
You've been singing it for years.

Red Tomatoes

Rolf Dieter Brinkmann

(Translated from the German by Hartmut Schnell)

The surprising effect
when you suddenly
see red tomatoes
on a corner, without

having thought of tomatoes
before at all. This is a
picture that knocks you out
on the spot, in the middle of

the day a closed fist, pressed
gently against both eyes.
By tomorrow something like this
will already look different, you think

and the tomatoes will be gone
then. Still, the imprint
lingers on both eyes, and you
don't quite know

what to do with it. As
for yourself you
decide to start all over
again in remembrance

of so many red
tomatoes as you've
never seen before
in a single pile.

Is The Grass Biased

JOSEPHINE CLARE

                              Is the grass
biased
do you notice   at last as you pass
the houses of the poor
how reluctant
              it grows here   in what
                      abortive patches
or walking beneath
                prospering trees   is there
or is there not
              a seething overhead   whisperings
              passed on ahead of you
up along the tranquil sunblotched street
                      your friends
do they look at you as before
or has your vision changed
                raw tentacles grown
                  does your presence
seem to inhale *their* air
is there so sudden less of *everything*
the standing in line   at the unemployment office
                each thursday at the ordered time
does it impoverish your blood
                or do you just *feel* weakened
when you step out of it
              into the street into the
                generous sunshine into
                an abundance
you search nervously
              for your sunglasses
suddenly this light is not meant for your eyes
any more   you need protection
                from it

Two Poems

WILLIAM HUNT

A Darkening Outing At Sea

The sun's horns shatter
and yet flow across the dark water,
like the melting we feel in love.

Someone is stretching out below
the cold surface of the unbreatheable.
His fingers lift up each wave.
He moves and moves
so that each wave rises in place.
We wait and watch
and he acknowledges that.

In groups of three and four
the children cry
mixed with the adults below deck
where everything sways.

 Now, imagine a lion on deck
whose gold hair is inserted
by the sun suddenly, ray by ray.
The gold wires thrum within us.

Later, the nipple
of the full moon is circled
with fire
and the lion goes
below deck to comfort the children.

No Longer May We Call

No longer may we call on those who once resembled storms
crossing a darkened horizon; we thought them spun out of trees,
furious with the vigour of their release from root-tangle,
clouds that dreamt aloud of the earth's shadow. Ballooned,
they spoke, as if with arms, they gestured. They even sang.
Gross, but intangible, a part of a thought that would not detach
from objects, which were in their case sun-weavings of foliage,
or in the cold days more obviously an uplift of yearning warmth
from bent, even then bending, limbs: a harshness of flesh
becoming earth, earthen, even as those who we called on emerged.
Great beings without names, we reach up now where once we
    saw you.
We learn now that we embody those forms we thought your own,
not that you live within us, but your warmth has become our
    gesture,
and the quieting storm's retreat is beyond our voices far within.

Two Poems

MELVIN B. TOLSON

Chittling Sue

On Central Avenue in Los Angeles
Chittling Sue's mother supported the family
By washing and ironing for the white folk.
With a dope-using husband who couldn't hold a job
And her children going to the dogs
Because she didn't have time to take care of them,
The mother became desperate.

One quiet Sunday after the church services
She served the family a big chicken dinner,
And Chittling Sue was the only one
Who didn't die of poisoning.

Grief-stricken for months,
The girl decided to go as far away as possible
From the haunted house on Central Avenue.
So she crossed the continent to Harlem
And went to work at a hole-in-the-wall restaurant.

When the Greek went out of business
Sue took over the place,
And it wasn't long before her chittlings
Became the talk of Lenox Avenue.
The black folk came from all parts of Harlem,
And the white folk followed.

If you haven't eaten in the Chittling Palace,
You've missed one of the delights of life.
Chittling Sue has five apartment-houses on Strivers' Row.

Harlem Big Shots, like Grand Chancellor Knapp Sackville,

Come to her to get the lowdown on business.
The little Greek is one of her cooks, when he isn't dead drunk.
And she pays him well.

But Harlem wants to know why Chittling Sue
Never goes to church,
Never attends a party,
Never has a sweet daddy,
Never visits anybody.

Brother Hester says
She's the same Chittling Sue
Who used to serve him
At the little Greek's hole-in-the-wall.

The Underdog

I am the coon, the black bastard,
On the *Queen Mary*,
The United Air Lines,
The Greyhound,
The Twentieth Century Limited.

I am sambo, the shine,
In the St. Regis Iridium,
The Cotton Club,
The Terrace Room of the New Yorker.

I am the nigger, the black son of a bitch,
From the Florida Keys to Caribou, Maine;
From the Golden Gate
To the Statue of Liberty.

I know the deafness of white ears,
The hate of white faces,

The venom of white tongues,
The torture of white hands.

I know the meek
Shall inherit the graves!

In jim crow schools
And jim crow churches,
In the nigger towns
And the Brazos bottoms,

Along Hollywood Boulevard
And Tobacco Road —
My teachers were Vice and Superstition,
Ignorance and Illiteracy . . .
My pals were TB and Syphilis,
Crime and Hunger.

Sambo, nigger, son of a bitch,
I came from the loins
Of the great white masters.

Kikes and bohunks and wops,
Dagos and niggers and crackers . . .
Starved and lousy,
Blind and stinking —
We fought each other,
Killed each other,
Because the great white masters
Played us against each other.

Then a kike said: *Workers of the world, unite!*
And a dago said: *Let us live!*
And a cracker said: *Ours for us!*
And a nigger said: *Walk together, children!*

WE ARE THE UNDERDOGS
ON A HOT TRAIL!

The Viewing

ELLEN TIFFT

Gerald stood in the front hall and looked out through the screen door. Have to keep tellin' myself; Irene's dead, her body's on the piano bench now the casket is, the funeral's tomorrow, can't get it through my head the last two nightmare days are real.

Lucky Erva tends to things, lucky I married her, just plain good luck. He looked out into the street, was it cooler or no, hardly, been like an oven all day. Nothing like July for heat.

Erva's tended to things, not Irene's mother, the fat lady of the Carnival, not her husband, oh Lord not him, Marcus, my brother, he's never tended to anything in his whole life. I've set him up in five businesses and five have failed, he never . . . made . . . a . . . go . . . of . . . anything. Well, lot a people out of work, Depression and all. Terrible.

Even Mrs. Toole the egg lady came in while we were all eating, talked a while on the side porch with Isobel and left. What a good neighbor Isobel is. Brought three dozen eggs too, was horrified when I tried to pay her for them, "not after a death," she said. "Hems, who's that?"

Oh it's the Marys, maids from across the street, look at that, don't know's I know them all dressed up if I hadn't seen, "Welcome, girls," that sounded condescending.

Erva came down the stairs and accepted the dish of baked beans, "thank you Miss Briggs and Miss Drawley, how nice of you. What pretty Bimberg sheers you have on, they're so nice for this hot weather, did you get them at Sheehan's?"

They nodded, pleased and pressed on in.

"You want to view the body don't you," she glanced up to where her daughter looked through the bannisters of the stairs, "Tobee, get dressed and come down, show the Marys to the side porch, I'll be with you in a sec."

"I am dressed," Tobee stood and smoothed her shorts and her string bean legs.

Gerald walked back slowly to the library and there was his mother in front of the casket. She dabbed at her eyes with her embroidered handkerchief. "No use to gettin' all 'motional about it now, Mother, it's in God's hands now, both her and her lover, we didn't turn the heater on and not light it."

"I wish I could really feel that, I'd like to think He engineered it all but I don't."

"Everybody's out on the side porch now, here let me take your arm, be careful of that step."

"I'm not an invalid, Gerald."

She went to Marcus and Delores who stood, held her hands for a little, "we'll go now," Marcus said, my he looked wrung through a ringer.

But they just came, Gerald thought, well; oh well. "I just asked them to step over for a little," he said, "they should get in early, the funeral tomorrow and all."

Marcus and Delores turned inside the library and stood in front of the casket. Gerald shut the door to give them a little privacy, should I offer them some hooch, no, don't want to get him started.

Erva came back in tried to pat Tobee's arm, she's been touchy all day, Tobee has, no help at all. She squirmed away now and they all sat silent. They could hear the peepers from down by the river. Someone mowed a lawn, all day the block's mowers had been going, so many people gawking in now toward the studio where the tragedy occurred. A train went by, Gerald pulled out his gold watch, wound it, "number five," he said, hoping someone would take the hint, go home.

"The train of the Phoebe Snow," Uncle Willis said and laughed.

"We'll have the family in the pantry as usual," Erva said,

"dear I hope there'll be enough *fruneral* chairs."

"Mr. Deets will tend to that Erva, the undertaker."

"Well how'll he know there'll be more people than we expected."

"Funeral chairs are always so stiff," Uncle Willis said.

"You don't like one of Mr. Deets' chairs, try one of his couches," Gerald said.

Everyone laughed.

Tobee hunched all up into a ball and pounded the floor in front of her.

"Tobee, listen," Isobel said, she tried to touch her but she writhed away, "it's wit like your father's that takes us poor mortals through such sad times." Tobee ran out.

There were several explosions and an old truck drew up to the curb. "That's not one of your brothers, Erva, that Irene's mother, the Fat —"

"Shh."

Isobel pulled the canvas curtains over, "we can't just stand here gawking."

"Take a ten ton derrick to extract her."

"She can barely shove along, Gerald you'll have to go out there, help her."

"Who'll help me?"

Gerald, walking through the living room, slipped on a small Oriental to a crouched position. Hems, nearly fell, we ought to get rid of these small Orientals, someone will break a neck some day, for sure. How'll she ever get through those doors, won't, I'll have to fasten back all four and fix the screen out too.

He did and then stood on the front porch. One foot pointed out the opened truck door, it seemed less a foot than a small rod with pounds of flesh pouring down over it, fifty pounds of flesh delivered on one foot, repulsive.

He went to the sidewalk and the open door, "Mrs. Prokoll, we're so sorry," he said. He shook her hand, rather his became wrapped in all the soft puddingy flesh of hers, his whole spine shuddered again.

She took two steps breathing heavily. Her breath made a

hundred small collapsing sea waves in the mounds of the flesh under a dress.

"—Here," he said, "—let me take your arm further. I know you want to come in and see your lovely daughter."

Her husband got out now and Gerald spoke to him. —"How are things at the Carnival?" Gerald said.

"A-okay" he said. "A-okay."

At the porch steps Mr. Prokoll took Mrs. Prokoll's arm and Gerald held one. He was as thin as she was big. Together he and Gerald worked her up all the steps. She leaned so heavily that sweat poured down onto Gerald's stiff collar, would melt it? Was the husband *doing anything*? Cheater! Gerald felt like saying to him you're cheating, you're just on for the ride.

When they finally got her to the top of the porch, Gerald undid his vest. She filled the whole doors, both sides. Puff puff.

Gerald and Mrs. Prokoll went through the living room on into the library. —"Where is everybody," she said with only half a second's glance at the casket. Gerald stiffened.

"—Why—uh—out on the side porch." She had hardly *looked* at her daughter. One brief glance. "—Where is everyone?" she said again.

"Out on the porch," he said. "Would you care to come out sit down a minute?" What *on*, he thought. Would the glider hold her? He hurried ahead and opened both sections of these doors too. She made her way through the vestibule, out to the porch and moved toward the glider as if she were docking.

She was so intent on trying to sit that she paid no attention to the introductions. Mr. Prokoll just stood beside her. He grunted hello. The glider gave a groan as she sat, the springs creaked, but it seemed to hold, would hold. Springs are smack dab on the floor, no wonder.

"I tried to make Irene keep her nose clean," Mrs. Prokoll said. Her breath came as if it were pumped with great effort. "I tried ta make her keep her nose clean but I never could. Not even when she was small. I kep my own nose clean myself, but I never could make her." Tobee had come back down to the porch. She sat now; amazed.

"Irene wouldn't do nothin' I ever ast her," Mrs. Prokoll said. "You know somethin'? I had her because of a bet. In a town where the Carnival played, they was this club, see, and they had this four hundred dollar bet with this other club that I couldn't get pregnant. See, 'cause I was such a fat lady. They said if I did they'd give him a hunert dollars. It was a joke. It was all a joke. I figured why the hell not. Hunert dollars, whaz that ta sneeze at? Ya know? So I had her, see. Odd Fellows, I think—was the name of the club. They had to pay him a hunert dollars, didn't they, Dad. We got it, still. Framed."

"A joke," Mr. Prokoll explained.

Tobee looked scared to death.

No one said anything. Mrs. Prokoll belched. A blast of hot air came way over to Gerald. He smelled it. Sickening. Spit came outside her mouth. Gerald noticed a crumb stuck there.

"They like to die laughing over it, this club. It was a joke, see, in that there club. So that's how Irene came to be. I tried to make her keep her nose clean but she wouldn't go straight. From the beginning she lied, cheated, stole, everything. When she got married I said 'Thank God, I don't have her no more.'"

No one said anything; still. They sat there; stunned.

Then, in the silence, Mrs. Prokoll stood up. "The mister 'n me ull run along now." Apparently she'd come to relieve herself of that speech and now she'd done it. And Gerald thought: Deliver me from evil.

As she moved toward the door, Gerald stood. It was Uncle Willis who talked, "Nice of you to come, Mrs. Prokoll, we appreciate your call. My wife stayed in New York because of a sick headache."

Feeling absent, manners come forward, Gerald thought, but he was glad Uncle Willis could say anything. Someone had to, had to be civil — though it was hard, Judas.

"I won't git to the funeral," Mrs. Prokoll barged through the library again, *not even glancing at her daughter.* "I'll be on stage then. I got my career to think of, after all."

"Oh yes, certainly, we under*stand.* Don't feel you hafta 'ness you want ta, 'ness you feel you should." The more said, the deeper he got in, Gerald felt. Might better shut up.

She lurched and leaned down the steps. Each time she landed the railing and the whole porch shook. The sidewalk rocked again as she crossed to the truck.

Gerald opened the door and then he and Mr. Prokoll tried to help her into the truck. They had to shove, Gerald thought of a soft rowboat, something. Finally the door could be shut.

When it was, Mr. Prokoll poked at his forehead and took off his cap. He examined the green visor, spit on a finger and shined it a little. "Gonna be a nice day tomorrow," he said. Then he drew out a stick of gum and offered one to Gerald. "I get it free from the pop stand," he said.

"Thanks," Gerald said and undid one limp spearmint. Funny time for gum, Gerald thought, I don't like it anyway, don't chew it as a rule.

They stood there and a large oily tear went down Mr. Prokoll's wood-carved face. Gerald jingled the change in his pocket. "We're *so* sorry," he said.

Mr. Prokoll's empty mouth shook and he threw out his lower jaw until it almost touched his nose, "so're we," he twitched as he pointed to his chest. Then he scratched his seat, his face still contorted.

"I wish I could do something for you."

"Nothing," Mr. Prokoll said and went behind the truck. He blew his nose and spit three times and then got into the truck. "Her'll be there tomorrow, I can't."

"I will not," she snapped.

"Yes you will," he said and jabbed viciously at the starter.

Gerald stopped in the vestibule, after all so many people without jobs, trying so hard, maybe she *had* to be the fat lady and that softened her brain. God I don't know. She hardly glanced at her beautiful dead daughter how *could that be.*

Back on the side porch there were chilly walls between himself and Erva, everyone sat there disconnected suddenly. He looked around very slowly, pained, sick, stricken. Grief doesn't bring people together it *separates* them, he thought.

"We all did it," Erva said quietly.

They all stared.

"We all did it; 'cept, Marcus and Delores, of course, *all* our hands are red except Marcus' and Delores'.

No one moved, no one even blinked.

"I did it," Tobee said. Erva just looked at her. "I planned that game."

"Yes that helped," Mother Stong said.

What about your scheme, Erva thought but didn't say. She hadn't told the scheme to Gerald so she was a conspirator.

"A failure of love, a failure to extend pure simple love to people who needed it, we are all guilty of that," Gerald said.

"But you *supported* them," Erva said. "That's a big *something.*"

"Very little."

"And Tobee you played with Delores some."

"Some," Mother Stong said and Erva's face slammed into a frown.

"You can't play much with a person you don't like, Cynthia Stong," Isobel said, "you know that, you're always urging a person to be himself herself, how is that making Tobee to be herself?"

"She should have compassion."

"Who's always saying pity is no good."

"*Compassion* is a different thing."

"How?"

"Well let's not get into that," Cynthia Stong said. "The terrible thing is one must make decisions and sometimes they're wrong."

Here it comes, the confession, Erva felt, and then Gerald will know I never told him about that scheme of Mother's.

"We killed them we're all murderers," is what Cynthia Stong said.

They all sat; silent, white; judged.

Gerald felt his chest constricted. "Tell us, dear Isobel, tell us we're not all guilty of murder, you will set us at our ease, it just happened that way, Irene having that awful mother and all, it just happened that way didn't it. We're not all that guilty, are we."

"We all did it," Isobel said.

"Then how will we bear it?"

She looked him very straight in the eyes. All her years of suffering were there. "We'll just have to endure."

Russell Lee

My Mother's House

Rose Graubart Ignatow

We came to my mother's house with the sagging wooden porch and bedrooms upstairs that had queer boarders during the Depression. There was one on Relief who filled his wastebasket full of tiny bits of torn newspapers.

A little girl answered the door and said in a friendly voice: "We are doing spring cleaning."

The house was occupied by strangers!

I turned to my husband: "My mother is dead," I told him.

"Let's go see your father," he said.

I was saturated with grief: "My father died before my mother."

— This visit was in a dream!

I remember real visits during the Depression when I witnessed my mother emptying that full wastebasket into the big can in the back yard. The flurry it made.

It aggravated her. Annoyed her further as bits fell outside the can and clung tenaciously to the cement walk. I'd coax them with a brush onto a dustpan for her — with a show of patience.

Yet, she was not unsympathetic towards the boarder. "You see . . . He has nothing better to occupy his time." And she gave me a pertinent stare that matched torn words.

I was hardly philosophical myself. I was waiting for my own weight of words to subside in me so I could speak to her less emotionally — about food.

My whole being seemed concentrated upon the problem of

food. We were on Relief. What to serve if we had company? People were our main relaxation. There was no money for other entertainments. I would lie awake nights figuring meals . . . Building menus around the Surplus Commodities . . . Dried apples, flour. Even salt butter and eggs some weeks . . . And bags of beans.

Before we got on Relief we used to go to my mother's house to borrow money for food. My husband's family was better off. They owned a brick house with a tenant upstairs. But his mother had a weak heart and we did not wish to worry her.

"You put too much salt in the soup tonight," my husband complained. "And not enough last time. You are becoming careless."

I was a fairly good cook when I had the proper supplies, so I said nothing. The soup had been made of dried split peas, water and an onion, all that was left of food in the house.

In the afternoon he had taken the last banana, the one I had saved for *the kid.*

He went down to get another one, hating himself as he walked past the grocery where he had taken a bottle of milk on credit. No one could ask him to go to that store again.

The Grievance Committee had presented our case. Getting on Relief was not easy. In the meanwhile we had to get some money. The only things we were taking on credit were milk, bread and eggs for *the kid's* sake. *The kid's* money had gone too. *The kid* shook the mailbox tin bank and it made no sounds.

"When the check comes," I kept saying. "There'll be even more pennies . . . "

"Check, check," he said to the tin bank. He liked the sounds without even knowing what *check* meant. Didn't ask, for once. Usually he asked too many questions. *Kids* of four will.

I, myself, had not been able to get a job and yet I still acted as if it was impossible for us to starve. It just couldn't happen. It seemed too silly. I couldn't think about it without laughing. Before anything like that happened we would borrow money.

We both knew that's what we had gone into Brooklyn for to my mother's house with its uneven wooden porch steps on which those boarders sat.

It was Sunday and lucky for us there was no agent in the change booth at the subway. With one nickle the three of us had pushed through the turnstile.

Neither his mother nor mine knew he had lost his W.P.A. job. The *pink slip* had come. And he couldn't get back on The Writers Project without getting on Relief first.

The first thing my mother did after we arrived was to begin complaining about all the payments she had to make that month. She blamed the boarders for her large electric and gas bills. And there was a general mumbling about how much meat cost. It seemed my mother was making it impossible for us to ask for a loan.

She asked us if we wanted a bite to eat. It was silly for us to think she was lukewarm in this invitation. She sometimes hated to see her kitchen messed up. With all her boarders coming in and out she liked keeping the house straightened up.

Luckily she decided to have some coffee after a while, so she put out some other food for sandwiches too.

At my mother's house, Pete, the shy Italian boarder, a man of forty, looked at my full form and stockingless legs and said to me: "Your husband no work yet?" And I could feel his thoughts . . . . Your skinny man without a job sleeping with you, and me, Peter, so husky and working . . .

Aloud he said: "If you not married, I marry you."

Pete worked as an operator on lumberjackets and snow suits. He played the trombone in a band for recreation. He always made it his business to be polite . . . to ask about your health, comment on the weather and inquire whether your business was slow or busy.

"Your husband's business . . . It's good now?" he had asked politely.

"No work, yet . . . " I said. (That's the way my mother was beginning to speak his English.)

"That's too bad . . . no very good. If he work on machine I take him in. No much work — but it's good even a little."

"Thanks Pete. No understand work on machine. Only typewriter machine. Make stories."

"Stories . . . I see . . . "

"What were you and Pete so chummy about?" my husband asked me.

"He wants to give you a job on a machine."

"Do you suppose a guy like me could learn to use a machine?"

But he was joking. "What day is it, anyway?" he asked.

"Worrying about rent?"

"No, we need a dispossess to get on Relief. It's just that I've lost track."

One's necessity must not affect others too much. It must have its form, must not be lawless and overreach propriety.

Necessity must be segregated, identified. Number 104.

"Number 104!"

That was our number. But our investigator was not in yet. She could not be found or she had not come in that day, or something like that. But a substitute was arriving from an upstairs department.

An old loft had been turned into a Relief Station. There were offices and desks for the personnel. And rows of wooden benches for the likes of us. There were policemen at every door to take away anyone who carried grimness too far. Society demands sincerity of its clients but not extremes.

A riot caught on in one of the cubicles and a policeman brought out the human flame.

The Welfare People were stalling us. At the Union for the

Unemployed the Grievance Committee was writing out demands: A BOY OF TWENTY IS WALKING AROUND WITHOUT
SHOES. WE DEMAND IMMEDIATE ACTION.

URGENT! A WOMAN OF SEVENTY IS SLEEPING ON THE
FLOOR. THE INVESTIGATOR HAS PROMISED THE SETTLEMENT
HOUSE WILL SEND HER A MATTRESS. WHY HAS THIS NOT BEEN
ATTENDED TO?

One woman was crying because she just had a tooth pulled.
She was holding her jaw. Another was smoking a tattered cigarette the man next to her had rolled and given her. One old
lady was using obscene language: she was feeling sorry for a
man who had carried the Surplus Commodity—tomatoes that
week—until his shopping bag began to leak and break. He had
lost almost all of his tomatoes.

One man was talking listlessly: "If I only had a job. Then
I could get my pay every week and not have to go through all
this."

The Grievance Committee had come with us to the Relief
Station to get an Emergency Food Order.

The policeman looked at us. His attitude said: there's no
point in talking to me about your troubles. I've got plenty of
my own with all of you.

"There's no service Saturday, as late as this," said the Social
Service lady.

"I don't give a damn about this," my husband said. "You
promised a check definitely last week. And you lied two days
ago; you told me it had been mailed. Well, do I get the Food
Voucher, or do I get arrested? Go ahead. Take me to court. I'll
tell the judge something about you desk hounds and your lying
promises."

"Just a minute . . . " The girl went into an office and came
out again. "There's a check for you. It's being mailed."

"I can't wait any longer. What I want is a Food Voucher.
And you know it."

She disappeared again. This time she appeared with a more

confidential air. "If we give you the voucher . . . you forfeit the check."

It was so obvious it sickened him, but this simple ruler mathematics of playing on people's faith was routine to them. This office equipment and well-meaning airs . . . Just an expedient gesture to see if it was food which prompted them.

"You can give me the Food Voucher."

"Just a minute."

She returned and brought out a voucher which had been made out for them some time ago.

He looked a little sheepish and a little proud with the voucher in his hand at last. Neither feelings were very definite in him. But they filled him like wine slowly drunk. It was drama warming him, bringing a glow into his first act, that moment when he heard his own strong, yet strange, voice with just that edge of desperation in it—it had vibrated in the room like a twang of a stringed instrument.

The policemen standing at attention near the doors were motionless like store dummies; especially when there was a woman client with a child by the hand . . . This combination seemed to make them especially still.

Food.

She was thinking specifically about the glory of food.

"Thank God we don't have to go to see your mother and listen to her speeches this week," my husband said.

I was too intense about all the food we'd buy to mind his disparagement of my mother and of that house in Brooklyn with boarders constantly leaving and new ones coming in. But Pete was still there. And he made me so uncomfortable. He, a shy man too. We wouldn't have to go to the house this week.

"We ask for five and she digs up three dollar bills and with each one a poverty soup recipe," my husband said too caustically.

"And we'll be able to get you a new ribbon for your typewriter. And a ream of white paper. You'll see . . . " I ignored his annoyance at my mother's ways.

At first he was irritated and thought I was a bit mad. It was only a Food Voucher—not money. I knew he was getting angry with himself and our situation because his ribbon had dimmed.

I went to a store, one of the smaller chain stores and called the head clerk aside and showed him the Food Voucher. I told him I had to have a few dollars in cash.

My voice had an urgency which displeased me. But I accepted it. Especially when he promised he would do his best for me.

Every once in a while walking through the aisles for cans or bags or boxes of food I felt something human touching me. It was the clerk, pretending to straighten cans and prices in my area, the one who had promised to do all he could . . .

I felt indignant and helpless as in a dream.

Rimsky, Nijinsky, and
a Pile of Wet Blankets

JAMES REISS

My mother-in-law, an old-guard Russian, is embarrassed
to tell me the Ukrainian word for chair means "under-the-ass."
Also, the Ukrainian word for skid means "fall-on-the-ass."
In the Ukraine there are no buts about it,
along with a lot of slippery ice.

Come to think of it, geographically
the Ukraine is sort of the gut of Russia, opening
out on the vast cloacal Black Sea. . . .
But my Chekhovian mother-in-law is embarrassed
by such talk and retreats to the livingroom stuffed chair.

I remain at the table, grinning, thoroughly *nye culturni,*
in love with the idea of language.
I wonder, what would the Ukrainians make of my rump roast?
And what about the diningroom rug?
Would they call it an "under-the-under-the-ass"?

Suddenly I get up from my vodka.
In my peasant's boots I step outside.
The Great Gate of Kiev looms in the front yard.
Under the Gate my gross wife has peeled off even her babushka.
We will make love here and now, skidding on icy cobblestones,
        landing on beautiful asses.

One Of Us

STANLEY PLUMLY

Think about ten years ago
when loneliness was simply
lack of company,
or later,
when it was three-,

four-sided crowds,
parties in the morning,
or the other side, and
the politics of talk
was like applause

above silence,
I think about now:
about the quiet,
the dark, the hard edges,
the purity in single words,

the few friends, like physicians,
and the women,
for whom the body broke
like bread.
I think about now

the way one thinks
about the future,
how the mind, all alone,
makes it up in order to deal
with what is coming.

The Rendezvous

CHARLES EDWARD EATON

The woman in the white dress sits on the red sofa—
It takes only a little expertise in blurring to suggest
That she is a swan floating on a pool of blood.

The arching neck, the little white hooded hat, the staring eyes
Such as might have been brought up out of the soul by a shoe
button hook
Go with the notion of well-creamed, well-turned, sanguine water.

She floats on the vivid possibilities of a connection.
It is as though I had her in mind long ago when I bought the
red sofa:
Things brim this way in the background until they flood.

Though one does not intend an indiscriminate invitation to the
furniture-minded,
Other women came, fat as partridges, standing heron-legged
beside the sofa,
But something placed in advance waits for the swan to track
forward like a bird in a shooting gallery.

It takes an unassuming courage to know when the time has come:
All I did was prepare the pool, a blood donation given to the
donor,
Sitting on the red sofa myself to get the feel of it.

Then one morning in the far reaches of the water something
stirred.
I kept tensely to one side, a shadow in the shape of a black swan:
She was insistently a woman, and then, and then, the gorgeous
bird.

Call in the ornithologists now to see the elegant, the odd,
The shadow and the substance that miscegenate—
I can rise, lustrous, black, streaming with the blood's powerful
   release

And go into another, quite an ordinary, room to drink a brandy.
The woman in white, impervious, improbable, has been known
   for years:
Spotless, detached, she sits on a sofa no one ever solicited for
   blood.

On Being Loved

FREDERICK ECKMAN

It is not like being the rails of a railroad track,
nor like a train thundering over the rails.

It is like being the train & the rails together,
the warm Ohio night, & the sweet haunting whistle,

& the right-of-way with its wild strawberries,
tiger lilies, tin cans, & soft gray cinders.

When she smiles at you with fifty-seven candles
behind her eyes, I want to tell you, friends,

it's better than owning all the railroads in America.
It's even better, I swear, than going to Cedar Point.

I love *her*, too. She has an infinite supply of candles,
& free passes on the train, & she tastes like wild

Cedar Point railroad tiger-lily strawberries. Honest,
she does. Loved by her, I am happier than a purple boxcar.

The Orphan Maker

WILLIAM HATHAWAY

In the midst of my life
I find myself in a dark wood
where I leave the children,
carefully collecting the trail
of crumbs, their sweet cries
growing dimmer in the gathering
night. And no shade will come
to lead me back to my little ones,
or even to aching contrition.

A new child grows in my side,
conceived in innocence and reckless
joy, it now swells and mutters
like an angry dwarf. Like a money-
belt of pain, a shameful brown
paper bag hidden in a banker's coat.

Dereglement des tous les sens
they say; "nobility of the mind."
No lyric flights can assuage
the inconsolable grief of children.
All my words lose heart.
Self-loathers have no right
to love and never do.
I must forgive your love, your
suffering, and hungerless eat
the bitter gruel that I've hoarded
from you, my lonely orphans.

In the deep woods a witch waits
in her quaint house of horrors.
She is your new cruel mother
children. Obey her and love her
for she is all the world's safety.
Goodbye, I will not come or write.

River Proposal

STEPHEN HARRIGAN

We found a place
where the shallow current
fell within its means.

Upstream the snakes were drowning,
coiling on the fence wire.
On the road the armadillos
mouldered in their broken shells,
buzzards dove into windshields.

In a garage
someone's flensed deer
swayed by its hind legs.

I could feel them all die
when I touched you,
I could feel them all die
and listen to myself say
It can't be helped, let them.

So beside this basin of small
turbulences
our human love came over us.
In the years to come
we would be dangerous
and unappeasable.

Martha Maverick

Montana, again

Andrew Grossbardt

This time you are not waiting
as the plane lowers
toward the valley I remembered

somehow greener. The pulp mill,
teepee burner open, sends its haze
toward town and the dying crops

burn brown in late summer sun.
I've come to the far end
of our deliberate arc

and the whole Montana sky
tilts with the descent. I come
with a picture—your head turned

to catch the sun that last morning
in the courtyard at San Miguel,
Patricia's woolen sweater,

flowers and gray stone—
and know I'll leave
with none to take its place.

I want to open up my heart
again, let all the sky
that's left pour in, but Jesus,

what is left is so brittle,
if I breathe it breaks. Tonight,
we'll meet, no longer lovers

or even friends, under a sky
that once seemed new
and say goodbye forever.

My Grandfather's Bones

WILLIAM JOYCE

Often my mother would remind me what a grand success my father could have been. He was the oldest of thirteen children. Unexpectedly, my father had to quit school and support the whole flock of them.

His own father was a crane operator at the local steel mill, Bog & Bliss. Just by pressing some little levers he could tilt a two-ton ladle filled with molten pig iron. One morning he climbed to his crane pie-eyed. All day he nipped from a thermos jug of cherry port. He didn't even hear the lunch whistle. He was dreaming of his dream back in Belfast. Thirteen children and twelve-hour shifts seven days a week weren't in it, that's for sure. He must have been dreaming the dream where the Statue of Liberty dissolved into a barmaid holding a pitcher of draught beer above her head. Every fourth pitcher she brushed her knee against the back of his stool. High atop the stool he thought how lucky he was to be out of the damp and the fog. No more dreary walks through McWain's pasture. No more midnight's chill weaving its way to the marrow of his bones after a weary round of the pubs. America was warmth and freedom. The dream was as high as he ever climbed. Everywhere he looked he saw the tongues of the open hearths licking the Irish fog. Women saved themselves for the day when they would have a good time. They dropped their Saint Christopher medals into a stein of lucky lager . . . a toast to the virility of John Thomas O'Rush. America was doing what you wanted to do when you wanted to do it.

Still my grandfather was doomed. Prophylactics weren't the

rage yet. The "pill" was still an aspirin. Thirteen children had cramped his style. All he saw was an endless row of open beaks squawking for papa to bring them one more worm. He was down on his patience. Everytime he lifted his wife's skirt he had to pay the city hospital fifty-two sixty. Enough was enough.

Everywhere he looked a soft, red glow was rising around him . . . rising through the floor of the crane cab . . . threatening to bear him away through the tin roof . . . and the layers of smog . . . through the bank of cotton-candy clouds . . . past the jets of semen that trapped him in a crane cab . . . to the pure blue sky and peace.

He yelled for another round. He watched the flutter of the barmaid's apron and thought of the handful he would grab the next time she came past. In the meantime, he gave the lever the final jerk of the day.

Heave-ho . . . the trestle car waited . . . the ladle tipped . . . just like tomato soup . . . bowl after bowlful . . . car roofs and cotter pins . . . stainless steel candle holders and tiny ball bearings . . . trolley tracks and gunsights . . . twelve hours later . . . crocked . . . enveloped by the glow from the bowels of the furnaces . . . my grandfather stepped from the crane. The barmaid smiled . . . the beer steins tinkled . . . the juke box flooded his ears with Yarmolinsky's wedding polka . . . "a two-step m' lady?" . . . what a fine rump . . . pleasingly plump . . . caressingly rotund . . . my grandfather reached . . . the barmaid sidestepped . . . her apron fluttered like a matador's cape . . . the bull with the crumpled horn flew past . . . and dropped . . . three stories down . . . to the crash of bear steins . . . and the hoof pounding of Yarmolinsky . . . plop, unnoticed . . . and the American Dream died in his liver.

For three weeks my grandfather was an enigma. My grandmother was in a virtual stew. At night she hid behind the door with a rolling pin in her right hand. She listened for John Thomas's footsteps coming down the street. She shined a flashlight out the window at every third passer-by. She figured he was off on one of his lusty capers, spooning it up with some trollop in the back of a taxi-cab. It never occurred to her that John Thomas couldn't afford taxi-cabs. For thirteen years he had been holding out on her. Of that she was sure. Her notion of compensation was intriguing. Steel mills were massive. Grocery stores were small. Therefore, steel mills paid more than grocery stores. One steel plant could cover two hundred acres. Their smoke stacks touched the sky. There was nothing to compare to it in Ireland. On payday she was sure he needed a shopping bag to carry all the money. What he didn't give to her, what he didn't booze, he buried in a dirt hole. The one book in the house clued her in on this. It was *Treasure Island*. She had one lady friend who could read. Every time my grandmother saw her on the street she called her into the house and made her read aloud from the financial sections of Stevenson, the digging and the counting. According to grandmother's philosophy of life, appearancess were deceptive because anybody who had anything kept it buried in a secret place. When my grandfather needed a taxi he simply dug some money out of the ground.

He never got any further than a taxi-cab with his pickups. They drove round and round the city. They kissed the whole time. Lovemaking for my grandmother was similar to stoking a coal furnace. It was a little chore that had to be done every so often just to keep the house from becoming chilly . . . hike up that skirt . . . whiff . . . wham . . . bam . . . thank you ma'am. The kissing part she liked though. She and my grandfather had done quite a bit of it in their courting days in the old country. She couldn't imagine any other enjoyment. Even in her wildest paranoia, she kept my grandfather kissing in the back of that taxi-cab till his tongue fell out.

Grandfather first appeared in the sheet pressing mill . . . as a grim joke on the steel industry. There was no way they could get rid of him . . . there he was floating down the rollers . . . not a body . . . just an impression, inverted of course, on sheet metal bound for a tank factory in Kenosha, Wisconsin.

Uncle Ed spotted him seven years later . . . crawling up the Alpine Highway. The paint had peeled off a single-turret job revealing the upper half of his father. That silly cherry port grin he always wore after an extended bender was still intact, along with his Van Winkle beard, and the fat black

mole in the middle of his upper lip. Nobody could understand
why Uncle Ed kissed the side of the tank. They thought he had
gone buggy with patriotism. The commander gave him a Good
Conduct Medal. He didn't have the nerve to tell them the truth.
Uncle Ed thought they would sandpaper his father away.

Uncle Tom got a bottom view of grandpa just after the war.
He was vacationing with his family at Lake Erie. He had just
gone in for a dip. His ears were plugged with sinusitis. He
didn't hear the outboard approaching. There was just time to
plunge and pray for the best. Out of the roar in his ears . . .
the loss of equilibrium . . . the wake rattling his dentures . . .
his feet stuck in the mud . . . the fear of bends in his abdomen,
he looked up. His father grinned from the bottom of the boat,
just for a second . . . through the ripples and the foam and
the translucent scum . . . the husk of a floating carp . . . the
rainbow oilslick . . . the kernels of popcorn . . . and the
corked wine bottle without a message in it. Uncle Tom plunged
to the surface. He churned full-steam through the water and
debris. He waved . . . he screamed . . . he foamed at the
mouth. The family of four faded away on their little outboard.
They thought it was all in good fun. They waved back and blew
kisses. They'd never looked at the bottom of their boat. They
couldn't understand a grown man hysterical with the vision of
something irrevocably lost but always searched for.

The foreman of the sheet pressing mill wasn't so taken in
with my grandfather's impression. Work was work. Business was
business. The show must go on. All the men protested. They
wanted to get a closer look. It might be somebody they knew.
The foreman remained adamant. A quota's a quota. Already they
were two tons behind. The foreman believed in life everlasting.
But he hadn't figured on a skeleton in his sheet metal.

The sheet metal carrying my grandfather was within six feet
of the water cooling department when the rollers rattled. The
housings shook. Gauges flew awry. Screws danced in their
threads. Bolts bounded from their moorings. Mechanics came
running with their tool chests. Something was jamming the
works. They removed the plates from the gear box. Complete
silence soared through the sheet pressing mill. Everyone tiptoed

closer to make sure their heart wasn't teasing their eyes. There before them . . . between the second and third gears . . . jamming the rotary mesh . . . clogging the central spindle . . . threatening the twelve-ton quota . . . fucking up the works . . . was the skeleton of my grandfather's right hand, the same one that had yanked crane levers for thirteen years.

The foreman was aghast. He thought someone had played a dirty trick on him. He threatened a full report. He snatched the hand from the gear box. He gave the men a dirty look. Then he ran pell-mell for the superintendent's office.

The superintendent hadn't been caught with his pants down. To the contrary. He'd been mixing it up in the nut-and-bolt department. He'd been inspiring the rank 'n file. Beside the file cabinet he stumbled on something hard. It completely threw him. He bumped his hip against a cotter pin. He stooped to investigate the culprit. He held it high in the air for everyone to see. The rank 'n file guffawed. Their superintendent looked so simple . . . standing there holding a bone . . . from the middle finger . . . high above his head. The second the super-intendent heard guffawing he turned pink with rage. Now he was sure the bone had been planted just for his visit . . . just to spook him . . . trip him up . . . let him know he wasn't wanted by the working man. He threatened an even fuller report than the foreman.

A full investigation was in the works. He threatened cutbacks in production . . . layoffs in personnel . . . kickbacks for those who would rat . . . he insinuated witchcraft. He blew on his thumb, tapped his temple, scratched his triple chin and farted. All the men in the nut-and-bolt department cheered. The super-intendent turned his back. He charged up the gangway. He tucked my grandfather's middle finger in his vest pocket. He ran ahead to consult with the production manager in charge of slag.

Already the production manager in charge of slag was rounding the corridor headed for the vice president in charge of drainage. A rib cage had exploded from one of his trestle cars full of slag. A sternum was found jutting out between the sixth and seventh ribs . . . with a Saint Christopher's medal tied around it . . . in a double half-hitch.

My grandfather had been known by his badge number. Alive, he was a born recluse. He didn't say "yea." He didn't say "nay," he didn't say "boo." He stuck to his own guns. Even when he peed you couldn't hear the tinkle. In any circle he would never make a splash. His drops fell like snowflakes. For months after his death, though, he was the conversational rage. He took the plant by storm. His foot fell out of a thermos jug in the wire and tube division. His right arm came up in a flush in the ladies' toilet. It caught an office worker by surprise. She was harvesting her bum-gut when she felt a tickle. She tried not to notice. Three months before he had made overtures to her. He asked her to join him for a Tootsie Roll in the company canteen. They would split it. She had lifted her nose in the air and sniffed. She only dated office men. Working men were so much cabbage. Grandfather avenged himself spectacularly. He got in her system and refused to let go. He wiggled up her colon. He played havoc with her small intestine. He made her urethra slide over. She had a sore ass for six months. She cried "wolf" only when her gall bladder got rubbed. Two maintenance men had to pry her cheeks apart. With a plumber's plunger and a pair of forceps they plucked out the avenger. While the lady pulled up her bloomers she thanked them three times. Then she snatched up the arm and bolted for the office of the maintenance head.

Everyone who had a piece of my grandfather met at the same time . . . in front of the timekeeper's office. Their heads were bowed . . . they were thinking of how they would explain their bones to the boss . . . of the reparations for their injuries suffered on the job . . . they were thinking of their status, too. They couldn't see around the oncoming corner . . . they were too occupied with themselves. All they could see was the tops of their shoes. Everyone collided at the same time. They hadn't seen the other thirteen bone carriers approaching. They all fell down. Grandpa flew in thirteen different directions. His sternum bounced off the superintendent's ear lobe. His knee cap stunned the foreman in the coccyx. He bounced off walls . . . he clattered along the floor . . . he jumped in people's laps and pinched their tooka-lookas. He was everywhere and nowhere. His revenge was catastrophic, apocalyptic, cabalistic, pantheistic, necrophilliac, solipsitic, metaphysical, and all a lie.

If only he had lived to see the day when I would revenge him. Living is the important thing. Legends won't do. Neither will reminiscence . . . my mother nearly made me puke with her soppy reminiscence. She gave me the bare bones of the story. It was up to me to piece things together. I did my best. It was too much. My foul concoctions drove me into fevers and night sweats.

My mother made my grandfather out to be a real pilgrim . . . the John Smith of Ireland . . . the seeder of maize . . . the diddler of Pochahanas of Belfast.

"Don't laugh Bosley, if it weren't for your grandfather you wouldn't be here," she said. Well, that was all right with me, I hadn't asked for as much. Things were bad enough without me being born.

What my mother really admired was my grandfather's virility . . . serving up thirteen children showed the makings of a real man. She was sure he had invented a secret formula, an aphrodisiac from onions or sour grapes. She wasn't sure which. All she knew was that my father had the secret and was holding out on her. I hadn't been born till they were forty. A real menopause baby. They thought they were over the hump. All those brothers and sisters had been a lesson to my father. Even the thought of a new-born child made him turn green. He and mother worked the rhythm method. The two dangerous weeks he taped his pecker to his right thigh. He used up so much black electrical tape, Levine, the druggist, finally made him a deal. There was a cylindrical bald spot in the middle of his groin. On my mother's forty-fifth birthday she broke the news to him . . . she hadn't flagged in six months. My father wasted no time. He tore off his vest . . . all the buttons rolled across the kitchen floor. He bent my mother over the kitchen sink, next to the garbage disposal, free-style . . . from then on it was free-style . . . three and four times a day, free-style . . . whenever he felt the urge . . . in bed or out . . . while she was peeling the potatoes . . . or dressing the turkey . . . he caught her in the strangest positions . . . bent over stoking the coal furnace . . . on her knees scrubbing the bathroom floor . . . up on a stool trying to swat a horsefly floundering in the chandelier . . . he was a regular demon . . . a fountain of youth . . a first class cocksman.

Mother was pleasantly surprised. She hadn't thought he had it in him. She went out of her way to make him happy . . . shining his shoes . . . dusting off his suit coat before he went to Tom's Bar . . . and serving generous portions of fried onions for dinner.

Two months later, she was pregnant. Her menopause didn't manifest for ten more years. It had all been a trick . . . to get me into the act. He never forgave her. He went back into hiding. Instead of passing out cigars when I was born, he bought a case of black electrical tape. All his friends walked around with that roll of tape in their pockets for months. None of them understood.

If it had been up to my mother, my grandfather and not Chistopher Columbus would have discovered the New World. It took a lot of courage to cross the Atlantic in those days, she said. The boats were something less than sturdy. Emigrants were crammed in like sardines . . . the wind was fierce, the waves colossal . . . the boat rocked the whole trip. It was impossible to spoon even two peas into your mouth. They kept rolling off onto your neighbor's lap. The trip was brutish. My grandfather bore up well. He comforted everyone. He surveyed the decks patting people on the back who were bent over the rail gagging. He supervised the vomiting from beginning to end. He was a seaman, a saint, an explorer, a father, a provider, a dare-devil, and the working man's working man all rolled into one. He was the epitome of freedom and courage and virility. Every day I got the same hog slough in school about the founding fathers. The idea was to give me a legacy . . . something to live up to . . . a legend . . . a sense of my roots . . . a guiding light . . . a trailblazer's spirit . . . the rock of ages . . . "Don't fire till you see the whites of their eyes" . . . "I have but one life to give" . . .

After two days my grandfather was assembled in front of the timekeeper's office . . . every bone was in its proper place . . . from clavicle to pelvis . . . from his rib cage to his tibia . . . all except his skull. They searched up and down the plant for his skull. They couldn't find it anywhere. The Saint Christopher's medal was draped over his knee cap. That was the only place it wouldn't slip off. The only identifcation they had were his shoes. They set them beside his skeleton for the next of kin to identify.

One morning my grandmother wandered into Bog & Bliss. This was her last hope. It had never occurred to her to check the mill, John Thomas's crane department. She feared all those men leering at her. Only on the advice of a neighbor had she come.

For the last three weeks she'd been hanging around taxi-cab stands. Each driver answered her desperate eyes with the same reply. "Sorry ma'am, hundreds of men with moles on their lips kiss in the back of my crate. What can I do?" When one of the drivers cast a lusty eye at her own fallen flanks, she gave up the taxi-cab idea.

Now John Thomas was laying at the bottom of some bar-stool. His real fidelity was invested in booze. She should have known. It took her another week to make the rounds of saloons, every rotgut shot-and-beer dive within a ten-mile radius. Surely he was laying in a puddle of cherry port rift. It was hereditary. John Thomas's father and the father before that couldn't hold their booze. She imagined the wildest catastrophes. Her husband had been bumped off by a cow catcher. My grandmother lumbered up the B & O tracks looking for his body. She scoured railroad embankments. When the neighbor told her about the fat wad of insurance money she could collect if John Thomas died on the job, she said, "I'll bet he swallowed a wine cork on his lunch hour."

She wasted no time getting down to the mill. The whole way she had visons of lace dresses, all the colors in the rainbow, one for every day of the year. And T-bone steaks. No more porridge for breakfast. Life was looking up.

America hadn't brought her any closer to John Thomas.

The kids came too fast. After work, he came home to pass out on the living room sofa. Sleeping alone came as a relief to my grandmother. They had ventured into the streets together only once in thirteen years . . . to a fireman's raffle . . . to try their luck at winning a cedar hope chest. All she could think about was lace dresses. Hundreds of them . . . to fill up that hope chest. Who knew . . . the insurance money might be waiting for her. Perhaps she should have brought a bushel basket. Thinking about all this made the air well up in her lungs like a gob of molasses.

Secretly she was torn to the gills over John Thomas. My grandmother had grown so used to seeing him alive she couldn't conceive of him in any other condition. Whiskey-blind morning or noon, John Thomas was hers.

When the public relations man showed her his skeleton and pair of steel-toed work shoes, she blinked and asked for a chair. For eight hours she stared at his skeleton propped in the corner of the timekeeper's office. The timekeeper tried to remove her but my grandmother refused to budge. Only once did she speak. His head, where was his head? The public relations man assured her it would turn up somewhere. He had every available man combing the plant for it. If need be, he would join the search himself. My grandmother nodded and turned back to her husband's skeleton.

Around her work went on as usual. Men with faces glowing like newborn devils shouted above the roar of the furnaces . . . trestle cars clanked their merry way down the tracks . . . ingots hissed in overgrown bathtubs . . . the whole plant rumbled like thirty-two volcanoes, a potpourri of hell and the Fourth of July . . . endless rivers of conveyor belts floating molten reeds around and around till they were the size of a paper clip . . . gargantuan sheets of steel . . . rolled quietly to their predesignated widths and heights. The whole world shuttled in its groove toward one more icebox, one more steely fruit courtesy of the lathe and Mr. Bessemer. There wasn't time for emotions. An ingot's an ingot. You can't get around it. Fifty million people were waiting . . . for one more appliance . . . one more contraption to make them feel a little more comfy . . . a little more at home with their hiccups.

The public relations man stuck a paper under her nose. Sign along the dotted line. Lucky she'd been counseled before hand . . . nothing doing! The public relations man skittered around the timekeeper's office. He's up on his angry broom. He bangs his fist on the desk. If my grandmother won't sign she'll never see a single nickel. He stumbles toward her. He shakes his finger under her nose. He's so fed up he might fly away. Grandmother keeps a wary eye. She clenches her penhand and shoves it in her coat pocket. The PR man backs up, his ten fingers raised to God Almighty. He tiptoes toward her and lays the paper under her nose again. Resting one hand on her shoulder, poppycock rolls from the tip of his PR tongue. He's all soft and oozy. It was all an accident he says. Only Grandmother isn't biting. She clenches her penfist all the tighter. He fingers his lapel. His Rotary button sparkles at fifty feet. His chartreuse tie is made of six windsor knots. It happens every day, he says. No use getting snotty. It's God's will. Men fall . . . we're all so busy . . . the company's just getting on its feet . . . nobody saw him go under . . . the company's not to blame . . . sign on the dotted line please.

My grandmother hasn't heard a word. She's been wondering how John Thomas likes his fried potatoes, well done or medium. She stares off into space. Liver and fried potatoes were always his favorite. What vegetable mixes nice with liver and fried potatoes? "What vegetable mixes nice with liver and fried potatoes?" she asks the public relations man. This really grabs his gander. Now he's sure he's got a looney on his hands. He peers suspiciously from the corner of his eye. There's no telling what she might do next. He's seen the abnormal variety before. It's enough to make him scram in the direction of the first aid room.

The PR man returned with a legion: a policeman, a doctor, and two men in white coats. Grandmother's standing by her husband now. She says she wishes to leave. All the men nod. One calls a cab. Another slips the fare in her coat pocket. They're afraid she'll create a stir . . . gain the men's sympathy. They try to usher her out the door. Grandma won't budge. She asks for a bag, a large one. John Thomas is coming home with her.

The public relations man is out the door and back with a bag in six seconds. SAFETY EQUIPMENT BOG & BLISS is stenciled across the front. He spreads it open. The other four men take a grip on grandpa. The two assistants have his legs. The doctor embraces the pelvic section. That leaves the rib cage for the policeman. He twirls his billy-stick. He grumbles between his missing front tooth. He doesn't like the looks. Convulsions on the altar . . . babies in taxi-cabs . . . frottagers on outbond trolleys, but this is a precedent. He's shook. In seventeen years on the beat, he's never come to the aid of a headless skeleton. They all take hold at once. "Easy does it," my grandmother cautions.

They count to three. On two there's trouble. Grandfather's right hand clatters to the floor. Two fingers fly loose and disappear under the timekeeper's desk. "Never mind," they say, "she can glue it back together when she gets the damn thing home. All right, let's count again." One . . . two . . . three heave-ho! Ooops! There goes his foot. Two toes bounce free and fly into the corridor. The public relations man retrieves them. He bends down to stick them back in place. Ooops! A kneecap clonks him on the head. The Saint Christopher's medal spins through the air . . . straight down . . . spins . . . glistens . . . wraps around the PR's neck . . . oops! there goes that clavicle . . . through the entrance where the neck was . . . and down the center . . . where his lungs should have been . . . and out the gap in the pelvic parts. It bounces all around the timekeeper's office. The PR's gagging. He can't undo the Saint Christopher medal. Grandma's in shock. She turns white. She coughs into her hemline. She staggers for a place to rest. John Thomas is real now. There'll be no fried potatoes . . . not tonight or ever.

Rapidly Grandpa disintegrated in their arms. They stood limp cradling what was left of him, while the bones fell at their feet. They were frozen. The PR's cries at their feet went unheeded. Grandma's gurglings drowned in their own spittle. The policeman, the doctor, the two attendants dropped their arms all together. What remained of grandpa fell in a thunderous clap at their feet. The widow's eyes rolled in their whites. This is too much! She faints across the timekeeper's desk scattering his charts to the four corners of the room. All the drawers in his desk rattle in their slots. PR's seventeen newly sharpened pencils fall to the floor and roll along like miniature reapers. Grandma's right leg develops spasms. It snaps downward. A khaki waste basket is caught in the line of fire. In a final burst of empathy grandma kicks the bucket.

Without a pulse . . . stripped of his nerve endings . . . minus his skull . . . grandpa proves a real character . . . a veritable spirit, heavenly . . . with a touch of the demon to boot.

It was impossible to get rid of him. When Grandma revived she was in the back of a taxi-cab. John Thomas was beside her. In the bag stenciled SAFETY EQUIPMENT. A quick peek inside told her he was still unassembled. The kids took care of that.

When she opened the front door they all cheered. "Mama's back, Mama's back." Then they spied the bag. They mobbed her. They wrestled the bag away. She was too tired to resist. Her whole body felt like a sponge. She plopped down in the middle of the floor. It had been a long day.

Around her there was mayhem. The kids had never seen a toy like this. It reminded them of an erector set. They spread the bones in a circle. Grandma's in the middle. My father leads the assault. He's the oldest and he's disturbed. He smells a raw deal . . . there were no directions in the bag. All the kids wait for my father to give the go-ahead sign. "Where are the directions?" he asks his mother. This makes her whimper. She mumbles something about "death." Death? "Death" is the stillness the cowboy makes when his spurred boots quit twitching. Kids never know anything.

My father thinks it's a stall. He rummages through her pocketbook to no avail. Further questioning only makes her whimper more. She keeps hearing whistles, boat whistles, the whistle calling her and John Thomas to board the boat for America. The kids hear it too, the seven o'clock mill whistle. Papa will be home any minute. They all run to the window to see if they can spot him.

My father has other ideas. He tells the rest: "Let's get the skeleton built for papa . . . surprise him with it . . . hide

it behind the door . . . so it falls on him when he walks in."
The kids really went for this idea. Already they thought my
father was a genius. He was always coming up with clever ideas
to hoax people. They jump up and down with glee. They ran
all around grandma tacking invention upon invention. They
formed two assembly lines, one for the upper half, one for
the lower half. The only problem comes when they try to fit
the legs onto the torso. They won't hold. There must be a part
missing. My father shakes the bag one last time . . . and the
Saint Christopher's medal jangles to the carpet. The missing
link discovered, they tie the legs to the torso once and for all.
That leaves only the head. For a moment there's panic. A
skeleton without a head is not a skeleton. My father turns to
my grandmother. "Where did you buy this?" he asks. She
doesn't hear. She's pulled John Thomas's baby picture down
from the mantle. Staring at it now, she's full of wonder at his
pink dimples. "Where's the guarantee? You've been had," he
says. "You know I'll bet he loved crushed apricots," is her only
reply.

This didn't cramp my father. He hustled upstairs to the
hope chest, the one grandpa and grandma won at the firemen's
raffle. That's where the Halloween costumes are stored. The
skeleton needs a mask. A cotton lamb's head serves fine. They
stuff it into the neck cavity. Then, standing on chairs, carefully,
they hoist the skeleton over their heads till it's poised on the
door frame. Some strips of black electrical tape balance it.
A skeleton doesn't weigh much. Everyone hides. Two sentries
are posted by an upstairs window. My father lies in wait . . .
for the enemy . . . behind the door . . . his pole balanced in
the breech. A slight nudge is all that's needed. When his father
opens the door all hell will break loose. He'll be smothered in
lamb's bones. He won't know what hit him. He'll think it's the
end of the world. A man's bones with a lamb's head . . . a
ghost come back to visit him . . . piggyback him through the
rest of his days. It wasn't often my father's father looked my
father in the eye. Now grandpa would have to compliment
him on what a clever trick he had devised. There was nothing
to do but wait.

Hours later they're still waiting. Curled in positions of sleep
. . . thirteen children . . . their limbs sprawled in all directions
. . . cocking their heads at each pair of passing footsteps on the
street outside. How could they know their father had ascended
after all . . . was looking down at them that very minute . . .
with lamb's eyes or the eyes of a B-29 wing flap. The kids without fear of death have made him live . . . a few more hours
. . . at least until the electrical tape gave way. At 6:57 a.m. the
mill whistle blew. My grandfather crashed to the floor. His bones
flew in every direction. The lamb's head landed beside grandma
asleep on the living room floor. This makes up her mind. She's
had enough. She collects the bones in the Bog & Bliss bag. The
kids don't understand. They think she's angry at them. They protest all the way to the coal furnace. "Please mama, one more
chance."

Mama plunges the stoker into the smoldering coals. Mama
dumps two shovelsful into the mouth of the furnace. The kids
leap around her begging forgiveness. One tiny flame leaps from
the coals. Grandma stokes again. Blue flames burst around the
fresh lumps. The crematorium is ready. Only John Thomas's
widow is having a hard time holding back the tears. John Thomas
wasn't such a bad guy after all. He had his good points. First
she jams the rib cage in. If only he hadn't boozed so. Next go
the arms. The kids are silent now. Gathered at the entrance
they smell something fishy. They notice the welling up in their
mother's eyes. The last bone disappears. There is complete reverence. No one says a word. The glow penetrates their faces. Their
eyes bulge to triple size. Their noses turn up, mouths hang open.
They resemble guppies in an undersized aquarium. "They aren't
burning, mama," one of the little ones cries. Grandmother turns
scarlet. She slams the furnace door. She grabs my father by the
neck. Fighting back the tears she says, "Come on, Arthur, it's time
you got a work permit."

Lewis W. Hine

Johann Gaertner (1793-1887)

GARY GILDNER

In the blue winter of 1812
Johann Gaertner, a bag of bones,
followed Napoleon home.
He was cold; Napoleon,
riding ahead under a bear
wrap, fumed at the lice
in his hair. —From Moscow
to Borodino, from Borodino
to the Baltic Sea, Napoleon
fumed and slapped, and glared hard
at the gray shapes
pushing at his face.
And maybe ate a piece of fruit
he did not taste. If he
cried, we do not know it.
But Johann Gaertner, 19,
a draftee, a bag of bones,
blew on his fingers
and bit them, and kicked at his toes.
And chewed and chewed
a piece of pony gristle.
And once, trying to whistle
an old dog into his coat,
swallowed a tooth.
God save Johann!, Johann
Gaertner, 19, cried,
moving his two blue feet
through bloody holes his eyes
kept staring and staring at . . .
And in the midst of all this
one night God appeared, hoary and fat,
and yelled at him in Russian,
Kooshat! Kooshat!—

and Johann closed his eyes
waiting for one of his sharp white bones
to pierce his heart.
When none did, he dragged them
past the mirror Napoleon
gazed and gazed at his rasp-
berry-colored chin in . . .
and past windy St. Helena
where his former leader was already lost
among the washed-up herring.
And Johann kept going,
picking up crumbs like a sparrow!—
no longer hearing that tooth
grinding against his ribs,
but starting to feel the sun
on the back of his neck
for a change, and loving the itch
and salty wash of sweat
everywhere on his chest.
                    And one day
holding up a jug of cool switchel,
he had swig upon swig upon swig
and felt his whole blessed mouth
turn ginger—
and he whispered a song
that came out *Ah, Johann* . . .
            Thus,
having stopped, he stepped back
and took in his fields of hay,
his acres and acres of feed,
and his six black bulls
bulging against the sky.
And sitting down he ate
the giant mounds of sweet
red cabbage his ample wife
set before him,
and the pickled corn,
and the mashed potatoes dripping
galaxies of gizzards, hearts,

and juicy bits of wing,
and yet another slice
of her salt-rising bread
spread with his own
bee-sweetened butter.
(Often Johann stretched out big
in the clover, listening to his bees,
churn, churn, they said, *churn* . . .)
And praising God while licking his fingers
he allowed for a wedge of her
sour cream raisin pie,
and a mug of steaming
coffee out on the porch,
where he liked to stick his stockinged feet
among the fireflies,
and feel the slow closing
of his eyes . . .
      And all of this
(including the hickory nut cake,
rhubarb wine, and the fine old fat-
bellied kitchen stove)
happened for many years
in little Festina, Iowa,—
where Anton Dvorak came to drink
local Bohemian beer
and hear the Turkey River;
and where rosy Johann Gaertner
dug down deep in the rich black dirt
to make his own hole
and one for his wife as well.

Two Poems

HILDA MORLEY

After The Moon-Walk

Moon, moon
   I want to talk to you
I want to dance a dance around you
   I want to stand in your light
There's noone here but me this night
   Noone is speaking
   Noone's listening
No need for you to stay in hiding tonight.
Everyone is asleep.
Moon Come out & show yourself
   You won't lose your secret
Moon moon
   I don't believe you've changed
You're still the watched for
   & the watching
   female,
   my bone's tissue
The light you make is webbed under my nails,
   breathing behind my skin.

The Tree

Seeing the trees lit up
now in the Xmas season,
   I remember the tree at
the end of the quay in Ibiza
where the breakwater ends: the restaurant
named for Rimbaud—El Barco Borracho,
a summertime tree,
   lit-up & shining those evenings
with bulbs of all colors

& we danced to the waltzes they played,
                                    our bodies
moving in joy,   with the music,
                    the smell of the food
                    the sky warm with stars
& holding each other inside that circle
of pleasures
              on the edge of the sea.

The Birth Of Venus In The Gulf Of Mexico

SANDRA LYNN

Please notice
her shell is the black scallop
that rides our turbid waters.
Botticelli wouldn't recognize her.
She has lost patience
with holding her long hair just so.
It now loops on the wind
and her—let's be exact—mons Veneris
is very much in evidence.
Her expression is not innocent
and is edged by a black border:
already something has died.

Asking

PHILIP LEVINE

Once, in the beginning,
on the last Sunday
of a lost August,
I sat on the Canadian shore
of Lake Huron and watched
the dark clouds go over,
knowing this was the end
of summer. There was a girl
beside me, but we
barely knew each other,
and so we sat
in our separate thoughts,
or I did anyway. I saw
how it would be, summer
after summer, working
toward a few days like this
when I came flushed
with strength and money,
my hands scarred
and hardened, my shoulders
and arms thick, and maybe
I would find a girl
or maybe I'd get drunk
and fight or growing older
just get drunk and sit
alone staring into a glass
the way my uncles did.
When I felt the girl's hand
on the back of my neck
I shuddered the way you do
when a cool wind
passes over you, and she
misunderstood and pulled
her hand away. I took

her hand in mine and said
something about having
drifted off and how odd
it was to know a season
had ended at one moment
and I had turned
toward winter, maybe
a lifetime of winters.
Then I thought of her
working week after week
in the office
of a small contractor
she said she hated
and going home to the father
she said she hated
and the mother who went on
about marriage and was
she ever going to get out,
and she just barely 22.
Almost 30 years ago.
She and I never saw
each other after we
got back to Detroit
in the smokey light
of early evening.
I let her out
a block from her house
and said I'd call her,
but knew I wouldn't
knowing what I did
about her life and how
she needed someone
I wasn't. I went back
to my room and sat
in the dark wondering
how can I get out.
I knew there must be
millions of us,

alone and frightened,
feeling the sudden chill
of winter, of time
gathering and falling
like a shadow across
our lives. Wondering
what was the answer.
Only a boy, still alone,
still solemn, turning
in the darkness
toward manhood, turning
as the years turned
imperceptibly, petal
by petal, closing
for the night,
the question still
unanswered, that question
never to be asked again.

Art Sinsabaugh

How the Boxcars Became Locomotives

DOUGLAS BLAZEK

For thirty-three summers they sat
listening to a mountain factory
their marvelous rust being carried off by bees

one day the farmer fumigated his field
and the bees took refuge in the boxcars
filling them with Motherhood Fuel

then a miracle happened
there was an earthquake
and the boxcars were swallowed by the earth

a geyser of honey resulted
sure sign of an engine letting steam
leading the planet toward its first child

Art Sinsabaugh

The Villanelle

DONALD HARINGTON

Regard the motion of the villanelle:
Its ins and outs and comely dips and sways.
A couple must unite to do it well.

The two of them will make a carrousel,
For dancing circles which are roundelays,
Around the motion of the villanelle.

They never touch until they bid farewell
And then they meet in passionate embrace.
A couple must embrace to do it well.

Impassioned in the dance's magic spell,
No single movement of a foot betrays
The comely motion of the villanelle.

Each step by step their movements parallel
And compliment the partner's dancing ways.
This couple must conspire to do it well.

The moment's coming when the rules impel
The dancers now to fuse in final phase:
Regard this motion of the villanelle:
Our couple have embraced and done it well.

What Love Meant for Isadora Duncan

From the French notebook of
COUNTEE CULLEN

Introduction and translation by Michel Fabre

In one of Countee Cullen's French exercise-books, now in the James Weldon Johnson collection at the Yale University Library, one can find the following piece scattered in episodic form among dictations, poems, short essays and translations. It is not surprising that Cullen should have been fascinated by Isadora Duncan: his conception of art as the expression of the spiritual in man, as the embodiment of a superior form of love comes close to her own views. Moreover, the evocation of the great dancer as a reincarnation of the Golden Age of the Hellenes perfectly tallies with the poet's deep devotion to classical literature and response to John Keats' "Ode to a Grecian Urn," for instance. It is even moving to reflect that Cullen penned this French essay on Isadora's conception of love in 1931, amid the despair and sorrow brought about by his unfortunate marriage to Yolande DuBois. In a contemporary essay reporting a Beethoven concert at the Salle Pleyel in Paris, he exclaims: "For a long time, I've had enough of love, enough of marriage."

Although research was unable to unearth the original English version of this piece, if indeed it does exist, there is no proof that Cullen authored it. It may be simply a translation. It is even possibly a slightly fictionalized reportorial piece. Let us not be mistaken: the words, even the structure of the sentences put in Isadora's mouth are unmistakably hers, as the style of her letters published in *Isadora Duncan's Russian Days and Her Last Years in France* by Irma Duncan and Alan Macdougall (1929) amply testifies. The chronological sequence of events is equally authentic: the dance festival at the Trocadéro alluded to in the essay took place in June, 1923 and Isadora's magnificent performance described at the end in the summer of 1926. This was in Nice, in "a theatre twice as big as the Rue de la Pompe with a stage, footlights, etc." — "a perfect gem," she wrote her sister on March 30, 1925.

The only period when Isadora Duncan could have been visited, depressed and penniless, in a dingy Berlin hotel room is the Fall of 1924. Upon her return from Russia in September, she stayed at the Eden, then at the Central, then in cheaper places until friends rescued her at the end of the year. Her biography reads:

From Berlin the news had gone out that Isadora Duncan was going to give out for publication all the love letters she had ever received in her life. As soon as she arrived in Paris, she was pestered by the representatives of the various sensational newspapers in America and England. She denied, however, that she had ever thought of doing such a thing; she was considering writing her memoirs and telling the story of her Art, she said. Her Art was much more important than her love affairs. And to all the fantastic offers for permission to reprint the intimate letters in her possession she turned a deaf ear. (p. 307)

Now, although it is quite possible that Cullen saw Isadora perform when he was "quite young . . . a reporter with literary ambitions" and again in Nice during the summer of 1926, either on his way to, or upon his return from the Holy Land, he never was, for all we know, in Berlin in 1924 to jot down Isadora's confession.

Yet "What Love Meant for Isadora Duncan" seemed to deserve publication. It is not only a fine association piece, the tribute of a great poet to a great dancer, the meeting of lofty hearts. Nor is it just another memory of the fascinating Twenties. In this culture where "most beings today spend some twenty-five to thirty years before they emerge from the actual lies and conventions that surround them," it should be read as an earnest message recorded by a noble mind.

—MICHEL FABRE

While she was dancing, that night, many years ago, she created for my young eyes all the beauty and all the grandeur that were the golden age of the Hellenes. A glorious Diana, a chaste Aphrodite. I was quite young at that time, a reporter with literary ambitions, and I fell beautifully in love, as I expected, with Isadora Duncan. Nearly two decades elapsed. What the evils of time have wrought upon me I cannot see, but I shall never forget the shock of seeing my goddess lying tall and withered, neglected, dishevelled, across a bed, in a second-class Berlin hotel room which she could not leave because she did not have the money to pay her bill.

She did not greet me. "If only I could have a drink, I would be able to talk to you," she said sadly.

I rang for the steward. He came grudgingly for lack of a tip. I asked her whether she preferred wine or a cocktail.

"Bring me a bottle of gin," she ordered in a suddenly firmer voice.

"Are you going to pay for this?" the steward asked me in too loud a whisper.

I pulled my pocketbook and he agreed.

She swallowed her gin straight, felt immediately refreshed and started, now ramblingly, now lucidly, to tell me all her present troubles.

"I am finished," she said. "I cannot go to France to sell my house — the French say I am a Bolshevik and they won't grant me a visa. I shall have to sell my love letters. They are all that I have left. I have more than a thousand. But it does not matter. After the difficulties I encountered because of my trip to Russia and my last tour of America, I have found out that I have no more friends in the world, so why should I hesitate to publish these letters? Oh, they are going to ruin a number of big reputations, but why should I bother? Would you like to see them?"

She moved her body, tied a negligé over the red, Greek-like garment that hung shapeless from her shoulders to her sandalled feet, stumbled across the room and opened a drawer. Her hair was dishevelled and a strange light shone in her magnificent eyes.

"These were written by d'Annunzio," she said, handing me a few blue sheets covered with a huge, rough handwriting, about twenty words per page. "And these by Gordon Craig." The letters had not been written but drawn, and each one was a work of art, like the words in old Japanese prints. Each page had been illuminated by ink and pencil drawings. Some were drawings with only a few words of text, others were words and paintings mingled into a single thing of beauty. "And these are from Lohengrin." Quite prosaic, the hard handwriting of a business-man. "Here are some by . . . well, I won't tell you his name now. He was my lover once, young and beautiful. Now he is married, has three children and does not write great poetry any longer."

I looked at the texts of a score of letters from former lovers. Although written by artists, by poets or by businessmen, the letters were all burning with the same passion that she kindled in men. The dates were at least ten years apart. Yet the feeling in all of them was the same. "You are just as beautiful and precious to me now as on the first day of our affair—you are the only woman in the world for whom my passion was not frozen by possession." The poet, the artist, and the businessman all expressed the same idea in sentences that simply differed in style and elegance.

"Those by Essenine are in Russian," she said. "You would not understand them, but they are just as beautiful as the others."

"Where is he?" I asked.

"Serge went to the Caucase in order to become a highwayman. He wrote me recently that he is mad with thrills. He said he'll become a thief and then he will truly write poetry."

"What about your divorce?"

"Well, it goes thus," Isadora answered. "In Russia, in order to get a divorce you have to apply before noon and neither Serge nor me were ever able to reach the police station before twelve. We lived at night and slept in the daytime. If the Soviets had had enough sense to open their divorce bureau at midnight, we would have divorced and probably married again several times."

She helped herself with a quarter of a glass of gin.

"I think I'll put all of these letters together in a book, which I'll call 'What Love Means to Different Men'—the poet, the banker, the playwright, the poor man, the lazy rich. I shall collect the letters under such titles. It is going to be an interesting volume, composed of truly human documents."

The chapter she dictated upon my advice ran thus:

I find this book difficult to write. I find it difficult to speak when I know that each word is going to be written down. I want this book to be something valuable for posterity. It will be worthwhile only if it helps people with their lives. I want to tell the truth about my loves and my art because everybody is brought up among complete lies. All our sustenance is derived from lies. We begin among lies and live about half of our existence among lies. Most beings today spend some twenty-five to thirty years before they emerge from the actual lies and conventions that surround them.

I am not an artist at all. Artists bore me to death. All the singers you meet speak of the A minor they are able to reach, all the violinists and pianists talk about the number of their concerts, and the writers about the size of their royalties. They don't give me any pleasure; these artists are stupid. The only artist present at a concert is the man who wrote the music they perform; at a play, it is the author of the text. Theatre people are mannered and egotistic. All artists in general are far too spoilt.

Art is not necessary at all. All that is necessary to make this world a better place to live is love, to love the way Christ did, to love the way Buddha did. That was the most marvellous thing in Lenin. *He* truly loved mankind. The others loved money, themselves, theories, power. Lenin loved his brothers. They tell me: "How can you be so enthusiastic about Lenin—he did not believe in God." I answer: "This is simply a way of speaking. Lenin was God, the same way Christ was God because God is Love and Christ and Lenin were Love, both of them!"

Do you love mankind? Lenin loved it. That is why he was supreme, because he really loved. When the world really realizes that thing, it will be wonderful, since most people do not really love anything.

This is the reason why I want to publish this book. Not for money but because I want to show mankind that it does not know how to love.

What men call Love is only hatred under a different guise. In flesh there is no love. I have had as much as anyone of the sort of thing men dare call Love. Men foaming at the mouth, men shouting that they would kill themselves if I did not love them. Love—trash. I had hardly stepped upon that stage than it began—all those professions of love. From every part I was surrounded by all kinds of men. What did they want from me? Now I know: their feelings were the feelings they had for a bottle of whiskey.

They would tell the bottle: "I am thirsty. I want you. I want to swallow you. I want to have you all." They told me the very same things: "I am hungry. I want you. I want to own you body and soul." Oh yes, in general they add the soul when they plead for the body.

Was that love? No, it was madness.

Love is the rarest thing in the world. Even the love of a mother is largely self-centered. A cat loves her kitterns up to a certain age. One talks about a mother's love as the most sacred thing in the world. Well, it is just as if you loved your own arms and legs. I did not want that kind of love. I wanted a pure, disinterested love; the love for mankind which Christ, Buddha and Lenin experienced.

When I was in Moscow I saw little children who slept huddled against each other under porches or on garbage heaps. Would such a thing be possible if there was love in this world? I took these children to my school and let them sleep there. After Lenin's death, the Soviet government would no longer allow this. Was that love? Have you ever been to the Eastern part of London? What did you see there? If you have not actually seen children sleeping in the street as they did in Russia, you must have seen them in a pretty terrible state. If there was any such thing as love in this world, would this be tolerated? Would people be able to go to their comfortable homes, knowing that there are children who live in such destitution? As long as little children are allowed to suffer, there will be no real love in the world.

Men have loved me, but the only love I have ever felt has been for children. All men of science, all doctors are surprised by what I have accomplished with children. First of all, I take them seriously. All children are very serious beings, in spite of the fact that their parents and their teachers treat them like ignorant and inconsequential animals. They come to me with all sorts of diseases—in their minds and in their bodies. Many of them have the rickets and bone diseases. When I started my first school in Berlin, Professor Stoffer came to see my pupils and when he saw them, he exclaimed, "These children are not for you. They are for me; they need medical treatment. This is not a school, but a hospital. You'll never be able to teach these children how to dance."

You should have seen how these children could dance by the end of a year! Simply because I let them do what they wanted. I let them dance, I did not ask them to dance. I encouraged them to dance better. That was all. It grew and flowered and blossomed out.

Of course, such love cannot be self-centered. It makes you feel like a kind of God, you know. Prometheus! It is wonderful to be able to shape human voices. I have taken children from the lower proletariat, powerless and sick and doomed to poverty and a premature death, the children of the men who dig ditches and break stones, and before I left for Moscow, they were dancing at the Berlin opera. When people saw them perform, they rose and clapped, weeping. And the men and women in the audience and the beautiful children on the stage felt a divine

Bourdelle

ecstasy, a part of the huge love the world needs and without which it will die.

In June we gave a festival at the Trocadero in Paris. From a box I watched my pupils dance. At certain parts of the program, the quivering audience rose and shouted with enthusiasm and pleasure. At the end, they applauded so long that the crowd looked as if they would never leave. I believe that such extraordinary enthusiasm for children who were in no way ballerinas or real artists was due to some hope in a new movement of mankind which I had obscurely foreseen. In fact, we were looking at the gestures briefly perceived in Nietzsche's vision: "Zarathustra, the light-bodied Zarathustra who flaps his wings, ready to soar, who beckons to all the birds, all ready, clear soul filled with joy!" We were looking at the future dancers of Beethoven's "Ninth Symphony." [Translator's note: this paragraph does not come after the preceding one in the manuscript, being separated by other texts. It seems, though, to belong here.]

Once you become interested in molding children's lives, you can never become truly interested in anything else. There is nothing greater in the world. I have never accepted an adult as a student, nor had a paying student. I worked only when I was able to work for nothing.

The world calls me a dancer. They say I revived the classical art of dance from Grecian times. But I am not a dancer. I never danced in my whole life. I hate all dance styles. All I can see in what is called a dance is a useless agitation of arms and legs. But I can understand dance in a social sense—the tango, for instance, the way they dance it in Buenos-Aires. There it is quite wonderful in the small, low-ceilinged bars; there it has a meaning. A man dances with the same girl all night long and if another man tries to dance with her he stabs the stranger in the back. This is the kind of dance based on sexual desire and on the right of property. We see all the external movement. But what of the inner movement? What of the spirit? I am not a dancer. I am interested in finding and expressing a new life form. The Greeks *did* live. Nowadays, we do not live. We derive about ten per cent from life. My aim was to teach children how to live, how to derive more from life, to urge them to always enjoy the moment and to shape life after their tastes and harmoniously.

I see only the ideal, but no ideal was ever a complete success on this earth. Ideals always bring calamities with them. People with ideals frequently become mad. You follow an ideal, you give it all your life and run the risk of becoming mad—what else is there to do? Every other possibility is just like a good meal. It helps you to while away time in a charming fashion and gives satiety to one of the main desires of the flesh. That is all.

Every two thousand years certain aspects in human affairs recur and certain forces are born again. Ideals become flesh. We have had Dionysos, and Christ and Buddha, and the greatest force of the present time is Lenin. I am convinced that in two thousand years people from all parts of the world will come to Lenin's tomb. It will become a holy place. He was the man in whom the new spirit lived, he was the rebirth of the face of idealism and the new religion. I am a kind of Cassandra and I prophesy from time to time.

I went to Russia because I am more interested in the future than the present. A practical-minded person going to Moscow will see hardly anything except calamity and catastrophe. Such a state of things followed the crucifixion of Christ and will follow Lenin. In the days to come, they will realize this. Now they can only see what is taking place. I can see the Ideal.

The following day the stenographer who had taken note of the preceding words brought me the copy and asked to be paid.

"I do not like her thoughts," she said; "besides I cannot afford to work for a woman who drinks gin."

I went to see Isadora and told her this. She poured herself another drink with a good-humored smile.

"I shall tell you how I have become like this," she said. "This is parental influence. Have you ever heard about the Kearny riots in San Francisco? They were the first bolshevik riots in America. My brother was a San Francisco banker. He was an honest and straight man. But the crowd came surging into the streets, shouting: 'Hang Duncan! Down with Duncan!' and they forced their way into our house, looking for my brother. My mother hid him in a closet and when the mob broke into her room and saw she was pregnant, they gave up their lynching. When my mother had let my brother out of the stifling closet, she collapsed and had to stay in bed for months. Then I was born. Now you can understand my strange and expensive tastes."

When I asked her to write another chapter of her book, she became suddenly indifferent to the project and tried to drop the subject.

"Look," she said, "you have already published a piece on the sale of my love letters. Well, I have received telegrams dealing with that. Certain people have been quite worried at the thought of the publication of these letters. I am sending a friend to France to see what is happening. I shall call you if I decide to proceed."

Days passed. No phone call came for me. I called and did not receive any satisfactory answer, but, generally, a curt word from the operator at the hotel where the Duncan bill was becoming larger every day . . .

A week later I went there. Everything was in turmoil. Smiling maids were packing a new trunk and Isadora, dressed in new clothes, was giving orders nonchalantly and happily.

"I am off for Spa," she said before I could speak, "where I shall take the waters. I have stopped drinking. I am too fat but I am going to lose weight in a short time. I am going to have another theatre. I'll go and spend the winter in Nice. Oh, you must come and see my *première*."

"What about your brother? And the letters?"

"Oh, all that is over. Publish my memoirs now? Who do you think I am? An old woman? Am I dead? Only the dead publish their memoirs! Well, I'll have plenty of time to write them when I am dead. Everything is different now. Life starts over."

That winter and still another winter elapsed, and summer came. I heard in Juan Les Pins that Isadora had returned to her theatre-workshop in Nice. I asked a friend of hers who was financing the theatre.

"It is a strange story," said the friend. "It appears that Isadora was once broke in Berlin and she told a reporter that she was preparing to publish her memoirs, including her love letters. Then she got very annoyed because that got into the news, but it was lucky for her because some man read the newspaper and cabled her that she was stupid, that she would ruin her career and that she should return to art. She would be given a studio if she wanted. Since then everything has been smooth for her."

The theatre was hung in dark-purple velvet. The stage, crowded with a hundred cushions was ready to accommodate the audience. A piano stood on the otherwise bare floor. Isadora

arrived in the same dress she had been wearing for lunch, a
Grecian dress, which would have been beautiful on a slim goddess, but which revealed rather than hid the huge breasts, long
belly and wide hips of a woman prematurely aged. Her arms,
once so expressive were thick and red; the flesh of her face
was sagging and her hair badly dyed in purple and henna.

She pulled the thin velvet cover off the piano and with ancient skill she threw a portion of it over her back and started
circling her body with the rest. At the same time her Russian

accompanist began to play. Then a strange thing happened. I
think it happened for all those present because we afterwards
confessed, each in a different way, the surprise and the thrill that
had possessed us when we had witnessed a miracle. Under our
eyes, a middle-aged woman, much the worse for her fights against
a hard and severe world, had suddenly become a thing of beauty,
something exalting, fairy-like. She did not dance the way she
had danced twenty years ago, when I had seen her "Song of the
Spring." She moved lightly, slowly. Her face became celestial
and changed expression with the music. Her arms, her legs and
her body swayed, her head rose and fell and in her eyes a light
seemed to shine, a light which rendered us entirely blind to the
fat ugliness of the aging flesh and the decaying human features.
This was not a dance, it was an interpretation of music as some
Greek artist might have presented it in front of Sophocles, in
order to convince him that irony and pity could be expressed by
dancing as profoundly as by the great tragedies, giving the audience the same cathartic feeling. This was a strange beauty we
were perceiving, a beauty into which "the whole soul has
passed with all its diseases." Not to Mona Lisa, who looks simple,
naïve and fixed in her posture, but to Mona Isadora should these
most romantic lines have been inscribed. For, that very afternoon,
the head of Isadora was "the head on which all the confines of
the world have come and whose eyelids are somewhat tired." In
her face, that day, I saw that "all the thoughts and all the experience of the world have painted and shaped, in what they
have the power to refine and express, the animal force of Greece,
the lust of Rome, the mysticism of the Middle-ages with its
spiritual ambition and imaginary loves, the return of the pagan
world, the sins of the Borgias."

Then the music ceased, Isadora stopped and the miracle
came to an end. The mystical circle was broken. There was
silence. We were too deeply moved to applaud or to cheer. We
simply rose and followed her home.

We are grateful to Mrs. Ida M. Cullen and to the James Weldon Johnson
Memorial Collection of Negro Arts and Letters, Collection of American Literature, The Beinecke Rare Book and Manuscript Library, Yale University for
their permission to publish this essay.

NEW LETTERS

A magazine of fine writing   *Edited by David Ray*

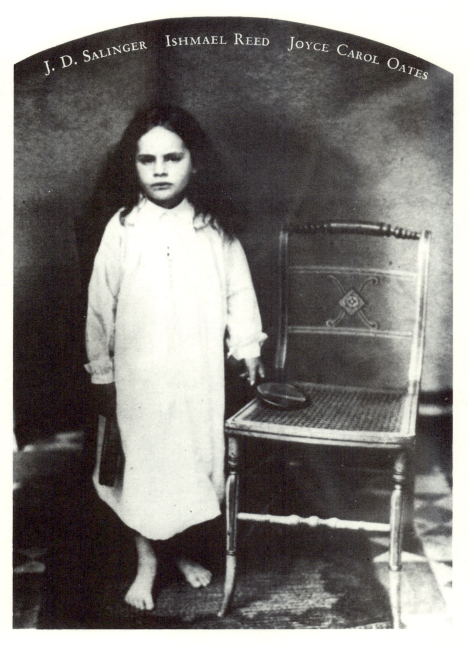

J. D. SALINGER   ISHMAEL REED   JOYCE CAROL OATES

Photographs by Lewis Carroll $2.50

NEW LETTERS

A magazine of fine writing
Edited by David Ray

Featuring

EACH NEW SPRINGTIME
EACH NEW SUMMER

A Novel by JAMES McKINLEY

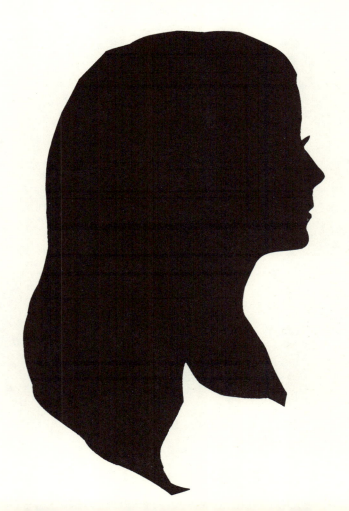

NEW LETTERS

A magazine of fine writing   *Edited by David Ray*

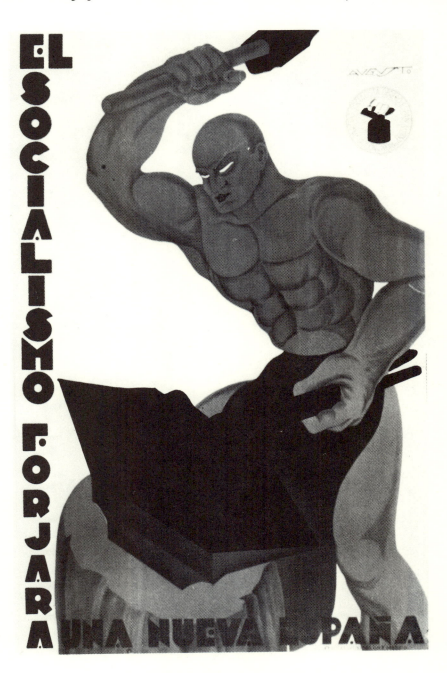

EL SOCIALISMO FORJARA UNA NUEVA ESPAÑA

Posters Of The Spanish Civil War

$2.50

Poetry By Diane Wakoski * Commentary By Marya Mannes

NEW LETTERS

A magazine of fine writing   *Edited by David Ray*

Fiction
Omnibus

Photographs by
Lewis W. Hine

Three Poems

HARRY ROSKOLENKO

View

Shapes change, buildings arrange, go
From wood to brick, stone, thatch,
In old and new countries, as variations
Derange the scene, take back things
Of another time to this — our time,
And we are housed now on hills of bricks,
On mountains of cement blocks, sculpting
The sky line that no longer has a line,
That no longer is the sky we used to know
When we knew another city of other shapes.

Shapes derange, buildings arrange, go
From things the hands did once
But no longer do as the hands did once,
As we did walking up the six-seven flights
To roofs, to pigeons, to fanciers of wings,
Birds that flew over the Brooklyn Bridge,
Then wheeled over the East River, flew on to
The Hudson River, seeing all of Manhattan
Grow into itself, then go on to other boroughs—
To make the wide swing-on-wing out to the
    Atlantic.

Nationalism

I'm so tired of being a Jew, an Arab,
Even an American . . . and all the flags
That spill our blood. Those Germans — Lord!
What was it they did 32 years ago?
What did Russia do when Stalin lived?
And France, England, Spain — name their crimes,
Name their colonies, name the years?

I'm so tired in the heart of all the parts,
All those orthodoxies that go with bullets—
Fired by boys, by men, by women — and bombs
Among the Irish when whiskey is so much better.
So tired of the latitudes of platitudes,
Sums of sentiment and the G.N.P.'s ghosts—
The First World, the Second, and the Third World.

Better not to develop; be like Iceland
Or some islands still lost in the South Pacific;
Be anything but a nation with a flag.
Burn them all! with the German going first,
Then the Russian — then our own bursting through air;
And we'll dance internationally. Dance! Dance! Dance!

Only God Can Make Me . . .

There are two trees so Australian out my window;
I see them as paintings done by Nolan, Tucker and Pugh,
And I remember so many scenes of "Dunmoochin's" early
    mornings,
Or the bush, the Nullarbor, Dandenongs — Australia.

Here, in Sausalito, before Manhattan chokes me again,
Two trees, and winds, and the Pacific, are my Madams;
My Mistresses, Bitches, beers — and so many other digressions;
Two trees, gums, laminated in grey, over bloody S.F. Bay.

Sheen, so young, Californian, without kangaroos and koalas,
They wake my mornings or keep me into the late midnight;
From my Australias, they come — for I live in two countries . . .
But only one, as trees, keeps me from insolence and violence.

Manhattan, what have you left in your angry stone and iron?
Ah, the ballet! The concerts! The intellectuals! What else?
Million-headed, dying, criminally-seized, fiscal-maddened!
Where are we all going? We've gone! Don't you remember,
    gone!

Two Poems

TED SCHAEFER

The Waltz of Nuclear Physics

"God does not play dice
with the world."
—Albert Einstein

The children on the ice
in their red mufflers
dance
without knowing it.
Even the wind is funny.
Their skates spit foxlike crystals
across the flats
of infinite chance, a black
freezer under laughter
where the fish
are suspended
and ringing like the telephone
in your grave.

Anxiety Pastorale

A Nazi in a Zeppelin
has anchored,
low,
between the stars and rows of corn.
We swallow our fear.
Up there
what's he thinking?
Tonight there's death on a neighboring farm,
its windows suddenly gold.

House

Raymond Roseliep

the surveyor
stops
to mount a cloud

on the trapeze net
of a monarch chrysalis
the architect's nose

the mouse just misses
the excavator's
scoop

the carpenter tilts
a dreaming ear to the bell
ring of nail

sky roofing
bird nothing but bird
over the roofer

the bricklayer
breathes into a mouth
of chimney

by broken water
the plumber's
coughing

on a leash his cat
dozes by the lunch pail
of the steamfitter

the contractor
reads blueprint detail
through dragonfly wing

with his trowel
the plasterer
swats flies

shooting star
still in the eye of
the electrician

the painter bids
the grasshopper
'Spit tobacco juice'

eating rose
pink by pink petal
the interior decorator

Another Barn Painting

SYLVIA WHEELER

Eyes dulled,
they paint the barn
pig colors
pink through mud crust,
clay
seeping out banks,
kaffir,
tassel bead dust,
or gravel down roads,
river birch buds,
fungus curling off old wood.

Mary Wilson

Rose's Wedding

SIMON PERCHIK

Who will forget the whiskey sours
the silver fountain
the blue, the yellow beacons
—a boat carved from ice
unable to pull abreast, a bride
a groom doomed by speed

—from my first wedding
crushed ice.
Did any guest survive?

My Vast Presumption

MOLLY PEACOCK

The balloon ride was his birthday present
three years ago. He never cashed the ticket,
I know, because periodically I'm sent
reminders in the mail. "I didn't take it,
not yet," he said for nearly a year. We don't
bring it up any more. I thought I'd try
a rescue, thought I should — the mire he was in,
his father, his job. Since we were kids, a lie
was a sin, still is. He's my favorite cousin.
I'd love to see him way up in the air
billowed over the farms below, the red stripes
teetering from cloud to cloud, from when to where,
far away from bleak here. "I'm not the type,"
he said from way inside his own balloon,
never waving, since never leaving home,
the faintly hysterical first goodby,
     "See you again, soon!"

Two Poems

HARLEY ELLIOTT

For Farmers

Surrounded by broken
pots and arrowheads
I walk the space where
earth dome houses stood.

The Kingdom of Quivira
neolithic farmers
tattooed arms beneath the stars
and a sight named Coronado
winding through the smoky hills

in a dazzle of crosses
and weapons on animals
with stone hard feet.
Gold squash and pumpkins shudder.

The man of metal
speaks of seven cities
made of gold
streets made of gold
gold temples clothes
and shoes of gold
gold idols rings
coffins plates the very
gutters made of gold.

The farmers stare
off at the sky
a high-pitched blue above
where wind and stone remain.

"We hear you stranger.
sit down
eat   drink.

That which you
desire is just
a little further on."

The Men Who Loved Everything

The men who loved everything
sat down in the road
golden and calm
in the late afternoon.

Saffron flowers quiet eyes
the men who loved everything
sat down in the road

they saw the tiny
ant in jeopardy
a milky blue earth
floating dead in its space.

Gasoline fills the air.
In the heat of the road
the men who loved everything

throw their light
to our eyes.

A Hero
In The Highway

JAMES SCHEVILL

(1)

Leaving Mexico City on the new highway north, I can't believe my eyes. The road turns incredibly sharply, proudly around the steep mountainside, a path to destiny like all Mexican roads rather than a mere highway. Accustomed to Mexican driving after many months I am tuned to surprises. Anything human or animal may turn up around the next corner. Still I gape and can't believe what I've seen. As a journalist I'm used to reporting crazy news even if it doesn't get published. Maybe there's a story here if I turn back.

(2)

An Indian is living in the middle of the highway. Impossible. There isn't any room. Cars and trucks smoke by him on both sides of the road. There he is on a narrow island of rocks. Somehow when they bulldozed the cliff for that curve they must have come upon one of those tiny, steep, impossible farms that Indians cling to. Perhaps part of the "slash and burn farm" slid into the roadway. More likely the crazy Indian slipped into a patch of land the road crew was working on and then he simply refused to leave. Why didn't they throw him out? Call the police if necessary. Maybe there is a story in this, even television—a last Indian living in the midst of a modern highway.

(3)

When I approach the Indian he throws rocks at me. A crazy man! "I am your friend!" I cry in Spanish, "*Amigo!*" He throws more rocks. Probably he doesn't even understand Spanish. After all there are a lot of illiterates in this country. I have an idea. I pretend to be hit by a rock and fall down as if badly injured. After a long wait he approaches me cautiously. As he kneels over me I grab his hand. "*Amigo!*" I cry. That much Spanish he can understand. Frightened he pulls away and tries to hide in his little hovel with a thatched roof. But he doesn't throw any more stones. When I enter the hovel he turns his back on me. Suddenly I decide the only way to win his confidence is to sleep there, to assure him of my companionship and my desire to understand his situation. We lie back to back, without speaking, like two motionless logs for the entire night. The sense of his tension makes me afraid to sleep. From such ordeals comes the beginning of understanding.

(4)

In the morning I begin to study the nature of this strange island in the highway. I get no help from the Indian. When I try to talk to him in the simplest Spanish or in the clearest international sign language, he grimaces at me with contempt. He won't even share his food with me, although he seems to eat hardly anything. According to what I've read about Mexican Indians it's unheard of that they don't share their food. To refuse a guest food gets your family into trouble with the gods. When I point to my mouth, pleading my hunger, he gestures toward the garbage and tin cans littering both sides of his highway island. As cars and trucks speed by the drivers often shout obscenities and throw their waste at us. If I stay here long I'll have to learn how to eat garbage. Is it worth it?

(5)

I've found a way to stay for a few days without eating garbage. As the cars speed by I kneel as if I'm praying before a rock shrine. Sympathetic passengers throw me food, fruit, even soft drinks. As I sit eating the Indian looks at me directly for the first time. Even if it's a wary look he doesn't turn away now. I think he has a new respect for me. But he won't eat any of my food when I offer him some.

(6)

I'm determined not to give up. Even though the Indian can't or won't talk about this crazy highway island, I've begun to appreciate his incredible achievement. It's not just that he's sitting here undisturbed on a chunk of federal highway property. It's what he's made of the barren property. He's built a hut on it even if it's only a crude, open Indian hut with a thatched roof. He's dug a deep well for brackish water that I stay away from. To protect the highway island from the pounding traffic he's even built stone walls and decorated them with a peculiar zig-

zag design like an Aztec ornament. An anthropologist once told me that this kind of design had to do with fire and lightning. Fire and lightning . . . There are a lot of storms up here in the mountains. None seems to hit us. Maybe this Indian does have some kind of magic. Still that's ridiculous . . . This morning we had a real thunderstorm and I found myself crouching next to the Indian by the zig-zag wall. The Indian had one hand placed tight on the zig-zag, so I put my hand on it too. We sat there as the storm crashed about us but never against us.

(7)

I've filed my first story. It seems to be changing things around for us. The Indian can't understand what's happened. The cars and trucks don't throw garbage at us any more. Now, besides food, beer, Coca-Cola, they throw us candy and god knows what. I almost got hit by a flashlight last night. I'm sleeping in a sleeping bag that a passing camper hurled over the zig-zag wall. The Indian still wraps himself up to sleep in a blanket, even though I offered him my sleeping bag and tried to tell him it's easy enough to get another. Today I actually heard cheers from cars going by in low gear. The Indian seemed scared. He's beginning to sulk and sit in his hut all day. I've got an idea to cheer him up, brighten this rocky highway island. Flags! I make a sign and hold it up. Soon we're swamped with flags. Mostly Mexican and American, but that's all right. I fly them side by side around our island. We're a real international frontier. We glitter with color. Somehow the Indian doesn't like the flags. I catch him tearing them down. *Why?* You have to respect flags. I'm teaching him the Spanish word for country, "Patria." He keeps repeating it over and over again. Maybe he's beginning to understand a little what it means to be a national hero.

(8)

Today I found it necessary to go into Mexico City to the Federal Department of Highways to try and get some background on the story. Maybe the engineers know something about the Indian, at least what tribe he's from. Since the Indian won't talk the story's going to die unless I can build up the facts. It's a real bureaucracy in the Highway Department. I see one official after another. "Sorry, Señor, I know nothing about an Indian." "You say there's an Indian in the highway. But it's impossible. That is one of our newest and best highways." Finally, in late afternoon, I get to the top official. At least he looks like the top official because he wears the most expensive clothes and white suede shoes. He apologizes profusely for the delay. Never mind. On his desk is a file. "Yes, Señor, we have a report here about an Indian in the highway. A minor affair. No problem. The engineers decided to leave him there. After all he is an Indian. The land belongs to the Indians. You have heard of 'Ejido' land?"

"You mean the new highway was built on land that belonged to the Indians?"

He doesn't bite. "All of our land, Señor, belongs to the Indians. It is a gift of our great heritage, the Mexican Revolution. If we need land for highways or housing we reimburse the Indians. We do not steal the land from them." He's looking at me sharply, critically now, Mexican to American, and I don't want to argue the point.

"Do you know what tribe the Indian belongs to?"

The official examines the report while I squirm. "No, Señor, the Indian evidently does not talk Spanish."

"Is there any indication why he wanted to stay there in that impossibly dangerous, barren place?"

"No. However, there is something interesting here. One engineer suggests that it may have to do with death."

"With *death*?"

"While bulldozing the cliff for the road the engineers evidently uncovered a grave. That brought the Indian to the site. After that he would never leave."

"Is there any indication what kind of grave? Was it a sacred ancestral grave of his tribe?"

"Who knows, Señor. The engineers brought in an anthropologist, but he couldn't decide. There weren't enough bones and no ornaments."

"Is there anything more in the file?"

"No, Señor. On the highways, if you know Mexico, it is best to leave Indians alone."

I try to get a closer look into the file, but he keeps sliding it away from me. It's a thick file too. If there were only some safe way to lift it for a while and photo-copy the contents. I bet there's a lot more important stuff in it than he tells me.

(9)

On the way back to the highway island I think about what to do. The story is getting clearer. The Indian is there to prevent the desecration of an ancient burial site. If I can only find more evidence of the burial site. . . . That might be dangerous if the Indian objects to my digging around. If I can only gain his confidence, get him to eat some of the free food he disdains, make him realize that he's becoming a national hero. Teach him the

Spanish word for hero, *Héroe*, maybe it'll get to him like *Patria*. With any luck it might be close to the word for hero in his ancient Indian language. The trouble is he's so silent he doesn't even seem to speak an Indian language. Still it's worth trying. Only a few words and he might begin to comprehend.

When he sees me, though, there's trouble. He starts to throw rocks again. I can't believe it. It's getting to be repetitious. Not that I expect him to welcome me back with a big embrace, but we were beginning to get along. "*Patria*," I cry at him. "*Héroe!*" But he keeps throwing rocks, not small ones either. Luckily the rocks are so big he gets tired after a while.

He goes into the hut to lie down. I go over and offer him some food and a soft drink to show him there's no hard feelings about the rock-throwing. Damn it, I've got to start again to win him over. He lies there rigidly, his back turned to me.

(10)

In the middle of the night I hear him stirring. Probably he has to go out and take a piss. He's always pissing on the road, never on the highway island come to think of it. Maybe that means something even though a family newspaper wouldn't be interested in it. I turn over in my sleeping bag and try to relax. Suddenly his short, thin figure is above me. What the hell? He's got a knife in his hand. It glitters in the moonlight shining through the open doorway. Desperately, quickly with my old army training, I grab his arm and hang on. Thank god I'm twice as big as he is, otherwise . . . It's still a real struggle because I'm on the defensive. Although I keep in good shape and exercise a lot it's like fighting a wildcat who's pounced on you. At last, sweating, I get into position to chop at his arm and the knife drops to the floor. The Indian flees outside and hurls himself down on the ground, rolling around in the agony of defeat. I pick up the knife. It's heavy hard stone covered with beautiful green jade. The handle is shaped in the head of a snake. Quetzelcoatl. By god, it's an ancient Aztec sacrificial knife. He was trying to cut my heart out. I can't believe it. Why else would he come at me with an old green stone knife like this? I've got to admit it's a beautiful knife. Did he get it from an old grave around here? Are there other treasures? Better keep the knife. It's safer. What a souvenir it'll make at home. Better stay awake tonight even though he'll probably never dare to attack me again.

(11)

Despite my frantic efforts to stay awake, I doze off in the early hours of the morning. I wake up with a start. A strange, eerie silence. No cars, no pounding of trucks, only birds singing outside of the hut. What's happened to the traffic? I grope my way outside wondering if the Indian has gone. A long line of silent cars and trucks clogs the highway. Has there been a terrible accident on the road? Why are they all staring at the highway island? Rows of people, businessmen in dark suits, tourists in sport shirts, truck drivers in heavy boots, all standing silently, solemnly staring at the one almost leafless tree in the corner of the highway island. As I approach I see the Indian hanging there, his body dangling from a noose. He's dressed in jeans, boots, white shirt, sombrero like one of those Judas dummies dressed like hacienda owners you see hanging from church doorways in Indian villages during Easter weekend ceremonies. The crazy fool! Maybe there's still time to save him. I rush up and cut him down. Useless. Too late. As I bend over him I draw back. Over his face is a white mask.

(12)

A year later I drive back to the highway island. It's a National Shrine now, celebrating The Unknown Indian. Everything has been polished up. The crude hut where we slept is a miniature museum full of Indian artifacts from the area. My contribution is the sacrificial knife which shines with its glowing green jade in a special case. I gave them the case too with an American lock so the knife would be more difficult to steal. Anyway peasants here are probably too superstitious to steal a sacred knife like this. My name isn't mentioned anywhere. That's what might be expected. I asked for the Mexican and American flags to be displayed together, but there's only a Mexican flag. Nothing much remains of the Indian. He hated being photographed, afraid like other Indians that the camera would steal his soul. Only his threadbare blanket is preserved in plastic in the hut. His grave is in the center of the highway island. The inscription says only: HERE LIES THE UNKNOWN INDIAN. The grave is topped with an enormous statue of a naked Indian warrior attacking an armored Spanish soldier in the Conquest. A famous Mexican sculptor was commissioned to create it. You can see it for miles down the highway. There's even a small parking lot next to the Shrine, although they had to narrow the road and curve it more to build the lot.

When I think about the Indian I'm glad that I helped to tell his story. It was a shame that I was only just beginning to communicate with him. I dream of his white mask sometimes. Did he think that he'd failed his people, that he was a Judas? No, that's ridiculous. It must have been the pressure of his poverty, his loneliness, the traffic that got to him and caused his breakdown. How could even an Indian survive for long in these barren rocks amidst all the pollution of these cars and trucks? Anyway he taught me a lot about courage and determination, even if he did blow his mind and attack me with that damn sacrificial knife. The one thing I regret is that I was never really able to get all the facts. Still I was lucky enough to deduce the major elements of the Indian's story even though he couldn't talk. In the end it was a real adventure. My stories about the Indian and how he came to be a hero are often reprinted in journalism anthologies. It's not every journalist who gets to create a Hero in the Highway.

Villanelle

JOHN NIST

Like twilight bleeding on a winter day,
smiles clack and gossip to the eye
black with birds of carrion prey.

I am sick of those pinched lips that say
a love so violent as ours will die
like twilight bleeding on a winter day.

I am sick of those lean hearts that say
our flesh will burn and blow about a sky
black with birds of carrion prey.

I am sick of those thin souls that pray
a love so violent as ours will die
like twilight bleeding on a winter day.

I am sick sick of all the dead can say
of our damnation in an envious eye
black with birds of carrion prey.

Despite the certainty of all they say,
my God, beloved, how easily they lie!
—Like twilight bleeding on a winter day
black with birds of carrion prey.

Soldiers

MICHAEL DOBBERSTEIN

> I above all promote brave soldiers.
> —Walt Whitman

The year my father was twenty-two he watched
The Japanese fighters climb gracefully
Out of the morning sun,
Saw them in perfect formation curve
The horizon over Hawaii.
The noise of their engines rose like a storm.

In his picture circa 1917 my great-uncle Arthur appears
Solid as a war bond and buttoned smartly up
To his chin in a mint-new Army uniform.

He is ready:
His gaze dead level,
His hair trimmed stiffly in a crew cut.
U.S. gleams on his collar.

After the Armistice people hoped for a better world.
When my father was born they said
This boy will never see war.

In his war Uncle Arthur had German cousins.
Their uniforms were similar.
No doubt in their photographs
They had serious looks on their faces.

Like him they also were very young.

Hurt in Korea my father still walks
Constantly with pain.
Ten years after Viet Nam my brother
Knows only the dreams
That fill his hospital room like smoke.
He dreams and dreams.

Uncle Arthur never got to the front.
In Dayton, Ohio he became a school teacher
And died in bed.
The German cousins he didn't fight had sons
Lost in the next war.

Descended from Prussians Uncle Arthur
Wanted to be stoic and severe.
He never knew my brother.

Morituri te salutamus, Uncle, Father.
My brother dreams
And the world catches fire: Ave Caesar.

Roger Pfingston

Old Women at Church

ANN STRUTHERS

Marcella prays silently for the man
who beat her that he may not suffer in hell
any longer. Twenty years is enough,
merciful mother, and I forgive him
except for the time he kicked me
and the baby was born thin and blue
like a coyote pup.

Rosita says prayers of thanksgiving.
The sheriff comes by asking for him
but he has not been back for ten years
and there is peace in the house and silence.
It smells of clean sand and dried strings
of peppers hanging from rafters. No more
bottle in the middle of the wild cards,
sick smell of whiskey and every man
with a knife or gun and short temper.

Old women dressed in black
beside adobe walls of the church
visit with each other while wind wraps
their long skirts against thin ankles.
They go home, cherishing their loneliness,
polishing it like smooth stones, strength
leaping inside the worn black shawls.

Consolation

Jim Barnes

Listen. That wind outside is yours:
your eyes ride it across jungles,
each yellow leaf a parachute.
You cannot go down:
the wind is for riding,
your eyes know.

Just listen. There is no dying in that,
though he is dead. The wind riddles
but it does not lie.
You can go on the wind
and come back here.

And listen. Take my hand. I offer
it to you to warm your breasts
while your dead airman's bones
talk to the wind we both know.

A Man Lies In White Linen

Morty Sklar

A man lies in white linen
lays on white linen his white head
and on his bed he kisses
the necks of his sons.
The paying of tavernkeepers
and priests becomes an act
like any other
and we are left
with one another

Mardi Gras Poem
(for Debbie)

STUART PETERFREUND

At the end of a perfect day,
the huge diesels begin hauling
their floats back from
Fat City, whirlwinds of ashes
following the flowers home.

We exchange a kiss, illuminated
by our own weak streetlight,
admitting that perfect days
come last; that the perfections
are in pawn until redeemed.
But we give our everything,
having discovered that everything
was ours to give away

Immigration Blues

Bienvenido N. Santos

Through the window curtain, Alipio saw two women, one seemed twice as large as the other. In their summer dresses, they looked like the country girls he knew back home in the Philippines, who went around peddling rice cakes. The slim one could have passed for his late wife Seniang's sister whom he remembered only in pictures because she never made it to the United States. Before Seniang's death, the couple had arranged for her coming to San Francisco, filing all the required petition papers to facilitate the approval of her visa. The sister was always "almost ready, all the papers have been signed," but she never showed up. His wife had been ailing when she died, he thought that hearing of her death would hasten her coming, but the wire he had sent her was neither returned nor acknowledged.

The knocking on the door was gentle. A little hard of hearing, Alipio was not sure it was indeed a knocking on the door, but it sounded different from the little noises that sometimes hummed in his ears in the daytime. It was not yet noon, but it must be warm outside in all that sunshine, otherwise those two women would be wearing spring dresses at the least. There were summer days in San Francisco that were cold like winter in the mid-west.

He limped painfully to the door. Until last month, he wore crutches. The entire year before that, he was bed-ridden, but he had to force himself to walk about in the house after coming from the hospital. After Seniang's death, everything had gone to pieces. It was one bust after another, he complained to the few friends who came to visit him.

"Seniang was my good luck. When God decided to take her, I had nothing but bad luck," he said.

Not long after Seniang's death, he was in a car accident. For almost a year he was in the hospital. The doctors were not sure he was going to walk again. He told them it was God's wish. As it was he was thankful he was still alive. It had been a horrible accident.

The case dragged on in court. His lawyer didn't seem too good about car accidents. He was an expert immigration lawyer, but he was a friend. As it turned out, Alipio lost the full privileges and benefits coming to him in another two years if he had not been hospitalized and had continued working until his official retirement.

However, he was well provided. He didn't spend a cent for doctor and medicine and hospital bills. Now there was the prospect of a few thousand dollars compensation. After deducting his lawyer's fees it would still be something to live on. He had social security benefits and a partial retirement pension. Not too bad, really. Besides, now he could walk a little although he still limped and had to move about with extreme care.

When he opened the door, the fat woman said, "Mr. Palma? Alipio Palma?" Her intonation sounded like the beginning of a familiar song.

"Yes," he said. "Come in, come on in." He had not talked to anyone the whole week. His telephone had not rung all that time, not even a wrong number, and there was nobody he wanted to talk to. The little noises in his ears had somehow kept him company. Radio and television sounds lulled him to sleep.

The thin one was completely out of sight as she stood behind the big one who was doing the talking. "I'm sorry, I should have phoned you first, but we were in a hurry."

"The house a mess," Alipio said truthfully. Had he been imagining things? He remembered seeing two women on the porch. There was another one, who looked like Seniang's sister. The woman said "we," and just then the other one materialized, close behind the big one, who walked in with the assurance of a social worker, about to do him a favor.

"Sit down. Sit down. Anywhere," Alipio said as he led the two women through the dining room, past a huge rectangular table in the center. It was bare except for a vase of plastic flowers as centerpiece. He passed his hand over his face, a mannerism which Seniang hated. Like you have a hang-over, she chided him, and you can't see straight.

A TV set stood close to a wall in the small living room crowded with an assortment of chairs and tables. An aquarium crowded the mantel-piece of a fake fireplace. A lighted bulb inside the tank showed many colored fish swimming about in a haze of fish food. Some of it lay scattered on the edge of the shelf. The carpet underneath was sodden black. Old magazines and tabloids lay just about everywhere.

"Sorry to bother you like this," the fat one said as she plunked herself down on the nearest chair, which sagged to the floor under her weight. The thin one chose the end of the sofa away from the TV set.

"I was just preparing my lunch. I know it's quite early, but I had nothing to do," Alipio said, pushing down with both hands the seat of the cushioned chair near a moveable partition, which separated the living room from the dining room. "It's painful just trying to sit down. I'm not too well yet," he added as he finally made it.

"I hope we're not really bothering you," the fat one said. The other had not said a word. She looked pale and sick. Maybe she was hungry or cold.

"How's it outside?" Alipio asked. "I've not been out all day." Whenever he felt like it, he dragged a chair to the porch and sat there, watching the construction going on across the street and smiling at the people passing by who happened to look his way. Some smiled back and mumbled something like a greeting or a comment on the beauty of the day. He stayed on until he got bored or it became colder than he could stand.

"It's fine. It's fine outside. Just like Baguio," the fat one said.

"You know Baguio? I was born near there."

"We're sisters."

Alipio was thinking, won't the other one speak at all?

"I'm Mrs. Antonieta Zafra, the wife of Carlito. I believe you know him. He says you're friends. In Salinas back in the thirties. He used to be a cook at the Marina."

"Carlito, yes, yes, Carlito Zafra. We bummed together. We come from Ilocos. Where you from?"

"Aklan. My sister and I speak Cebuano."

"Oh, she speak? You, you don't speak Ilocano?"

"Not much. Carlito and I talk in English. Except when he's real mad, like when his cock don't fight or when he lose, then he speaks Ilocano. Cuss words. I've learned them myself. Some, anyway."

"Yes. Carlito. He love cockfighting. How's he?"

"Retired like you. We're now in Fresno. On a farm. He raises chickens and hogs. I do some sewing in town when I can. My sister here is Monica. She's older than me. Never been married."

Monica smiled at the old man, her face in anguish, as if near to tears.

"Carlito. He got some fighting cocks, I bet."

"Not anymore. But he talks a lot about cockfighting. But nobody, not even the pinoys and the Chicanos are interested in it." Mrs. Zafra appeared pleased at the state of things on her home front.

"I remember. Carlito once promoted a cockfight. Everything was ready, but the roosters won't fight. Poor man, he did everything to make them fight like having them peck on each other's necks and so forth. They were so tame, so friendly with each other. Only thing they didn't do is embrace." Alipio laughed, showing a set of perfectly white and even teeth, obviously dentures.

"He hasn't told me about that, I'll remind him."

"Do that. Where's he? Why isn't he with you?"

"We didn't know we'd find you. While visiting some friends this morning, we learned you live here." Mrs. Zafra was beaming on him.

"I've always lived here, but I got few friends now. So you're Mrs. Carlito. I thought he's dead already. I never hear from him. We're old now. We're  old already when we got our citizenship papers right after Japanese surrender. So you and him. Good for Carlito."

"I heard about your accident."

"After Seniang died. She was not yet sixty, but she had this heart trouble. I took care of her." Alipio seemed to have forgotten his visitors. He sat there staring at the fish in the aquarium, his ears perked as though waiting for some sound, like the breaking of the surf not far away, or the TV set suddenly turned on.

The sisters looked at each other. Monica was fidgeting, her eyes seemed to say, let's go, let's get out of here.

"Did you hear that?" the old man said.

Monica turned to her sister, her eyes wild with panic. Mrs. Zafra leaned forward, her hand touching the edge of the chair where Alipio sat, and asked gently, "Hear what?"

"The waves. Listen. They're just outside, you know. The breakers have a nice sound like at home in the Philippines. We lived in a coastal town. Like here, I always tell Seniang, across that ocean is the Philippines, we're not far from home."

"But you're alone now. It's not good to be alone," Mrs. Zafra said.

"At night I hear better. I can see the Pacific Ocean from my bedroom. It sends me to sleep. I sleep soundly like I got no debts. I can sleep all day, too, but that's bad. So I walk. I walk much before. I go out there. I let the breakers touch me. It's nice the touch. Seniang always scold me, she says I'll be catching cold, but I don't catch cold, she catch the cold all the time."

"You must miss her," Mrs. Zafra said. Monica was staring at her hands on her lap while the sister talked. Monica's skin was transparent and the veins showed on the back of her hands like trapped eels.

"I take care of Seniang. I work all day and leave her here alone. When I come home, she's smiling. She's wearing my jacket and my slippers. You look funny, I says, why do you wear my things, you're lost inside them. She chuckles, you keep me warm all day, she says, like you're here, I smell you. Oh, that Seniang. You see, we have no baby. If we have a baby . . . "

"I think you and Carlito have the same fate. We have no baby also."

"God dictates," Alipio said, making an effort to stand. In a miraculous surge of power, Monica rushed to him and helped him up. She seemed astonished and embarrassed at what she had done.

"Thank you," said Alipio. "I have crutches, but I don't want no crutches. They tickle me, they hurt me, too." He watched Monica go back to her seat.

"You need help better than crutches," Mrs. Zafra said.

"God helps," Alipio said, walking towards the kitchen as if expecting to find the Almighty there.

Mrs. Zafra followed him. "What are you preparing?" she asked.

"Let's have lunch," he said, "I'm hungry. I hope you are also."

"We'll help you," Mrs. Zafra said, turning back to where Monica sat staring at her hands again and listening perhaps for the sound of the sea. She had not noticed nor heard her sister when she called, "Monica!"

The second time she heard her. Monica stood up and went to the kitchen.

"There's nothing to prepare," Alipio was saying, as he opened the refrigerator. "What you want to eat? Me, I don't eat bread so I got no bread. I eat rice. I was just opening a can of sardines when you come. I like sardines with lotsa tomato juice, it's great with hot rice."

"Don't you cook the sardines?" Mrs. Zafra asked. "Monica will cook it for you if you want."

"No! If you cook sardines, it taste bad. Better uncooked.

Besides it gets cooked on top of the hot rice. Mix with onions, chopped nice. Raw not cooked. You like it?"

"Monica loves raw onions, don't you, Sis?"

"Yes," Monica said in a low voice.

"Your sister, she is well?" Alipio said, glancing towards Monica.

Mrs. Zafra gave her sister an angry look.

"I'm okay," Monica said, a bit louder this time.

"She's not sick," Mrs. Zafra said, "But she's shy. Her own shadow frightens her. I tell you, this sister of mine, she got problems."

"Oh?" Alipio exclaimed. He had been listening quite attentively.

"I eat onions, raw," Monica said. "Sardines, too, I like uncooked."

Her sister smiled. "What do you say, I run out for some groceries," she said, going back to the living room to get her bag.

"Thanks. But no need for you to do that. I got lotsa food, canned food. Only thing I haven't got is bread," Alipio said.

"I eat rice, too," Monica said.

Alipio reached up to open the cabinet. It was stacked full of canned food: corn beef, pork and beans, vienna sausage, tuna, crab meat, shrimp, chow mein, imitation noodles, and, of course, sardines, in green and yellow labels.

"The yellow ones with mustard sauce, not tomato," he explained.

"All I need is a cup of coffee," Mrs. Zafra said, throwing her handbag back on the chair in the living room.

Alipio opened two drawers near the refrigerator. "Look," he said as Mrs. Zafra came running back to the kitchen. "I got more food to last me . . . a long time."

The sisters gaped at the bags of rice, macaroni, spaghetti sticks, sugar, dried shrimps wrapped in cellophane, bottles of soy sauce and fish sauce, vinegar, ketchup, instant coffee, and more cans of sardines.

The sight of all that foodstuff seemed to have enlivened the old man. After all, food meant life, continuing sustenance, source of energy and health. "Now look here," he said, turning briskly now to the refrigerator, which he opened, the sudden light touching his face with a glow that erased years from his eyes. With a jerk he pulled open the large freezer, cramped full of meats. "Mostly lamb chops," he said, adding, "I like lamb chops."

"Carlito, he hates lamb chops," Mrs. Zafra said.

"I like lamb chops," Monica said, still wild eyed, but now a bit of color tinted her cheeks. "Why do you have so much food?" she asked.

Alipio looked at her before answering. He thought she looked younger than Mrs. Zafra. "You see," he said, closing the refrigerator. He was beginning to chill. "I watch the papers for bargain sales. I can still drive the car when I feel right. It's only now my legs bothering me. So. I buy all I can. Save me many trips. Money, too."

Later they sat around the enormous table in the dining room. Monica shared half a plate of boiling rice topped with a sardine with Alipio. He showed her how to place the sardine on top, pressing it a little and pouring spoonfuls of tomato juice over it.

Mrs. Zafra had coffee and settled for a small can of vienna sausage and a little rice. She sipped her coffee meditatively.

"This is good coffee," she said. "I remember how we used to hoard Hills Bros. coffee at . . . at the convent. The sisters were quite selfish about it."

"Antonieta was a nun, a sister of mercy," Monica said.

"What?" Alipio exclaimed, pointing a finger at her for no apparent reason, an involuntary gesture of surprise.

"Yes, I was," Mrs. Zafra admitted. "When I married, I had been out of the order for more than a year, yes, in California, at St. Mary's."

"You didn't . . . " Alipio began.

"Of course not," she interrupted him. "If you mean did I leave the order to marry Carlito. Oh, no. He was already an old man when I met him."

"I see. We used to joke him because he didn't like the girls too much. He prefer the cocks." The memory delighted him so much, he reared his head up as he laughed, covering his mouth hastily, but too late. Some of the tomato soaked grains had already spilled out on his plate and on the table in front of him.

Monica looked pleased as she gathered carefully some of the grains on the table.

"He hasn't changed," Mrs. Zafra said vaguely. "It was me who wanted to marry him."

"You? After being a nun, you wanted to marry . . . Carlito? But why Carlito?" Alipio seemed to have forgotten for the moment that he was still eating. The steam from the rice touched his face till it glistened darkly. He was staring at Mrs. Zafra as he breathed in the aroma without savoring it.

"It's a long story," Mrs. Zafra said. She stabbed a chunky sausage and brought it to her mouth. She looked pensive as she chewed on it.

"When did this happen?"

"Five, six years ago. Six years ago, almost."

"That long?"

"She had to marry him," Monica said blandly.

"What?" Alipio shouted, visibly disturbed. There was the sound of dentures grating in his mouth. He passed a hand over his face. "Carlito done that to you?"

The coffee spilled a little as Mrs. Zafra put the cup down. "Why no," she said. "What are you thinking of?"

Before he could answer, Monica spoke in the same tone of voice, low, unexcited, saying, "He thinks Carlito got you pregnant, that's what."

"Carlito?" She turned to Monica in disbelief. "Why, Alipio knows Carlito," she said.

Monica shrugged her shoulders. "Why don't you tell him why?" she suggested.

"As I said, it's a long story, but I shall make it short," Mrs. Zafra began. She took a sip from her cup and continued, "After leaving the order, I couldn't find a job. I was interested in social work, but I didn't know anybody who could help me."

As she paused, Alipio said, "What the heck does Carlito know about social work?"

"Let me continue," Mrs. Zafra said.

She still had a little money, from home, and she was not too worried about being jobless. But there was the question of her status as an alien. Once out of the community, she was no longer entitled to stay in the United States, let alone secure employment. The immigration office began to hound her, as it did other Filipinos in similar predicaments. They were a pitiful lot. Some hid in the apartments of friends like criminals running away from the law. Of course, they were law breakers. Those with transportation money returned home, which they hated to do. At home they would be forced to invent stories, tell lies to explain away why they returned so soon. All their lives they had to learn how to cope with the stigma of failure in a foreign land. They were losers and no longer fit for anything useful. The more sensitive and weak lost their minds and had to be committed to insane asylums. Others became neurotic, anti-social, depressed in mind and spirit. Some turned to crime. Or just folded up, in a manner of speaking. It was a nightmare. Antonieta didn't want to go back to the Philippines under those circumstances. She would have had to be very convincing to prove that she was not thrown out of the order for immoral reasons. Just when she seemed to have reached the breaking point, she recalled incidents in which women in her situation married American citizens and, automatically, became entitled to permanent residency with an option to become U.S. citizens after five years. At first, she thought the idea of such a marriage was hideous, unspeakable. Perhaps other foreign women in similar situations, could do it — and have done it — but not Philippine girls. But what was so special about Philippine girls? Nothing really, but their upbringing was such that to place themselves in a situation where they had to tell a man that all they wanted was a marriage for convenience, was degrading, an unbearable shame. A form of self-destruction. Mortal sin. Better repatriation. A thousand times better.

When an immigration officer finally caught up with her, he proved to be very understanding and quite a gentleman. Yet he was firm. He was young, maybe of Italian descent, and looked like a salesman for a well-known company in the islands that dealt in farm equipment.

"I'm giving you one week," he said. "You have already overstayed by several months. If in one week's time, you haven't left yet, you might have to wait in jail for deportation proceedings."

She cried, oh, how she cried. She wished she had not left the order, no, not really. She had no regrets about leaving up to this point. Life in the convent had turned sour on her. She despised the sisters and the system, which she found tyrannical, inhuman. In her own way, she had a long series of talks with God and God had approved of the step she had taken. She was not going back to he order. Anyhow, even if she did, she would not be taken back. To jail then?

But why not marry an American citizen? In one week's time? How? Accost the first likely man and say, "You look like an American citizen. If you are, indeed, and you have the necessary papers to prove it, will you marry me? I want to remain in this country."

All week she talked to God. It was the same God she had worshipped and feared all her life. Now they were *palsy walsy*, on the best of terms. As she brooded over her misfortune, He brooded with her, sympathized with her, and finally advised her to go look for an elderly Filipino, who was an American citizen, and tell him the truth of the matter. Tell him that if he wished, it could be a marriage in name only. For his trouble, she would be willing to pay. How much? If it's a bit too much, could she pay on the installment plan? If he wished . . . otherwise . . . Meanwhile He would look the other way.

How she found Carlito Zafra was another story, a much

longer story, more confused and confusing. It was like a miracle, though. Her friend God could not have sent her to a better instrument to satisfy her need. That was not expressed well, but it amounted to that, a need. Carlito was an instrument necessary for her good. And, as it turned out, a not too unwilling instrument.

"We were married the day before the week was over," Mrs. Zafra said. "And I've been in this country ever since. And no regrets."

They lived well and simply, a country life. True, they were childless, but both of them were helping relatives in the Philippines, sending them money and goods marked Made in U.S.A.

"Lately, however, some of the goods we've been sending do not arrive intact. Do you know that some of the good quality material we send never reach our relatives? It's frustrating."

"We got lotsa thieves between here and there," Alipio said, but his mind seemed to be on something else.

"And I was able to send for Monica. From the snapshots she sent us she seemed to be getting thinner and more sickly, teaching in the barrio. And she wanted so much to come here."

"Seniang was like you also, hiding from immigration. I thank God for her," Alipio told Mrs. Zafra in such a low voice he could hardly be heard.

The sisters pretended they didn't know, but they knew practically everything about him. Alipio appeared tired, pensive, and eager to talk so they listened.

"She went to my apartment and said, without any hesitation, marry me and I'll take care of you. She was thin then and I thought what she said was funny, the others had been matching us, you know, but I was not really interested. I believe marriage mean children. And if you cannot produce children, why get married? Besides, I had ugly experiences, bad moments. When I first arrived in the States, here in Frisco, I was young and there were lotsa blondies hanging around on Kearny Street. It was easy. But I wanted a family and they didn't. None of 'em. So what the heck, I said."

Alipio realized that Seniang was not joking. She had to get married to an American citizen otherwise she would be deported. At that time, Alipio was beginning to feel the disadvantages of living alone. There was too much time in his hands. How he hated himself for some of the things he did. He believed that if he was married, he would be more sensible with his time and his money. He would be happier and live long. So when Seniang showed that she was serious, he agreed to marry her. It was not to be in name only. He wanted a woman. He liked her so much he would have proposed himself had he suspected that he had a chance. She was hard working, decent, and in those days, rather slim.

"Like Monica," he said.

"Oh, I'm thin," Monica protested, blushing deeply, "I'm all bones."

"Monica is my only sister. We have no brother," Mrs. Zafra said, adding more items to her sister's vita.

"Look," Monica said, "I finished everything on my plate. I've never tasted sardines this good. Especially the way you eat them. I'm afraid I've eaten up your lunch. This is my first full meal. And I thought I've lost my appetite already."

The words came out in a rush. It seemed she didn't want to stop and she paused only because she didn't know what else to say. She moved about, gaily and at ease, perfectly at home. Alipio watched her with a bemused look in his face as she gathered the dishes and brought them to the kitchen sink. When Alipio heard the water running, he stood up, without much effort this time, and walked to her saying, "Don't bother. I got all the time to do that. You got to leave me something to do. Come, perhaps your sister wants another cup of coffee."

Mrs. Zafra had not moved from her seat. She was watching the two argue about the dishes. When she heard Alipio mention coffee, she said, "No, no more, thanks. I've drunk enough to keep me awake all week."

"Well, I'm going to wash them myself later," Monica was saying as she walked back to the table, Alipio close behind her.

"You're an excellent host, Alipio." Mrs. Zafra spoke in a tone like a reading from a citation on a certificate of merit or

something. "And to two complete strangers at that. You're a good man."

"But you're not strangers. Carlito is my friend. We were young together in this country. And that's something, you know. There are lotsa guys like us here. Old timers, o.t.'s, they call us. Permanent residents. U.S. Citizens. We all gonna be buried here." He appeared to be thinking deeply as he added, "But what's wrong about that?"

The sisters ignored the question. The old man was talking to himself.

"What's wrong is to be dishonest. Earn a living with both hands, not afraid of any kind of work, that's the best good. No other way. Yes, everything for convenience, why not? That's frankly honest. No pretend. Love comes in the afterwards. When it comes. If it comes."

Mrs. Zafra chuckled, saying, "Ah, you're a romantic, Alipio. I must ask Carlito about you. You seem to know so much about him. I bet you were quite a . . . " she paused because what she wanted to say was "rooster," but she might give the impression of over-familiarity.

Alipio interrupted her, saying, "Ask him, he will say yes, I'm a romantic." His voice held a vibrance that was a surprise and a revelation to the visitors. He gestured as he talked, puckering his mouth every now and then, obviously to keep his dentures from slipping out. "What do you think? We were young, why not? We wowed 'em with our gallantry, with our cooking. Boy those dames never seen anything like us. Also, we were fools, most of us, anyway. Fools on fire."

Mrs. Zafra clapped her hands. Monica was smiling.

"Ah, but that fire's gone. Only the fool's left now," Alipio said, weakly. His voice was low and he looked tired as he passed both hands across his face. Then he raised his head. The listening look came back to his face. When he spoke, his voice shook a little.

"Many times I wonder where are the others. Where are you? Speak to me. And I think they're wondering the same, asking the same, so I say, I'm here, your friend Alipio Palma, my leg is broken, the wife she's dead, but I'm okay. Are you okay also? The dead they can hear even they don't answer. The alive don't answer. But I know. I feel. Some okay, some not. They old now, all of us, who were very young. All over the United States of America. All over the world . . . "

Abruptly, he turned to Mrs. Zafra, saying, "So. You and Carlito. But Carlito, he never had fire."

"How true, how very very true," Mrs. Zafra laughed. "It would burn him. Can't stand it. Not Carlito. But he's a good man, I can tell you that."

"No question. Dabest," Alipio conceded.

Monica remained silent, but her eyes followed every move Alipio made, straying no farther than the reach of his arms as he gestured to help make clear the intensity of his feeling.

"I'm sure you still got some of that fire," Mrs. Zafra said.

Monica gasped, but she recovered quickly. Again a rush of words came from her lips as if they had been there all the time waiting for what her sister had said that touched off the torrent of words. Her eyes shone as in a fever as she talked.

"I don't know Carlito very well. I've not been with them very long, but from what you say, from the way you talk, from what I see, the two of you are very different."

"Oh, maybe not," Alipio said, trying to protest, but Monica went on.

"You have strength, Mr. Palma. Strength of character. Strength in your belief in God. I admire that in a man, in a human being. Look at you. Alone. This huge table. Don't you find it too big sometimes?" Monica paused perhaps to allow her meaning to sink into Alipio's conciousness, as she fixed her eyes on him.

"No, not really. I don't eat at this table. I eat in the kitchen," Alipio said.

Mrs. Zafra was going to say something, but she held back. Monica was talking again.

"But it must be hard, that you cannot deny. Living from day to day. Alone. On what? Memories? Cabinets and a refrigerator full of food? I repeat, I admire you, sir. You've found your place. You're home safe. And at peace." She paused again this time to sweep back the strand of hair that had fallen on her brow.

Alipio had a drugged look. He seemed to have lost the drift of her speech. What was she talking about? Groceries? Baseball? He was going to say, you like baseball also? You like tuna? I have all kinds of fish. Get them at bargain price. But, obviously, it was not the proper thing to say.

"Well, I guess, one gets used to anything. Even loneliness," Monica said in a listless, dispirited tone, all the fever in her voice gone.

"God dictates," Alipio said, feeling he had found his way again and he was now on the right track. What a girl. If she had only a little more flesh. And color.

Monica leaned back on her chair, exhausted. Mrs. Zafra was staring at her in disbelief, in grievous disappointment. Her eyes seemed to say, what happened, you were going great, what suddenly hit you that you had to stop, give up, defeated? Monica shook her head in a gesture that quite clearly said, no, I can't do it, I can't anymore, I give up.

Their eyes kept up a show, a deaf-mute dialogue. Mrs. Zafra: Just when everything was going on fine, you quit. We've reached this far and you quit. I could have done it my way, directly, honestly. Not that what you were doing was dishonest, you were great, and now look at that dumb expression in your eyes. Monica: I can't. I can't anymore. But I tried. It's too much.

"How long have you been in the States?" Alipio asked Monica.

"For almost a year now!" Mrs. Zafra screamed and Alipio was visibly shaken, but she didn't care. This was the right moment. She would take it from here whether Monica went along with her or not. She was going to do it her way. "How long exactly, let's see. Moni, when did you get your last extension?"

"Extension?" Alipio repeated the word. It had such a familiar ring like "visa" or "social security," it broke into his consciousness like a touch from Seniang's fingers. It was quite intimate. "You mean . . . "

"That's right. She's here as a temporary visitor. As a matter of fact, she came on a tourist visa. Carlito and I sponsored her coming, filed all the necessary papers, and all she had to do was wait another year in the Philippines, and everything would have been fine, but she couldn't wait. She had to come here as a tourist. Now she's in trouble."

"What trouble?" Alipio asked.

"She has to go back to the Philippines. She can't stay here any longer."

"I have only two days left," Monica said, her head in her hands. "And I don't want to go back."

Alipio glanced at the wall clock. It was past three. They had been talking for hours. It was visas right from the start. Marriages. The long years and the o.t.'s. Now it was visas again. Were his ears playing a game? They might as well as they did sometimes, but his eyes surely were not. He could see this woman very plainly, sobbing on the table. Boy, she was in big trouble. Visas. Immigration. Boy, oh, boy! He knew all about that. His gleaming dentures showed a crooked smile. He turned to Mrs. Zafra.

"Did you come here," he began, but Mrs. Zafra interrupted him.

"Yes, Alipio. Forgive us. As soon as we arrived, I wanted to tell you without much talk, I wanted to say, 'I must tell you why we're here. I've heard about you. Not only from Carlito, but from other Filipinos who know you, how you're living here in San Francisco alone, a widower, and we heard of the accident, your stay in the hospital, when you were released, everything. Here's my sister, a teacher in the Philippines, never married, worried to death because she's being deported unless something turned up like she could marry a U.S. citizen, like I did, like your late wife Seniang, like many others have done, are doing in this exact moment, who can say? Now look at her, she's good, religious, any arrangement you wish, she'd accept it.' But I didn't have a chance to say it. You welcomed us like old friends, relatives. Later every time I began to say something about why we came, she interrupted me. I was afraid she had changed her mind and then she began to talk, then stopped without finishing what she really wanted to say, that is, why we came to see you, and so forth."

"No, no!" Monica cried, raising her head, her eyes red from weeping, her face damp with tears. "You're such a good man. We couldn't do this to you. We're wrong. We started wrong. We should've been more honest, but I was ashamed. I was afraid. Let's go! Let's go!"

"Where you going?" Alipio asked.

"Anywhere," Monica answered. "Forgive us. Forgive me, Mister. Alipio, please."

"What's to forgive? Don't go. We have dinner. But first, let's have *merienda*. I take *merienda*. You do also, don't you? And I don't mean snacks like the Americans."

The sisters exchanged glances, their eyes chattering away.

Alipio chuckled. He wanted to say, talk of lightning striking same fellow twice, but thought better of it. A bad thing to say. Seniang was not lightning. At times only. Mostly his fault. And this girl Monica . . Moni? Nice name also. How can this one be lightning?

Mrs. Zafra picked up her purse and before anyone could stop her, she was opening the door. "Where's the nearest grocery store around here?" she asked, but she didn't wait for an answer.

"Come back, come back here, we got lotsa food," Alipio called after her, but he might just as well been calling the Pacific Ocean.

Mrs. Zafra took time although a supermarket was only a few blocks away. When she returned, her arms were full of grocery in paper bags. Alipio and Monica met her on the porch.

"*Comusta?*" she asked, speaking in the dialect for the first time as Monica relieved her of her load. The one word question seemed to mean much more than "How are you?" or "How has it been?"

Alipio replied in English. "God dictates," he said, his dentures sounding faintly as he smacked his lips, but he was not looking at the foodstuff in the paper bags Monica was carrying. His eyes were on her legs, in the direction she was taking. She knew where the kitchen was, of course. He just wanted to be sure she won't lose her way. Like him. On his way to the kitchen, sometimes he found himself in the bedroom. Lotsa things happened to men his age.

Sunday Afternoon

G. S. SHARAT CHANDRA

She was not in the balcony
　　not near the fountain
　　nor under the palm fronds
　　　sipping tequila

Ah, her calf high boots,
　　the ebullience of her
　　　recrossed thighs . . .

Why do I think of piranhas
　　on a turquoise ocean floor
explosion in the bakery
　　across the street?

I've no poetic education
　　that's why

She was not at the fruit stand
　　not at the penny arcade
　　nor at the museum of arts
　　　sipping capuccino

with her handbag
　　between her knees . . .

If Michael Angelo had seen her knees,
　　gleaming alabaster,
　　open oyster shells . . .

Not hiding behind the angel
　　in the cemetery
　　nor at the open air
　　concert
　　not at the bus stop

It's restful to know
    she's not anywhere
    someone might find her,
    some busybody, sun in the eye
      who has no newspaper . . .

Auto-

DENNIS SCHMITZ

by law death enters
    at the mouth
also by law the driver exits

    turning off the key.
the wife or husband who is left
    imagines upholstery:
the navel machine-punched,
the eye oozing kapok.
the kids of course

    cry. a married aunt
will take them, will drive
    them to the end

of her life without accusation
    (sometimes neglect equals
apology, sometimes
the sideroad dissolves to prickly

Three Poems

RICHARD JONES

In her lenity
There were legions
At their leisure
Watching

In her numbness
There were legions
At their leisure
Watching

In her constitution
There were wordlings
Mute and molting

In her jailings
There were rapists
Escapists
Dopers lifers killers

But in her guts
There were legions
At their leisure
watching television

Levels of abstraction
Jellied in my head
Like a second hand friend
Telling a second hand story
Of the review of a poet's line
On recording tape
Of the television videotape
Of a painting
Of the photograph
Of the reflection of
A shadow sobbing

Old Lady

I saw a pulchritudinous girl
most lovely in this or any other
world

She flirted signs   read
I am eighty-three

At that
she was more graced
than goddess
and far
far
far
too good
for me

Two Poems

VICTOR CONTOSKI

Unhappy Couple

They came
like Magi

bearing between them
a box in a velvet cloth.

Among shepherds and oxen
they knelt
in silk mantles.

We offer you the unhappiness
we have made between us
like a child.

It is all we have.
We want you to share it.

The Message

The books are bent,
their pages loose.

Hands come apart.
Fingers flutter down.
Hair falls.

Tongues wrap themselves
around seeds.

A bob white
in the far field.

The unseen
sings
to the unreal.

The River

Joyce Carol Oates

How do you drive the river,
how do you navigate—
Ice broken like pavement,
wind a torment of fine dry stinging snow—

(The old car's steering wheel so cold
your flesh flies to it, and clings—)

How do you navigate the ice-shards of vertebrae
fallen everywhere in heaps
how do you steer the narrow swift channel
proclaiming it is your choice—

Always the same, the same voice,
the same loneliness, the voice
urging behind the mirror,
the loneliness, the wonder—
how do you drive the river,
how do you keep the wreck afloat,
how can you bear the pain
of your silly fingers stuck to the wheel—

Some Nagging Irrelevant Thoughts on Sex

Elizabeth Von Vogt

When I was thirteen I had a vision of sex and innocence. It didn't teach me a thing, having nothing whatever to do with knowledge. I *knew* what men and women did together, I had had my solitary nighttime lusts, and had daily devoured, with my eyes, the handsome boys of the sophomore class. I had even shrewdly noted male couples along Lexington Avenue in New York and the butchy girls on Thompson Street in the Village. What's more, I had learned already to snicker at them.

But only visions pierce the soul with meaning. And in the act of piercing, a touchstone is born, against which all the knowledges and experiences of later life are stacked.

I lived in a big, broad, sunny room on East Fortieth Street with my mother and sister. We all three slept in this room, cooked on a hot plate, sat in front of a fireplace, and practiced the arts of such living in front of a wall of windows that let in all the upper light of the outside world (a world of five stories high), and in turn, exposed our own silly lives before that world. I hated school that year and feigned sickness almost every morning and got away with it far too much. Instead I dreamed in front of the wall of windows. I had little life except in that large room and on the one lone walk I was allowed to take, the short one north to Grand Central Station.

I spent every evening there. I'd go about five o'clock when the people crowded the concourse. I'd stand on the balcony at the Vanderbilt Avenue entrance, and look down fascinated, riveted to the throngs crisscrossing endlessly, magically over that magnificent floor. The gigantic room with its unceasing, flowing life became the setting for an otherwise fruitless eighth grade year. There was the outsized American flag suspended over the entrance to the waiting room. There was a new car displayed at one end of the room, while the glaring, fiercely happy outlines of the Kodak family radiated high over the opposite end. There were the black triangular marquees of the tracks lining the north side—The State of Maine, The Merchant's Limited to Boston, the trains for the Berkshires, for Poughkeepsie and Cape Cod. And over all there was the grand, merciful dome, an ersatz sky of silver constellations and a greeny-turquoise blue, a superbly fake Grand Central blue utterly alien to any natural or even Venetian heaven. I stood there on more evenings than I would care to count—stood leaning on the chilly marble balustrade, glued to the turmoil below. I think I sensed some vague community, some coherence in the panorama of people arriving and departing the vast room, that escaped me on the streets. I watched and reveled in the watching. I loved the room and the humanity that momentarily passed and touched together under its phoney sky. And sometime during those strange vigils of that year I got a vision of men and women, of sex, of lovers, that seemed to shape some surviving attitude.

One night during that cocktail hour watch, instead of just seeing the usual mass at its best, released and relaxed, I singled out couples. I noticed along the way that most people formed a twosome—that people were, when you could observe them thus from benevolent heights, mostly united in these separate units of male and female. It struck me abruptly from everywhere that men and women came together at the information booth in endless embraces, that they walked together arm in arm to trains and ticket windows, that they clasped each other's waists in ludicrous poses as they strolled aimlessly across the concourse, that they could be spied in all the locales of the room, talking earnestly or not talking but waiting with their bags and their tacit connection. Of course there were people alone and men together and women together, but these others were at once swept away for me by the discovery that literally and ridiculously shook my thirteen year old being—the momentous revelation that people, that life itself must obviously arrange itself into these eternal combinations of two, that there was absolutely no escaping the prevailing formula. And moreover, this fated arrangement seemed to be the very most that life could give, for otherwise why would all humanity be so obsessed by it? The repeated couples in the station, the variety of ages, looks and classes, and the monotonous uniformity of the simple combination—male-female—over and over, telegraphed a message to my straining puberty. The privacy within the public, the mystery of two alone amidst the city's thousands, and finally the beauty of bodies that touch and cleave to each other among the desolate throngs of commuters—this was clearly the destiny of our human life. This then was the fantastic secret that lay at the end of the impossible few years ahead of me.

Well, I went there every night for awhile pursuing the obsession, I guess until the discovery lost its exultation and I put on the more certain knowledge of adolescent sex and probably a quotient of pain with it that made the aspect of these men and women a bitterness to the silly girl who couldn't yet experience the secret. But I won't forget the image, the breakthrough to my consciousness of the immensity of the man-woman thing. How I stared at one after another of the numberless couples, futilely trying to divine the meaning of their touches, their looks, trying to read what they were really saying to each other with those intimate gestures, both the warm and the indifferent ones. But nothing came to me except maybe an aura, a magic almost unendurable. There seemed to flow through that room a spell of desire, a stream of caresses, touches, of simple *connection* that bore the very essence of life along its course. It wasn't a bad vision to get. The look-out on that balcony made me want only the real thing—to me, the supremely *adult* thing I saw moving over that concourse.

———

Since then I've had the "adult" thing. In fact, I didn't waste too many years getting to it. And since then there have been a Kinsey Report and a sexual revolution. There have been adulterous triangles and *ménages à trois*; there have been all the combinations of love in *Another Country*, *Thérèse et Isabelle*, *The Boys in the Band* and *Murmur of the Heart*. "Gay Love" along with "Latin Eagles" defaces the walls around my neighborhood, and on the block where I drop my laundry, there are in succession a Lesbian Feminist Center, a bookstore called "Idyl Pleasures," and on the corner "Little Jim's," a drag bar for gay Latinos. I've had my own brush with complex sexuality and have discovered enough contemporary ambivalence in myself to have shot that silly Grand Central vision all to hell.

And as if to buttress the pervasiveness and the long coming on of the new sexual cast of characters, my little story took place in a small Michigan town in 1956.

That was my one year in the real provinces. I was teaching at a tiny sectarian college in a remote outpost of a town in central Michigan. It was exile and I'm sure I was vulnerable to Siberian pitfalls, the big threat to equilibrium and character obviously being boredom. And I was miserably, drastically bored—bored right off in September to the limit of drama and daring. I remember an earnest conversation in the college snack bar with

a young dean about differences in background, about the cosmopolitan fate that I now sensed precluded sanity in the provinces. There was no doubt. I was twenty-three, smug and naïve. It was a bad scene.

But of course I hung on and curiosities and vitalities surfaced. I found a slumside of town apartment and invested it with the charm of harried neglect. I bought an old black Chrysler, my first car. And by October, a cold and particularly sparkling one far off there in the middle of Michigan, I had discovered the forms of passionate sexual exoticism as they should appear in exile—intensely, intimately, tacitly. Because they wore a thin disguise of conventionality in Presbyterian Alma, they became more involving than they had ever been as side shows on the side streets of Manhattan. Just as they were more timid of exhibition, they were also more penetrating of the nooks and crannies of that pious college drawing room.

I met Bill B., a new language teacher, the first week out. And a meeting with Kay (I can't dredge up her full or proper name, and I apologize to her for this, a final cut over all the years) occurred barely three weeks later at some pitiful function acquainting new teachers with old ones, Kay being one of the latter. She seemed somewhere in the vague vicinity of her late twenties to middle thirties, but Bill was fond of declaring as the year ripened and rotted, that this was but another pathetic sham, that Kay was forty and nearing oblivion. So within a month there and despite arrogant proclamations of imminent flight, I had established my first independent residence in life, and had found two friends with whom I tasted relational intricacies never before known to such a callow New Yorker as myself.

Bill was forty-ish and approaching the terrible truths of some brink of annihilation. He taught French, had studied at the Sorbonne, had been in the Army and vaguely in World War Two. There had been a distant, short-lived marriage that had left him sentimental and falsely, comically bitter (I soon learned that he really didn't like women). The post-war period had brought him to Columbia graduate school, Greenwich Village, cocktails at four P.M. and even, he snickered sibilantly and with the irony of those hippest early fifties, a shot or two of morphine picked up along Madison Avenue, "you know." And finally defeated by the competition of the Eastern establishment (and we found common ground here), he had retreated back across the flattened hills of Ohio to anonymity in miniature colleges, and summers of possible eroticism abroad. He had gone to Ada, Ohio, for a year or so, and was now moving inexorably up the line toward the Arctic regions of society, the move to Alma being but a way station on the road to total effacement. He used to say over our pathetic four o'clock cocktails, "From Ada to Alma to Sault St. Marie," the last being a dim college of the nether regions of Michigan's upper penninsula. Of course, I had no intentions of making such a trek, and he must have felt momentarily revived by my brashness. And certainly I was kept from acting out any silly desperation by Bill's wit, jaded and sour though it turned after a couple of drinks, and his eagerness for companionship in that physical and spiritual tundra. The mutual reinforcement to be found in *his* having gone to San Remo's (where I went to "school") and *my* knowing the West End Bar at Columbia was not to be resisted. The same sense of exile founded on the same self-disappointment added a positive zing to the ordering of dry martinis in highway taverns. We pulled together at once.

But I soon found Bill numbing from the advancing cold of his life. He was drinking way too heavily of weekday afternoons while he awaited the arrival of an ancient mother who hovered over his shaky passage through the years, hovered ominously and damagingly, I gathered. I found him adrift in the chilling Alma desert, at forty with too many unfulfillments, too much anger and heat and sarcasm for the temperature of his age— in short, with too much unlived life on his hands, especially the idle hands of exile. I early concluded, with the harshness and simplicity of youth, that Bill was queer. And he was, but the corridors of his emotional life had steered him away from a confrontation with that fact. He faced mother and martinis instead of boys most of the time. And since I seemed willing to face them with him on those fading, sharp October afternoons, he conceived a need for me.

The complexity of the need and the forms it took can only be imagined. He made no passes. To face the deep revulsion they would cause would have been too much. At forty dissembling with the body must become impossible. But he surrounded me. He monopolized every afternoon for those make-believe cocktails, and the afternoons became roadhouse dinners that he paid for with the fine generosity of desperation. The dinners then lengthened into liquored late nights, until he had extracted the meat out of every one of my off-campus hours. I soon knew that he must have me with him every minute. The body of a woman must have filled him with dread and its acompanying loathing, though he had paid obeisance to it in the past. He must have fondled continental boys in countless Augusts, never admitting the *idea* of such caresses. And now, he loved me for whatever complexities it meant. I could never have stated it, but I felt its meaning. Possession, control, reassurance, the sucking of one soul into another. If Alma was a camp of exile, Bill's peculiar lust was becoming a birdcage within the prison cell. And me, I loved nobody, and within the gilded cage, soon learned the uses to be made of the jailor. In short, I grew complacent in the security of his compulsion for me, and sought with true deviousness, the avenues of freedom. I met, *we all* met, Kay at the said innocuous tea.

I had never attended even remotely to her type, eyeing them only across the tourist and sex barriers at San Remo's on Mac-Dougal Street. But in Siberia, and I felt I was there, one is thrown in with all sorts of prisoners and one is open to the various lessons they can teach.

Well, Kay was the girls' gym teacher. She was butch on sight, with sporty clothes and tight muscular calves above the bobby socks and sneakers. She lisped slurringly with a slight speech impediment, her short brown hair was swept up and back, casual and efficient. I knew what she was at a glance. She would not have had it otherwise, as she functioned on multi-levels within the steadfast community. But the inclination to fun and freedom led me to savor her extreme good-nature, the glasses of wine she would sneak to me at the impossible social functions, and the all-hour ease of her garage apartment—cramped, cozy and promising of at least the fringes of a more daring life. I began to urge sleep upon Bill earlier in the evenings, or even afternoons, as the martini glasses piled up around our elbows at the dreary, sordid roadside taverns. I would get away from him, finding my way more and more to Kay's digs. I began to savor her cheap, fruity wine, the amusement of her open but still guarded talk with me, the favorite girl athletes who would inevitably "drop by," and even the tall, soft, sibilant boy who might also "show up." She had a circle (she eschewed the company of faculty), and I delighted to imagine the variety of activities with which the members entertained each other.

But Kay began to cultivate me. I soon felt the cultivation growing. She would begin to get rid of the circle after business talk about the coming game, a show, a dance they were supervising, and after curious veiled comments. She more and more

urged my staying on into the later Alma hours. She pressed more wine (I delighted to realize that she must have begun to supply it for these evenings), she talked more closely, the conversation now acquiring the tone of jocular, warm confidence. I talked of Bill. She sympathized and in the most direct, friendly manner. She knew Bill. She guardedly hinted to me that she pegged him as queer, that he could be up to no good with me. How wonderful, I thought, they had spotted each other at once —some initial introduction at one of those early progressive dinners. Kay in turn, confessed to a hopeless, though passionate male love, a boy in Pennsylvania with a mysterious illness to whom she "flew off" every possible weekend. I caught the accents of her growing desire for me—in a chair drawing closer, in the eyes too riveted and unmasked. She too was beginning to show another angle of love.

So there I was between Bill and Kay, neither laying a hand on me (and I was far from virginal by that year), but both enforcing upon me nevertheless the bonds of possession and domination. Without a touch from either I reacted, and not without pleasure from both quarters, to the sensuality of their friendly overtures to me. They wanted me, and the complex ends which I served never disturbed the positive feeling of well-being this produced in me. I began to go almost willy-nilly from one to the other, mercilessly extracting my own kick from their futile desires. Bill would buy me dinners. Kay would serve me dinners, candlelit and *entime*. I liked them both immensely. I amused myself.

But of course at last they reached their own limits of endurance. They began to have clandestine, lacerating meetings of their own. Reports of these would surface in conversations, and I imagined the fury with which they must assault each other for "using me." And of course, as doom would fashion it, they each began to attack the other to me. One would declare the other "dike," "fag" and "over the hill." They each devalued the love (concern) of the other. In sum, they began to abase themselves before me. And I became more deeply embroiled and uncertain.

Finally I guess some dim sense of responsibility began to gnaw at me. I thought I should dispense some favors and begin some journey toward honesty. I began to weigh the love of each and was startled to feel too often that the woman's love seemed clearer than the man's. I became grateful to her and even planned and baked a chicken dinner of my own for her one night to which she came reticently and left disappointed. What a tease I was becoming under their care! But on the other hand, I felt a kind of trust in Bill, his drunkenness and excess, that I usually reserved for men. I began to discover how heterosexual I was, in that the area of difference between us—man and woman— seemed to establish patterns of relating—seemed to be an area I could rely on.

But as they each clutched harder at me, I began to back away from both. At the first turning of the stair of their vulnerability I turned icy and cruel. I used one against the other. I became secretive with them, leading each one to believe that I was more intimate with the other, but also that I saw through the adversary. I was contradictory. But to redeem my role in this a litttle, my behavior was some measure of my confusion at the hands of their loves.

And so the pattern continued for awhile, but *la ronde* could only begin to run itself down. After all, I loved neither of them. And I awoke sometime in the deadening November days to the positive shock of how easy and tempting it would have been to use them even more successfully with the instrument of my body. At that I pulled back. Who knows what dangers and charities can surface in the psyche of a young girl?

Scenes were becoming sour, even bitter. One night after a roadhouse cocktail hour and dinner among the farmers and their brassy, genial bar girls, Bill sat on my couch and let the rising demon push him to extremity. Forging into new territory, he kissed me. He pulled me around the sofa and spit out a mixture of sarcasm and affection between hard, wounding kisses and liquored sobs. Drunken and driven, he lacerated me with sexual moves. It was hopeless. I felt the convolutions of his lust in his own hostility that surfaced to defeat him. The fear *I* felt (a just reward for my conduct with him) could not match the near-terror in Bill's eyes as he faced the truth of his revulsion at the lips and breasts and thighs he was attempting to maul. The impasse had been reached. He left exhausted from combat, not sex. Such moments force people to step back from each other. The cocktail hour pretty much closed itself out after that night.

One afternoon, a last bright one about two o'clock, I wandered into Kay's garage, calling casually for her. The kitchen was still, the silence curiously draining the rooms of the mystery and intrigue of the "circle." There was no answer, and as I looked indifferently around not especially sorry at Kay's absence, I caught sight of her in the tiny, dark bedroom, spread out naked under a careless sheet, napping. Her head lay face downward in the bend of a bare arm. Her rest was simple, beyond torture and ambiguity. She was a woman napping, in all reasonableness, at two of an afternoon. I don't know why, but I felt a revulsion, a disgust at myself, *awake* before her sleeping form. It was a moment when an image struck home as no analysis ever could. How clearly had I disturbed, could I even now, destroy her rest! I left, foregoing her wine and company for the desolate hours, and don't remember going there much again.

A while ago I read *The Captive* of Marcel Proust. I wandered lost amid the fine variety of tortures Marcel pursues over Albertine, Charlus over Morel. There in Proust were all the crooked angles of sexual passion characteristic of our own time. Is Albertine kissing her girlfriend Andrée, or flirting with Marcel's own chauffeur? Surely here is contained the cruelest ambivalence of sexual jealousy. For when a lover doesn't know whether his love is yearning after the bodies of boys or girls, the old element of control, of physical imprisonment even, must become a mania. The lover seeks more and more futilely to dominate as the means to dominate become less and less effective. Can he or she be trusted with *anybody*? Betrayal, peril and helplessness-in-love are raised to a higher mathematics as the combination of their forms becomes infinite. So the passionate Proustian heart is never shattered along pure, simple lines. Impossible for morality to follow its intricate fissures.

Something in *The Captive* then called forth the memory of my Michigan interlude. I felt Marcel's peculiar, exquisite torments—I understood Bill. I re-discovered Kay in the priceless humanity of Charlus standing blasted before his lover in the Verdurin's living room. And in the white Balbec sunlight that opened up *all* the scenes of life alike, but blasted the explanations into silence, I found *myself* exposed in the figure of Albertine. All the elements were there. The depth of sexual layers; the age, the dominance, the futility of my pursuers; the cruel number of opportunities for emotional betrayal on all sides; and at the crux of the scene, the uses of sensual power. For though it was never touched during that exiled autumn, I have never felt that my sex was a more potent instrument. There were too many options. By withholding here with a man who was probably homosexual, but who was often then telling himself he wanted me, I seemed to keep Bill poised, pivoting between need and frustration and revelation, one compelling the other. With Kay, acting straight in the late evenings appeared to enhance those multi-levels tensions of her life. My goodness! To shake her hand, to touch a wrist in the emphasis of intimate conversation, to pat a shoulder, was to open up an abyss of interpretation for her. "Liz is straight. She's smart, young, hip. She's warm, affectionate, close . . . " The agony of possibility within impossibility. And so in all this nothing happened. There were no "caresses in the bushes, kisses at the door." But the atmosphere in any meeting between one of these two and myself was laden with a sensual power that oughtn't to belong to any twenty-three year old. Albertine had this power. Morel did.

I learned anew from Proust as he traced, never obscured, the line between body and heart. Suddenly the simplicity that proselytizes to us that *all* love, no matter the physical form, is the same, is dealt a death blow. Love for Marcel, Albertine and Charlus (as for Bill and Kay and me) could not be as it was for Anna Karenina, Heathcliffe or our grandfathers. There is too much paradox. On the one side lovers become too vulnerable, too dominant, desperate, helpless. Their beloveds have turned the tables on them. Pursued, they manipulate. The most quintessential type of modern love story then houses the most destructive irony—love transmuted into power. Master and slave, old and young, beauty and beast, gay and tough. It becomes a dynamic of ceaselessly changing roles. The end result? With all *that* power how could I love Bill or Kay or anybody? Something in their ambiguity tipped the old balance. We could not meet from positions of equality.

I begin to sense a new type of heartbreak in the contemporary sexual milieu Proust foresaw and we inhabit. Perhaps even a tragic flaw. The old reciprocity of love seems gone, the old forms by which it *could* flourish (though it needn't), blighted by sexual ambiguity. OK. The price the heart seems to have to pay for its new freedom.

But after all, I don't entirely trust these latter day insights. Because behind it all I make out a pimply, pubescent girl staring down with longing on Grand Central Station. D. H. Lawrence said you can't trust the mind. All the rational discourse may be just such a trick of the mind. Don't listen. The words may be the perfect cloak devised by the mature reader and intellect to hide the hurt of an adolescent vision compromised by life. Fatally compromised, but still calling the tune.

The Betrayal

JOHN UNTERECKER

This morning there were three dead warblers under the window:
a darkness singing.

It was as if I had forgotten your name.

Two Poems

LYN LIFSHIN

Channuka Madonna

burns too fast

gets brighter
throughout
the week

her wick waiting
for the match
that will burn
her to nothing

Jealousy

like a little dirt
under a fingernail
that pushes the nail
from your skin,
a little garden
burning knives grow in

Bread

for E. L. Mayo, 1904-1979

Robert Dana

Not Wonder in its white wrapper
with yellow, red, and blue balloons,
or Colonial, or Sunbeam,
those breads of air
you can accordion down to a slice,
limp cake that won't
take peanut butter without tearing,
a cheap cloth of crust.

No.

Real bread.
Its crumb tight,
grist for cheese, *wurst*, or hard sausage,
a mop to thick, steaming soups;
braided loaves, or long French ones
to be cut with a pocket knife,
or rounds with gashed tops,
grainy, and brown, and water crusted,
with a haze baked on them
you can sink your teeth into.

In that soft ratcheting
of sifter against screen,
any afternoon we can find the time,
we can make ghosts of our hands
in the silk of flour;
and in the beer of yeast,
be sure of the one ingredient necessary

to three risings and kneadings
on the cracked board,
until the greased tins
are finally dusted with granules
of white cornmeal,
and even the sleeps of this house
sweeten with this art.

Old Irishman, my father,
you with your Saturday sleeves rolled up,
and smelling powerfully of Lucky Tiger like whiskey,
you knew all about it,
the making of bread.

Your Special Chair

DANIEL CURLEY

                    lives in the corner
of the kitchen. It has had a hard life.
Although it is one of the dining room set,
it is at best a poor relation,
scratched, stained, and spotted with paint.
Something has also happened to its finish—
perhaps at one time someone thought
of refinishing it and despaired
or died or sold out to the highest
bidder. Now it lives in reserve,
in support for your dark times.
It knows you at three a.m.
It knows your gin and your cigarettes.
Sometimes it wears your clothes haphazard
as if trying to hold up its end.
Sometimes its feet are clogged with dust.
Sometimes in the morning I can
hear its joints whimpering.

Plague

MALCOLM GLASS

The low hills moved in,
dust rising behind them
to stripe the cloudless sky
with a border of tan
haze. In the binoculars
we could see the land
flowing toward us like
tidewater.

       Word had gone
out on the radio. We were
ready: boarded up,
the chimney sealed.

        Now
the binoculars showed
the ground gray, roiling,
swimming faster down
the slope.

      When we could see
their eyes, we went into
the darkened house to wait
for the earth to cover us,
the thousands of claws
and teeth swarming
the sides of the house,
screeching across the roof.

"Rat plague," Ian called it.
"The house is alive
with them, like a swarm
of bees."

Some of them
consumed the bags
of poisoned wheat, but that
scrap of death would make
too little difference.

Beyond us, in one corner
of the desert, they would
finally turn on each other
and leave us holding
the land still again.

Luther Smith

Hans-Peter Otto

The New York Game

WILLARD MANUS

They were playing a game of ball in Central Park; some grown men were doing a rinkydink number out there, with the batter having plunked a blooper into right-center and the runner on first, a roly-poly in a pink-on-purple uniform with COCO emblazoned across his jiggling titties, trying to survive the voyage to third. From the stricken look on his face as he swept pachydermously around second, he was risking a cardiac arrest as he ran, head tilting, mouth wheezing for air. The right-fielder could have bowled the ball to third and got him, but cut loose instead with a throw that soared high and far enough to induce rain from the overhanging clouds. The peg not only cleared third, the onlookers behind the bag, but rolled all the way down the greensward toward the Carousel, scattering frisbee players and sunbathers like an errant torpedo.

The two teams were members of the Broadway Show League. The performers and backstage hands from the various shows around town got together to compete for a trophy every year. Actors on spikes: I knew all about them. Four or five years ago, *Holiday* magazine had assigned me to write a piece about softball in New York.

Write us a nice, offbeat article on the city game, they said. You know the scene, you've played ball in the schoolyards and playgrounds from Bedford-Stuyvesant to Pelham Bay. Tell us what it's really like out there, how it differs from the softball most Americans know. Write it from the inside, make it as strong and true as you can. Give us the excitement, the tension, the challenge of the game. Put it all down—the yelling and laughing, the betting, the smells, the heat, the atmosphere. Give us the real thing, Samuels.

So I gave it to them, did I ever. They'd inspired me to do my best, to write honestly about something I knew well. It was a rare and lucky assignment. I wrote the piece with joy and ease, five thousand words in two days. "Softball in the Summer— Everyman's Sport in New York."

The article began with a description of Sunday morning in New York. Sunday morning in summer meant softball. It meant getting up at dawn, just as I'd done yesterday, and going downstairs and waiting on the corner, the city silent and sleeping, the sun edging up into the robin-blue sky, for Teddy Jones to pick me up.

Ted drove a Chevy pickup truck around New York. He kept 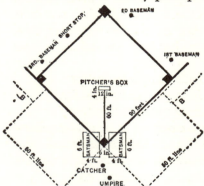 a big box of old, rusty tools and junk in back, and for fifteen years now had parked wherever he pleased—in front of the school he taught at, in the center of Times Square, on the corner of Madison and 45th, on the sidewalk opposite Yankee Stadium—without ever once having drawn a ticket.

Yeah, there was Ted, his gear bag and a sackful of White Tower donuts and coffee on the seat beside him, and the dashboard blaring WLIB: the church service from Rev. Adam Clayton Powell's Abyssynian Church, with Sister Thorpe and fifty cooking gospel singers wailing and tambourining Down By the Riverside, down by the—

"How's my man?"

"Wasted. You?"

"Wiped out. I was up most of the night with the old man. Had to take him back to the hospital. His foot's bad, turning gangrenous. I'm afraid they may have to amputate it."

"That's a bitch. I sure hate to think of Amos sufferng like that."

"He thinks he's going to die, Ted. He thinks it's all over for him."

You could forget all that, though, once you reached Col. Charles Young park on 145th and Lenox. You could forget your sick and dying father, your bastard of a boss, or your bullshit job for a few hours anyway. Here, in the park, on this boxed-in slab of asphalt, the game offered forgetfulness and escape. Here a man who was a construction laborer, a postoffice clerk, a failed writer could shed all that, could divest himself of poverty and obscurity for a few quick hours. As much as we did excitement and sport, we craved amnesia out here. Sweet obliviousness.

That's why we changed our clothes, slipped into gaudy, multi-colored uniforms with the name HARLEM LORDS stitched across our chests. And why our opponents were usually called the DUKES, the ROYALS, the KINGS, the CHIEFS. We were failures and fools on weekdays—but on Sunday we were boss, we were ten feet tall, the biggest baddest motherfuckers this town had *ever* seen.

"Hey, Len, how you doin, what's happenin, baby?"

"What's shakin, Ted. You ready to play some ball, Slick? You ready to show what you're made of, you cocksucker?"

Oh yes, uh-*huh*, it was eight o'clock on a Sunday morning in Harlem, time to strut your stuff and shoot the shit and play the dozens. And as you warmed up, as you played catch and fielded grounders and hit a few to right and some to left, you began to feel good. Good to be here in the sun, alive and about to play the best, the quickest, the toughest team game there was.

Softball. Softball in the city. *Holiday*, you asked for it and you got it. You got a description of Charles Young park, that huge parade grounds of a field with ballgames going on simultaneously in all four corners of the rectangle, with the public housing projects and the apartment houses rising up around it and the smell of the nearby Harlem River in the air and the stands filling slowly with the first onlookers, neighborhood faces, folks on their way to church, team backers, small-time gamblers, girl friends, wives, winos.

They were all coming out, some to catch the local heroes in action, others to meet their friends, show off their Sunday best, exchange some gossip, drink some beer, flirt with the chicks, and maybe even make a few bucks betting on the game.

The betting was a big part of the action, *Holiday*. This was New York, it was Harlem, where gambling was part of life. The best part of life.

"Let's get it together, let's put some money in the hat."

As the home team, we were obliged to stake out the kitty first. Junior went around collecting, first from the team, then the onlookers—"Ten for you, Len, OK, I got you—twenty for you, Wrinks—gotcha, baby—gotcha written down—" —and then we went out for infield drill, this time under the eyes of our opponents, who had just arrived. The BROOKLYN MA-JESTICS they called themselves and they were a smart-looking team, togged out in brand-new green and white uniforms, tight stretch pants and V-cut jerseys with square, big-peaked caps. They'd come in from Bed-Stuy with a tough rep and they had a giant of a pitcher warming up on the far sideline. Built like a pro tackle or defensive end, this dude was about six-five and 250 pounds, and when he swung his long arm up and around in the windmill style and cut loose with the ball, it looked like a white pea as it shot toward the catcher, who kept his mitt stiff and flat so that the ball went *thowockkkkkkkk* when it hit, the sound reverberating like a shot around the stands and ring-ing out over the field. ZOCK, ZOCK, ZAT, that cat could throw, listen to that monster hit that leather, how would we ever hit that motherfucker, he sure throws *hard*, don't he, he goin to break our *bats*, man.

It was all part of the psychological warfare that was going down now. So was the routine Ted and I put on. It was an act we'd perfected over the years and which we dusted off whenever we faced a new team. Teddy took infield wearing this ridiculous Coney Island beanie, and when he threw it was with a slightly limp-wristed motion that made you think, "Hey what the fuck— is that some kind of *faggott* out there?" Cauz when he bent for a ball he also stuck his rump out in a provocative way that made you giggle and snicker even more. *Whooeee, ain't he cute!*

Then there was the shortstop, me, the only white boy on the field, looking like one scared ofay in the midst of all these big, tough blacks. The cat's nervous, he's tight, he's a lame, they muttered as I lunged at every ball and bobbled every throw and fired every peg wildly.

"Come *on*, short," our manager Junior howled convincingly from behind home plate. "Throw it straight, stop wearing us out, man!"

The idea was to look so bad that the MAJESTICS would become cocky and over-confident ("They look like shit out there, we're gonna *waste* them") and want to increase their betting on the game, from five hundred to maybe a thousand bucks. The hustling went back and forth right up until game time, culminating in a burst of verbal abuse that could stand as the quintessence of animadversion.

"Hey, is that all you people can come up with, a lousy six hundred dollars? You ought to change the name of your team from the *Majestics* to the *Dickless Wonders*."

"Whooee! Listen to those boys, they sure do *talk* a good game, don't they? Ain't it a shame you can't play softball with your mouth: those boys would be champs."

"You doin some heavy bullshittin yourself, farmer. Why don't you put your money where your mouth is?"

"Now you're talking, you faggotts, now you're making some sense. Looka here," cried Wrinks, the team coach, as he high-stepped up and down the sidelines, his knee-high sequinned riding boots winkling in the sunlight. Wrinks was also wearing a Captain Blood slouch hat with a fantastic yellow feather, a bolero cape, and a purple and pink satin jump suit. He owned an ebony walking stick which he now jabbed at the opposition. "Look what I got here in my pocket!"

Wrinks had pulled a roll of greenbacks out and was peeling ten dollar bills off and flicking them at the MAJESTICS' feet:

"Here 7-8-9-10 big ones that says you assholes are gonna get your brains kicked in out there. Well, come on, how come you all so silent now—I can't *hear* you all of a sudden—shit, maybe I got water in my ears—maybe this ain't enough for you. Well lawrd knows there's lots more green behind me—uh-huh—here it is—show me yours, motherfuckers—come on, lemme see it—show us what you got, rednecks—conversation time is over—it's time to put up or shut up, you turkeys, you jive-ass Mississippi chitlin-eaters!"

Holiday, poor white Anglo-Saxon *Holiday*, you got more than you bargained for, didn't you? You got your faces shoved right down into the streets, the armpit of black America. Crazy coons in gaucho gear, profanity sizzling the asphalt, illegal betting in the open, postal clerks and janitors and ex-jailbirds for players: what a raw slice of life.

It wasn't the kind of life *Holiday* was used to portraying. The magazine preferred chatty, amiable pieces about cruising down the Rhine, or dining out at the Four Seasons, or visiting backstage at *Aunty Mame's*. There were no slums, no jive-ass black folk playing the dozens in *Holiday's* world. As for softball, the only game *Holiday* knew was the one played out in small-town America: bright-green grass, stadiums, industrial teams with brand-names on their jerseys. Episcopalian softball.

But my assignment cut across the magazine's grain. My editor, a new boy on the block, fresh out of the Columbia Journalism School, bubbling over with ideals and honesty, said clearly that I was to write about the game I knew, the New York game. Full speed ahead and damn the restraints. Tell it like it is, man.

Ok, *Holiday*, thank you, *Holiday*. Way ta go, fellas.

*　　*　　*

I could no longer remember the game I'd written about for *Holiday*, but it couldn't have been very different from the one we'd played yesterday against the BROOKLYN MAJESTICS. The game and the scene were still the same, part and parcel of neighborhood life in Harlem. Charles Young park was a kind of public square or promenade, not just a ball field. It was a poor man's sporting and social club, a place to meet and gossip and relax of a Sunday morning. You could also see the best softball in the city—maybe even in America—played there, from dawn to dusk, by a collection of extremely gifted amateur athletes.

That's why I'd been reluctant to try my skills out again, after having been away from New York for three years. There were some damn good ballplayers competing against each other, for high stakes. You were expected to play well if you went out on the field; incompetence could lead to personal humiliation and financial disaster for the team. This pressure, and the knowledge that I was nowhere the player I used to be, made me feel stiff out there, tight as an overwound alarm clock. My hands felt heavy and clumsy, nothing left of the old quickness and sureness.

On the first play of the game I made an error, on a simple ground ball that even my Uncle Bozzie could have handled. Then the next man hit a single, sending the runner to third, from where he scored on a fly ball. A few innings later I came up to bat with a man on third and two out. Not only didn't I bring him in, I didn't even tip a single pitch. The MAJESTIC's big fastballer just over-powered me. Go back to Europe, you turkey.

But Ralph, our third-string pitcher, had caught his stride and was having one of his better games, throwing curves and risers with accuracy, fooling the opposing batsmen easily. We got him some runs early on, when Butch hit a triple with the bases loaded; and in the fifth Teddy, Mr. Slick himself, punched home two more with a single. And so I began to relax; along about the sixth inning I suddenly began to feel like my old self again.

With a man on first and one out, the batter drove one in the hole between short and third, a hard-hit ball that came off the bounce with a wicked topspin. That, *Holiday*, was one of the things that gave the city game its quick, special character. Ground balls came shooting off the asphalt or concrete like skimmed stones, at a velocity you never faced playing on dirt and grass. And the distances were so short that the slightest bobble would give the batter first base. I'd screwed up some earlier chances, but this time my body responded and I came alive. Darting to my right, I backhanded the ball, and, wheeling, fired a hard peg to Ted, who relayed it just as fast to first; the whole play taking but a couple of seconds, bang bang, double play.

It brought everyone in the stands up ("Oh yass, now *that's* the way to play the game") and made our guys yell, and I felt about fifty feet tall, not just because I'd made the play, but because I'd felt *good* doing it; oh, yeah, it was indeed like old times out there.

"Hit it to me!" I yelled at the next batter and goddamn if he didn't, a high Baltimore-chopper. Even in my prime as a semi-pro player, this kind of ball always gave me trouble. If you hung back and played it safe, waiting for the big bounce, chances were the runner would beat it out. A nervy shortstop, though, charged the ball, risking an error on the always-tricky short hop, firing underhand on the run to beat the man, one of the prettiest plays in the game.

Well, I played that chopper the way it should be played and threw a strike to first, socking Butch's mitt with a whack they could hear all the way to the Triboro Bridge. Next thing you know, the whole team was ganging up on me on the sidelines, yelling, "Way ta go, Leonard, those were *money* plays, mother-fucker, you still the boss out there, baby. Give me five and five *more*, jim!"

All right, I was back into it, was stomping around like my old self out there. The sun had moved further overhead and was heating everything up; that August-in-the-city heat that came at you from above and below, *Holiday*; it poured down on you and hit the asphalt and soaked and softened it, sending a tar smell up into your nose. The baking heat was part of the city game too, *Holiday*, and so was the tar-smell. This was tar city, *Holiday*, and we were its tar-babies, children of the old asphalt jungle. That sticky, gritty New York air lay on your skin like a pestilence and no matter how often you rinsed your mouth out, it still tasted of burnt rubber. Soon it grew so hot that your jersey turned soggy and stuck like mud, the sweat running down your face and stinging your eyes.

By mid-day the only way to catch a pop-up was to turn away from the white, brutal glare of the sun and catch the ball side-ways, over your shoulder. As the morning went on, getting hotter by the hour, more and more people began to turn out, nearly all of them black: families with kids, crapshooters and card-players, subway conductors and jazz musicians, salesgirls and whores, churchgoing folk in their Sunday best, youngbloods in their zoot suits and reep pleats.

The most sensational entrance of all was made by Sister Thelma, manageress of the HARLEM TOPHATS, our second-game opponents. Thelma owned a string of black bars and brothels, and she entered with a whoop and a waddle, shaking her huge hips and flashing her diamonds as big as the ritz, and hollering across the field, "Hey, Wrinks, I got a thousand dollars here that says you can't beat my boys."

"A thousand?"

"Is that all you got to say? What's the matter, man, you wear your tongue out hustling small-timers this morning?"

"Sugar, I hate to think how you done wore down that tongue of *yours*," was Wrinks' rejoinder. It broke the park up.

But Thelma came back fast and sassy. "That may be, but I sure didn't do it going down on you. The last time I tried that, I came up with a mouthful of pussy!"

Sorry about that, *Holiday*, but you did ask for the real thing, didn't you?

Poor, poor *Holiday*. Charles Young park just wasn't its scene. There had never been any talk of pussy in its pages. Neither had there been any fat madams with rocks on her fingers, or car-washers in Captain Blood hats. What an embarrassment for you, *Holiday*. What a problem. The Broadway Show League was more your world; chorus boys and celebrities. Nice clean well-mannered white folk running around aimlessly and goofily in the sun—like those two out there now, thundering after a fly ball with such Anglo-Saxon intensity that they forgot to call for the ball and ended up crashing into each other like cars at a demolition derby.

It was the third time somebody had got hurt during the course of the game. An inning ago, the third-baseman of HELLO, DOLLY! had stopped a line drive with his thumb, and COCO's catcher had become crippled with a charleyhorse from bending. And now this collision: blood spurting from noses, soiling those pretty pink uniforms. . . .

What a difference from yesterday's second game in Harlem, the one against Lefty Long. That was softball, the real thing, not a single mistake or misplay for six tight innings. Long was as good as ever, still able to throw hard when he had to, but mostly working his risers and drops, varying his speeds, making sure that no two pitches were alike. Long, a tall, thin, solemn-faced Negro had been doing this for twenty-five years, throwing strike after strike in his shrewd, unemotional, masterful way. A hospital orderly during the week, he picked up 50-100 bucks a game pitching on weekends for the likes of the TOPHATS or for the CAFE DE CREMA team in the Saturday Latin-American league.

The game against Long was New York softball at its best. Neither team got a single basehit in the first six innings, not an unusual occurence in a game of this caliber. Long was brilliant, but so was Howard Koren, our strong right hand. Both men kept sitting the batters down, one after the other, strike three, *you're out.*

A lot of money was riding on the game, nearly two thousand dollars. Everyone was yelling it up, players and onlookers alike, but the excitement would have been there even if we'd been playing for peanuts. This was *sport* and anyone who knew anything felt it: the tension, the rapture. To be part of a game like this was a trip; it was like being *high,* only better.

Over the years I'd had my share of hits against Long, but today he'd fooled me twice, found me over-eager, lunging at the ball. I'd grounded out twice and, as clean-up man, it had hurt the team. They'd slotted me there out of blind faith, remembering some of my previous successes against Long, forgetting I'd been away, living in a country where they kicked balls instead of catching them. Goddamn it, they were all living in the past, trading on nostalgia and sentiment. Bunch of romantics—why wouldn't they grow up?

"Who needs it?" I said to Teddy. "We're too *old* for his shit, man."

"If you believe it, then you're too old to live," was his rejoinder.

He was first up in the bottom of the seventh and last inning and I knew, with prescience, that he'd hit his way on. I'd watched him so often, knew him so well as an athlete, that his actions and responses had become predictable. I could tell what he was going to do even as a husband can anticipate his wife's words before she speaks.

He was standing by the side of the plate watching Long finish his warm-up pitches, looking as cocky and calm as ever, grinning a little, enjoying the challenge. It was the same look he'd worn on his face the day he got married, ditto the night he went on the Ed Sullivan Show to accept his All-American basketball award: the nonchalant untroubled Theodore Jones, Mr. Slick himself, number one devotee of the Cool School, class of '52.

Long threw and Teddy hit, he wasted no time stroking a clean sweet line drive into centerfield and as he ran to first, he looked back over his shoulder at me, as if to say, I knew it and you knew it and now it's up to you. Just like old times, baby. Just like it used to be.

There had been a hundred, *five* hundred, games like this in which things had ended up in a similar way. Teddy on base, in the late innings, looking for me to drive him in, to win it. It was only a quick flash that he'd given me, but I read a lot into it; saw the proud joy of reconciliation there, yet a hint of sadness too. We'd won so many games together at a time like this. We'd win this one too; we both felt it, but at the same time we both knew that it might not happen again.

Teddy knew as well as I did that we weren't so tight any more, that time and distance had loosened our bonds. It hurt, of course, and somehow it would hurt even more if I hit one off Long and won the game. That was the strange thing about the moment, knowing that even if I came through it would wound, simply because the glory might be final, the victory climactic.

The number two hitter popped up and, trying to pound a Long riser to right field, the number three man went out on a soft fly ball. So here we were. Where we'd been before and where, maybe, we'd never be again.

Long threw me a strike, a curve ball which I swung at and missed badly. But I was trying to set him up. I'd gone out in front of the ball on purpose. Wrinks scowled and yelled from third, "Easy, Len, not too eager, baby."

Lefty threw another curve ball, high and outside. I practically ran out of the box before checking my swing, again wanting to look nervous and over-eager. Lefty threw yet another devilish curve which went over, inside, just above the knees, the umpire calling it a strike. I stood griping and bitching away, glowering ferociously at Long, who looked back at me unemotionally, face hardened in its usual deadpan expression. Inside, though, I was

as calm and lucid as he. I knew in my bones that I had him
fooled.

Ninety-nine times out of a hundred a pitcher in a spot like
this would cut loose with his best pitch, a curve or a riser, with
a lot on it. But Long was different from all the rest. He could
not be read as you read the others. With a lucidity bordering on
the clairvoyant, I seemed to know exactly what he was going to
do. What courage he had, what a great pitcher he was.

After flashing Teddy our old, private hit and run sign, I was
crouching and waiting when Long threw the change-up.

The ball came in floating like a balloon and I hit the shit
out of it, clean and hard into left-centerfield, and by the time
the ball was relayed, Ted was home, the game was over.

Goddammit, maybe I'd never win a Guggenheim or the
National Book Award or the Nobel Prize for Literature, but
this moment, except for the twinges I felt about Teddy, was
almost as good. Hell, it was every *bit* as good.

*　　*　　*

That's what I wrote for *Holiday.* It was all there in the
piece I turned in. But a week later the article was back on my
desk with this note from the editor attached to it:

"It's a helluva well-written piece, Len, but after careful con-
sideration we feel that it concentrates too much on the neighborhood game, the idea of softball as a poor people's game. We'd
like a little more glamour and glitter in the piece. Take it and
rewrite it and work in some of this."

Attached to the memo was a cutting from the *Herald-Tribune*
about the Broadway Show League opening and how Paul Newman and George C. Scott and Robert Ryan and some of the
bunnies from the Playboy Club played once a week through
the spring/summer season on the 63rd Street diamond.

"But these people can't play softball," I told the editor.
"They're worth a mention, but that's all. You can't really call
what they play softball."

"Yes, I agree with you, but what can I do, Len? My boss
thinks the piece is a little too *ethnic*. Clean it up a bit, Len. Give
it a little more sophistication."

So I went home and ripped the heart out of the article. I took out the blacks and the bookies, took out the smell of tar and sweat, took out the hookers and the winos. In their place I put Paul Newman and Central Park and the Playboy Bunnies, and *Holiday* sent me a return check for seven hundred and fifty dollars. It was the biggest sale I'd ever made and my mother called to congratulate me.

Later that night I put the check in the oven, turned up the gas, and burned it to a crisp.

Now, remembering all that, I watched as the batter bounced a slow booper-dooper grounder to HELLO, DOLLY, who swiped at it, juggled it, and then threw it fifteen feet above the first-baseman's head.

Way ta go, DOLLY, I muttered. Way to go, *Holiday*.

Collected Poems
E. L. MAYO

E. L. Mayo's poems shine with a wit and wonder and
intelligence that make them truly remarkable.
—ROBERT DANA

A *New Letters* Book

Ohio University Press/Swallow Press
Scott Quad, Dept. FRDR
Athens, OH 45701

Ohio University Press/Swallow Press
Scott Quad, Dept. FRDR
Athens, OH 45701

India

An Anthology of Contemporary Writing

Edited by
DAVID RAY and AMRITJIT SINGH

1983   277 pp.   6 x 9   illus. $10.95